WATERLOO

GREAT BATTLES

WATERLOO

ALAN FORREST

OXFORD
UNIVERSITY PRESS

OXFORD
UNIVERSITY PRESS

Great Clarendon Street, Oxford, OX2 6DP,
United Kingdom

Oxford University Press is a department of the University of Oxford.
It furthers the University's objective of excellence in research, scholarship,
and education by publishing worldwide. Oxford is a registered trade mark of
Oxford University Press in the UK and in certain other countries

First Edition published in 2015

Impression: 1

Published in the United States of America by Oxford University Press
198 Madison Avenue, New York, NY 10016, United States of America

British Library Cataloguing in Publication Data
Data available

Library of Congress Control Number: 2014948241

ISBN 978–0–19–966325–5

Printed in Italy by L.E.G.O. S.p.A.

FOREWORD

For those who practise war in the 21st century the idea of a 'great battle' can seem no more than the echo of a remote past. The names on regimental colours or the events commemorated at mess dinners bear little relationship to patrolling in dusty villages or waging 'wars amongst the people'. Contemporary military doctrine downplays the idea of victory, arguing that wars end by negotiation not by the smashing of an enemy army or navy. Indeed it erodes the very division between war and peace, and with it the aspiration to fight a culminating 'great battle'.

And yet to take battle out of war is to redefine war, possibly to the point where some would argue that it ceases to be war. Carl von Clausewitz, who experienced two 'great battles' at first hand – Jena in 1806 and Borodino in 1812 – wrote in *On War* that major battle is 'concentrated war', and 'the centre of gravity of the entire campaign'. Clausewitz's remarks related to the theory of strategy. He recognised that in practice armies might avoid battles, but even then the efficacy of their actions relied on the latent threat of fighting. Winston Churchill saw the importance of battles in different terms, not for their place within war but for their impact on historical and national narratives. His forebear, the Duke of Marlborough, fought four major battles and named his palace after the most famous of them, Blenheim, fought in 1704. Battles, Churchill wrote in his life of Marlborough, are 'the principal milestones in secular history'. For him 'Great battles, won or lost, change the entire course of events, create new standards of values, new moods, new atmospheres, in armies and nations, to which all must conform'.

Clausewitz's experience of war was shaped by Napoleon. Like Marlborough, the French emperor sought to bring his enemies to battle. However, each lived within a century of the other, and they fought their wars in the same continent and even on occasion on adjacent ground. Winston Churchill's own experience of war, which spanned the late nineteenth-century colonial conflicts of the British empire as well as two world wars, became increasingly distanced from the sorts of battle he and Clausewitz described. In 1898 Churchill rode in a cavalry charge in a battle which crushed the Madhist forces of the Sudan in a single day. Four years later the British commander at Omdurman, Lord Kitchener, brought the South African War to a conclusion after a two-year guerrilla conflict in which no climactic battle occurred. Both Churchill and Kitchener served as British cabinet ministers in the First World War, a conflict in which battles lasted weeks, and even months, and which, despite their scale and duration, did not produce clear-cut outcomes. The 'battle' of Verdun ran for all but one month of 1916 and that of the Somme for five months. The potentially decisive naval action at Jutland spanned a more traditional 24-hour timetable but was not conclusive and was not replicated during the war. In the Second World War, the major struggle in waters adjacent to Europe, the 'battle' of the Atlantic, was fought from 1940 to early 1944.

Clausewitz would have called these twentieth-century 'battles' campaigns, or even seen them as wars in their own right. The determination to seek battle and to venerate its effects may therefore be culturally determined, the product of time and place, rather than an inherent attribute of war. The ancient historian, Victor Davis Hanson, has argued that seeking battle is a 'western way of war' derived from classical Greece. Seemingly supportive of his argument are the writings of Sun Tzu, who flourished in warring states China between two and five centuries before the birth of Christ, and who pointed out that the most effective way of waging war was to avoid the risks and dangers of actual fighting. Hanson has provoked strong criticism: those who argue that wars can be won without battles are not only to be found in Asia. Eighteenth-century European commanders, deploying armies in close-order formations in order to deliver concentrated fires, realised that the destructive consequences of battle for their own troops could be self-defeating. After the First World War, Basil Liddell Hart developed a theory of strategy which he called 'the indirect approach', and suggested that manoeuvre might substitute for hard fighting, even if its success still relied on the inherent threat of battle.

The winners of battles have been celebrated as heroes, and nations have used their triumphs to establish their founding myths. It is precisely for these reasons that their legacies have outlived their direct political consequences. Commemorated in painting, verse and music, marked by monumental memorials, and used as the way points for the periodisation of history, they have enjoyed cultural after-lives. These are evident in many capitals, in place names and statues, not least in Paris and London. The French tourist who finds himself in a London taxi travelling from Trafalgar Square to Waterloo Station should reflect on his or her own domestic peregrinations from the Rue de Rivoli to the Gare d'Austerlitz. Today's Mongolia venerates the memory of Genghis Khan while Greece and Macedonia scrap over the rights to Alexander the Great.

This series of books on 'great battles' tips its hat to both Clausewitz and Churchill. Each of its volumes situates the battle which it discusses in the context of the war in which it occurred, but each then goes on to discuss its legacy, its historical interpretation and reinterpretation, its place in national memory and commemoration, and its manifestations in art and culture. These are not easy books to write. The victors were more often celebrated than the defeated; the effect of loss on the battlefield could be cultural oblivion. However, that point is not universally true: the British have done more over time to mark their defeats at Gallipoli in 1915 and Dunkirk in 1940 than their conquerors on both occasions. For the history of war to thrive and be productive it needs to embrace the view from 'the other side of the hill', to use Duke of Wellington's words. The battle the British call Omdurman is for the Sudanese the battle of Kerreri ; the Germans called Waterloo 'la Belle Alliance' and Jutland Skagerrak. Indeed the naming of battles could itself be a sign not only of geographical precision or imprecision (Kerreri is more accurate but as a hill rather than a town is harder to find on a small-scale map), but also of cultural choice. In 1914 the German general staff opted to name their defeat of the Russians in East Prussia not Allenstein (as geography suggested) but Tannenberg, in order to claim revenge the defeat of the Teutonic Knights in 1410.

Military history, more than many other forms of history, is bound up with national stories. All too frequently it fails to be comparative, to recognise that war is a 'clash of wills' (to quote Clausewitz once more), and so omits to address both parties to the fight. Cultural difference and even more linguistic ignorance can prevent the historian considering a battle in the round; so too can the availability of sources. Levels of literacy matter here, but so does cultural survival. Often these pressures can be congruent but they can also be divergent. Britain enjoys much higher levels of literacy than Afghanistan, but in 2002 the memory of the two countries' three wars flourished in the latter, thanks to an oral tradition, much more robustly than in the former, for whom literacy had created distance. And the historian who addresses cultural legacy is likely to face a much more challenging task the further in the past the battle occurred. The opportunity for invention and reinvention is simply greater the longer the lapse of time since the key event.

All historians of war must nonetheless, never forget that, however rich and splendid the cultural legacy of a great battle, it was won and lost by fighting, by killing and being killed. The battle of Waterloo has left as abundant a footprint as any, but the general who harvested most of its glory reflected on it in terms which have general applicability, and carry across time in their capacity to capture a universal truth. Wellington wrote to Lady Shelley in its immediate aftermath: 'I hope to God I have fought my last battle. It is a bad thing to be always fighting. While in the thick of it I am much too occupied to feel anything; but it is wretched just after. It is quite impossible to think of glory. Both mind and feelings are exhausted. I am wretched even at the moment of victory, and I always say that, next to a battle lost, the greatest misery is a battle gained.' Readers of this series should never forget the immediate suffering caused by battle, as well as the courage required to engage in it: the physical courage of the soldier, sailor or warrior, and the moral courage of the commander, ready to hazard all on its uncertain outcomes.

HEW STRACHAN

ACKNOWLEDGEMENTS

Let me begin with a confession. Though I write about armies and war, soldiers' writings and military memory, I am not, in the strict sense of the term, a military historian. But then battles are not only about tactics and strategy. They are part of European culture and have an afterlife in which they are woven into the narratives of the nations that fought in them. Waterloo was the battle that finally brought peace to Europe, that ended Napoleon's dreams of hegemony, and that went on to form a central plank in Britain's military identity during the Victorian era. There was so much of Waterloo that lay beyond the confines of the battlefield and which forms the central core of this book.

The path that leads to that battlefield is a well-trodden one, and I at once acknowledge my debt to those historians who have taken it before me. Studies of battlefield tactics are, of course, legion, and my debt to others here will be evident to any reader. I am indebted, too, to the valuable work of those who have published military memoirs of Waterloo or collected in anthologies the first-hand accounts of soldiers involved. They provide much of the raw material for this study.

Some of my fellow historians have had a more direct input, those friends and colleagues who have provided comments on the proposal or with whom I have had an opportunity to discuss the battle during the past months. In this country they include Michael Broers, Charles Esdaile, Philip Shaw, and Jeremy Black, who generously shared with me some of their expertise on the Napoleonic Wars and Waterloo, as well as Hew Strachan, the series editor, for his patience in nurturing the project. I have given lectures on the French memory of Waterloo in London, Southampton, and in Canberra; my thanks go to the organizing committee of Waterloo 200, to the Australian Army History Unit, and to the organizer of the Wellington Lecture, Chris Woolgar. I have also taken the opportunity to discuss drafts of various sections of the book in seminars at universities in London, Warwick, and St Andrews, which provided both lively discussion and valuable feedback: Michael Rowe, Guy Rowlands, and Mark Philp were kind and informative hosts. My thanks go, too, to Jordan Girardin who kindly let me read his master's thesis tracing Napoleon's march north from Antibes after his return from Elba.

I owe a special debt to those colleagues with whom I have worked on collaborative projects on war over the years, and in particular to Karen Hagemann and Étienne François with whom I edited a collective volume on *War Memories* in 2012. On the French response to Waterloo I have benefited from lengthy conversations with Thierry Lentz, Jacques Garnier, Jean-Marc Largeaud, Natalie Petiteau, and Jacques-Olivier Boudon. In Amsterdam and Paris Annie Jourdan has been a staunch ally and a source of invaluable expertise, both on the Napoleonic legend generally and on the memory of Waterloo in the Netherlands in particular. Lotte Jensen helped guide me through Dutch literary and artistic references to the battle, and Philippe Raxhon has shared some of his expertise on Belgian memory. Peter Hofschröer kindly drew my attention to relevant German sources on the battle and sent me copies of pertinent documents; we also walked part of the battlefield together. Geraint Thomas helped ensure that my coverage of Waterloo memories in the British Isles did not overlook Wales. Without all of them this book would be the poorer, besides being much less fun to write.

I have been fortunate, too, in being involved with the preparations for the Waterloo Bicentenary in 2015, both here in Britain, through engagement with the work of Waterloo 200, and in Belgium, where I have served on an international *comité scientifique* advising on the new museum and visitor centre at Waterloo. It has been a rewarding and invigorating experience. Yves Vander Cruysen shared his huge enthusiasm for Waterloo as well as his knowledge of the battle's resonance across the globe, and Philippe de Callatay was a superb guide to the riches of the Wellington Museum on Waterloo's high street. Thanks are also due to Alastair Massie at the National Army Museum in London, and to the staff of the British Library at Boston Spa. At Oxford University Press, Matthew Cotton has been the most encouraging and trusting of editors. I only hope that he can feel that a fraction of his trust has been rewarded.

The book is for Rosemary, who has had to live with both Napoleon and Waterloo for far too long, and is, as always, my first and most critical reader.

ALAN FORREST
York, August 2014

CONTENTS

LIST OF FIGURES

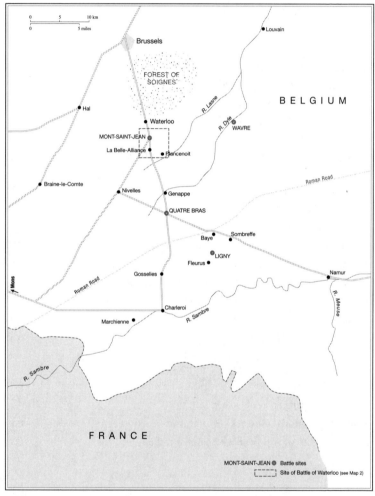

The Waterloo campaign: the main sites around the battlefield

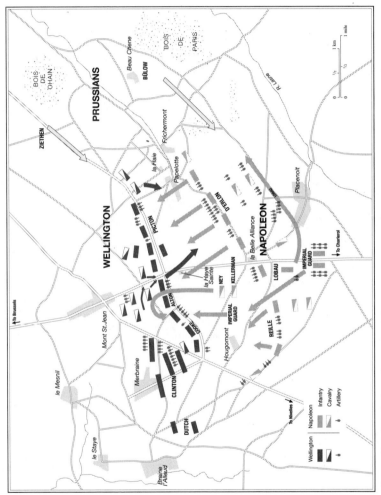

The Battle of Waterloo: the opposing armies

1

Introduction

The Battle of Waterloo led to Napoleon's second abdication and established the Duke of Wellington's reputation as one of the great British military commanders of the modern era.[1] It was also the last occasion on which Britain defeated France, her most persistent adversary over the centuries, in a major land war. But should Waterloo be considered a great battle from a military perspective? Wellington appeared to resist the triumphalist call in 1815 to turn Waterloo into a great military epic. He was unwilling to gloat on the morning after a struggle in which so many brave men, on both sides, had been killed, and when, amongst the British officers who had fallen, were men he had counted as his friends. He was dismissive of the many attempts to recount the battle as a single triumphant narrative. 'The history of the battle', he insisted, 'is not unlike the history of a ball! Some individuals may recollect all the little events of which the great result is the battle lost or won; but no individual can recollect the order in which, or the exact moment at which, they occurred, which makes all the difference as to their value or importance.'[2]

Waterloo was a murderous encounter, fought between a French army recruited after Napoleon's return from Elba and the Allied forces of Britain, Belgium, and the Netherlands, commanded by the newly ennobled Duke of Wellington, and of Prussia, under General Gebhard Leberecht von Blücher. Napoleon's army was necessarily more French in its composition than those he had commanded in recent campaigns, since the states that had been his allies before 1814 had either abandoned him or had rallied to the Allied side. But in military terms little had changed. The weaponry at Waterloo was little different from that of the mid-eighteenth century. Flintlock muskets were the principal firearm for both sides. The armies also fought with swords and fixed bayonets, and, of course, with cannon; Napoleon was an artillery officer who never forgot the value of field guns or the damage that could be inflicted by concentrated fire. There were modest numbers of rifles in the British army and in the Prussian units, and pistols and carbines—shorter and lighter than muskets—were used by the cavalry.[3] The soldiers still wore brightly coloured uniforms, easy to identify by friend and foe alike. Waterloo saw the clash of two eighteenth-century armies at war.

The armies of the Napoleonic era were considerably larger than in earlier wars, with much of continental Europe now using some form of conscription; but the greatest change was in the command structure and in the deployment of the troops on the battlefield. In the French army greater use was made of staff officers: by 1809 there were some twenty officers answering directly to the Emperor as well as several hundred serving Berthier, his chief of staff.[4] Waterloo evolved, however, rather differently from Napoleon's earlier battles like Jena and Austerlitz. Massed forces were deployed by both sides within a very limited space, a recipe for terrible losses and fearful casualty rates. In the end, Waterloo would be a victory for careful planning and defensive deployment, areas at which Wellington excelled. It was won by stolid resistance and courage in the face of concentrated fire, and, once the Prussians joined the combat, by vastly superior numbers.

It was not an easy victory for the Allied armies. Wellington famously wrote that 'it was the most desperate business I ever was in; I never took so much trouble about any Battle; and never was so near being Beat'.[5] The two sides may have been fairly evenly matched in terms of the quality, but once their armies merged the Allies enjoyed considerable numerical advantage. Strength numbers are necessarily somewhat imprecise and changed over the four days of the Waterloo campaign, but the Anglo-Dutch army of Wellington numbered some 95,000 men and Blücher's Prussians a further 124,000, giving a total of nearly 220,000 on the Allied side. Lined up against them were the 124,000 troops that Napoleon had been able to muster.[6] Neither army had been fully prepared for the campaign. Napoleon's troops had been raised hurriedly and in circumstances of some desperation; and the marshals at his disposal were not of the quality of those in his earlier campaigns. Wellington also complained about the troops that he was given to command, insisting, perhaps rather too dramatically, that he had 'got an infamous army, very weak and ill-equipped, and a very inexperienced staff'.[7] For much of the day the two armies slugged it out, inflicting terrible casualties and leaving the field strewn with corpses to be stripped and plundered in the cold light of the following morning. It was an experience that few who lived through it could recall without a shudder, a feat of endurance and a tribute to their courage and resolution. Even Wellington had trouble coming to terms with the scale of the destruction or the sacrifice of human life. 'Thank God,' he wrote on the day after Waterloo, 'I don't know what it's like to lose a battle; but certainly nothing can be more painful than to gain one with the loss of so many of one's friends.'[8] In later years he looked back on the battle with a shudder of regret, seeing it as 'a terrible battle' or 'a dreadful day'.[9]

It was, of course, a decisive victory, the battle that inflicted Napoleon's final defeat. Waterloo brought an end to a generation of war in which millions of soldiers had lost their lives, civil society had been undermined, and agriculture and industry across Europe had been disrupted to serve the war economy. The war had not been contained within Europe; it had spread to North Africa and the Near East, to North America and the Caribbean, to produce what the American historian David Bell has dubbed 'the first total war'.[10] In contrast, Waterloo heralded an era of relative peace among the Great Powers, an era that would only be broken in the Crimea in the 1850s. Britain, certainly, thought this worth celebrating, and those British regiments that had fought in the battle would regard it as one of their most glorious moments, to be treasured amongst their most cherished battle honours. But across Europe Waterloo's status was more

uncertain, its afterlife less assured. That afterlife is the major focus of
this book: the cultural history of the battle, its memory and commemoration, what Jenny Macleod has called, in the context of the Gallipoli
landings in the First World War, its 'heroic-romantic myth'.[11]

Britain was the country which most strongly identified with the
battle. The fact that Britain emerged from the conflict with its reputation enhanced and its world empire secured served to accentuate the
mood of triumphalism in London and around the country: Britain, in
a real sense, was the winner in the wars against Napoleon. There is
little reason to doubt the enthusiasm of the British public for Waterloo; there was throughout Britain a welling-up of patriotic sentiment
in the moment of victory. But that enthusiasm faded as unemployment rose and poverty set in, condemning many of those who
returned as heroes to long years of misery and idleness. Wellington
himself became a divisive figure who was more and more associated in
the public mind with the landowning elite and with a sectarian brand
of conservatism that showed little understanding of the needs or
interests of the industrial working class. He went on to have a prominent political career and to serve his country as prime minister in a
deeply conservative administration. For many, especially in the North,
he would prove a difficult man to forge into a national hero.

In any case, Britain already had its hero from the Napoleonic Wars,
an unambiguous figure on whom all could agree, in the person of
Horatio Nelson. It did not need Wellington, however much the British
government sought to gain kudos by associating with him, and
however much Wellington himself in his later years wished to play
on his historic role. Nelson was, for the English especially, a far more
authentic hero—a naval man, first and foremost, in a country which
had always looked to the navy as its principal line of defence in war;
an admiral who had won scintillating victories over the French at the
Nile and Trafalgar, victories that owed much to his bold tactical vision
and his willingness to take calculated risks; a hero who had lost an eye
in the service of his country and who was mortally wounded at
Trafalgar. Nelson was everything that a hero-figure should be—the

author Joseph Conrad wrote that he 'brought heroism into the line of duty'[12]—and, like Napoleon, he had devoted a great deal of time and energy to the kind of self-publicity that established his reputation in the public eye. Since the time of the Spanish Armada, the Royal Navy had been held in higher esteem by the British public than the army, and it seemed only fitting that the country's hero should be a naval man from Norfolk, one of the heartlands of the country's seafaring tradition. Arthur Wellesley, born in 1769 at Dangan Castle in County Meath and a scion of an Anglo-Irish noble family, might seem poorly equipped to compete.[13]

Though Britain would claim it as an archetypically British victory, epitomized by the unflinching courage of the troops under fire, there were more foreign soldiers in the Allied army—Dutch, Belgians, and especially Germans—than there were men of British stock. The British army had not, of course, been affected by France's revolutionary ideology and was still a traditional eighteenth-century army, its officers largely drawn from the landowning gentry, its regiments recruited on a regional basis across the country, with the Celtic fringes of Scotland and Ireland especially heavily represented. It also continued to employ foreign troops in substantial numbers, in particular German soldiers who were seen as specialists in light cavalry and skirmishing tactics. The King's German Legion (customarily abbreviated to the KGL), formed largely of men from George III's Hanoverian possessions, contributed as many as 30,000 troops to the British war effort, most of whom were recruited after the French occupation in 1803 which forced the dissolution of the previously independent Hanoverian army.[14] Though Peter Hofschröer may exaggerate when he talks of the Waterloo campaign as a 'German victory', there is no denying that the German part in it was very considerable.[15]

Yet Waterloo figures surprisingly little in German memory of the Napoleonic Wars, where it was discussed simply as the final battle of a long campaign in which Blücher and his army played a defining role. That they had done there is no reason to doubt. The arrival of the Prussians on the battlefield in the afternoon of the conflict proved decisive, providing much-needed reinforcements and the benefit of fresh legs at a time when the British forces were visibly tiring. Moreover, it was the agreement reached by Wellington and Blücher on the eve of the battle, and the Prussian general's promise to send his army into action, which enabled Wellington to plan his defensive tactics. The relatively low-key celebrations in Berlin and the modest place accorded to Waterloo in German war memory may therefore seem surprising. Blücher himself, of course, was widely commemorated, but the praise that was lavished upon 'General Vorwaerts' (literally 'General Forwards') was less for his leadership in 1815 than for his role two years previously in the Battle of the Nations at Leipzig. In German eyes, Leipzig was the really significant encounter, the moment which signalled Napoleon's defeat. It had a unique place in German nationalist mythology, as the moment when German kings and princes rallied to the side of Prussia in a united effort to free Germany from Napoleon's tyranny. In truth, those who fought in the battle—and there were 175,000 on the Allied side alone—fought for their states and princes rather than for any broader concept of Germany, but that mattered little. Leipzig, not Waterloo, would remain the vital battle for Germany and for Europe.[16]

For France, too, the memory of Waterloo would be an ambiguous one. Countries have little reason to commemorate national defeats, far less to celebrate them. And Waterloo was undeniably a defeat, the defeat of a regime and an imperial ambition as well as of French arms. For most Frenchmen, however, it was not the turning point of the Napoleonic Wars. That had come earlier, in the Peninsular War, during the Russian campaign, or at Leipzig. The war was already lost with the 1814 campaign and the surrender of Paris; Napoleon had abdicated and been exiled to Elba; the Bourbons had returned to the throne; and the European order had been restored at the Congress of Vienna. The Hundred Days had come as a sudden—and, for some, very unwelcome—surprise, raising once again the spectre of war, conscription, and renewed fighting. Even in the army, where Napoleon's support was strongest, not all had been pleased to welcome their Emperor's return. Many saw Waterloo as an unnecessary battle, born of Napoleon's refusal to accept that his Empire was finished or to understand that the rest of Europe would not choose peace while he was still at large.

In the longer term, however, Waterloo did little to damage Napoleon's reputation or his appeal to future generations. His daring escape from Elba captured the nineteenth-century imagination, and there was in his indomitable dreams and ambitions something of the heroic that appealed to artists and poets and which came to epitomize the Romantic age. If Waterloo was a defeat, it was a heroic defeat, a desperate throw of the dice by a beleaguered Emperor. Napoleon, not Wellington, was the central figure in this drama, and he would remain so for the successive generations of tourists who have visited the battlefield over the years. Not all these visitors were French. They flocked from all over Europe to look out over a battlefield that was curiously civilized and accessible, and most chose to view it as Napoleon had done, from the ridge from which he had surveyed his legions. Even British writers could not refrain from expressing a grudging admiration for the man whose dreams lay shattered on the Belgian turf. As a heroic defeat Waterloo haunted their poetic imagination and helped to shape Napoleon's legend across the nineteenth century.[17]

2

From Vienna to Waterloo

The Revolutionary and Napoleonic Wars, which had engulfed most of Europe and a large part of the colonial world and had left the armies of Europe exhausted, formally ended on 31 March 1814 as the Allied troops finally closed in on Paris. Napoleon himself was in no mood to surrender, yet two days earlier, in a powerfully symbolic gesture, he had ordered the Empress to leave the capital and take his son to a place of safety. They went first to his palace at Rambouillet, to the south of the city, and continued from there to Blois in the Loire valley, before leaving France altogether for the relative security of the Austrian court.[1] The move was seen as seriously weakening the Emperor's negotiating hand, and it was the moment when his marshals took the executive decision to offer no further resistance. Back in Paris Marmont, who had been defending the city from the heights of Montmartre, surrendered the capital and agreed to an armistice, even marching his troops over to join the other side in case Napoleon tried to countermand his orders. It was the same story across the French provinces. In Lyons, Augereau abandoned his headquarters to the advancing Allies. Bordeaux had already fallen: on 12 March Mayor Lynch had handed the keys of the city to the royalists and the city declared for Louis XVIII. In the opinion of Napoleon's commanders, he had little choice but to lay down his arms. Paris had been left exposed, without fortifications, and to have carried on fighting would have incurred huge civilian losses and the likelihood that much of the city would be left shattered and in ruins. Napoleon himself took little part in the decision to surrender; even as Marmont acted, he was waiting near Fontainebleau with an army of 60,000 men and appeared intent on fighting on. But those of his marshals who were with him at Fontainebleau, among them close advisers such as Ney, Oudinot, and Macdonald, were of one mind, refusing to march on the capital or to risk firing on Parisians. The *Campagne de France*, the rearguard action to defend French territory from invasion, was, as far as they were concerned, over, and with it the war was lost.

In truth, the 1814 campaign was not one that Napoleon could realistically have hoped to win following the debacle he had suffered at Leipzig the previous year. By early February his position had seemed desperate, with enemy armies occupying French territory and poised to attack Paris. But he recovered something of his youthful flair, and from the middle of the month his army suddenly seemed stronger, administering a series of minor reverses on the Prussians which culminated in the defeat of their advance guard at Craonne. But his troops were raw, inexperienced, and weary, and increasingly he found himself fighting a rearguard action, dependent on the successes of others (Davout in Hamburg and Soult in southern France) and on the intervention of local peasant partisans who took up arms to disrupt the Allied advance. Further encounters in March ended in defeat, and, still worse from his point of view, his tactical plans fell into Prussian hands. It was this that finally persuaded the Allies to advance directly on Paris and that helped persuade the French marshals that the war was irreversibly lost.[2] The political leadership agreed, and on 2 April the Senate presented Napoleon with a fait accompli, proclaiming the Emperor formally deposed and inviting Louis XVIII to ascend to the throne. The French political class was prepared to work with a Bourbon restoration; it only remained for the victorious Allied powers to decide on the terms of a peace settlement that would be acceptable to the rest of Europe.

Napoleon had fought on in the expectation that he would be able to negotiate from a position of strength, and so to improve on the terms that had already been proposed to him at Frankfurt before he embarked on the *Campagne de France*, but by refusing to make peace

Figure 1. Delaroche,
Napoleon 1814

when it had been offered, he had effectively passed the initiative to his opponents. In the negotiations that were opened at Châtillon in early February the Allies had still showed themselves divided, with Russia taking an increasingly hard line towards France while Austria, and Metternich in particular, seemed willing to make serious concessions and to negotiate with Napoleon as a future European partner. But Napoleon's intransigence and the continuation of the war made such generous terms less and less likely. The Emperor showed an increasing lack of realism over the peace terms he could hope to achieve: as late as mid-March he was still talking of natural boundaries, of the River Scheldt as France's northern frontier, and of establishing a regency for the Empress until his son reached the age of majority, terms which his opponents were determined not to concede.[3] By then, the Tsar was convinced that there could be no lasting peace with Napoleon still in power: he had to be seen to have been defeated, Alexander insisted, before France could be offered any settlement. The Allies allowed themselves to be persuaded; indeed, it was principally to accommodate Alexander and to prevent the Austrians from making a separate peace that the leaders agreed to move the peace talks to Paris. At Chaumont in March 1814 they took the decision that would help determine the shape of the post-war world: binding them to a new alliance, providing the subsidy for another year's war if it proved necessary, and committing them jointly to maintain the peace of Europe for the next twenty years. With this agreement the Congress System was born, and months of protracted negotiations began over the detail of the treaty settlement as it would affect all the warring parties.[4]

Congress Europe

The settlement reached in the months that followed would push France's boundaries back to those of 1 November 1792 and would reimpose Bourbon rule, a legitimist restoration that suited the Allies more than it satisfied the French people. There would be no Napoleonic restoration, no acceptance of the Empire, no admission that Napoleon's son might succeed to the throne. What mattered was that Napoleon must be removed from France and from political power for ever. On 6 April he apparently accepted his fate, signing a letter of abdication in return for a number of somewhat nominal concessions: he was allowed to keep his imperial title, was given sovereignty over the tiny island of Elba, and was to be paid an annual income of 2 million francs by the French government. Honour, it was felt, had been preserved, and the threat to European peace which Napoleon had presented had been finally removed. A fortnight later, on 20 April, he left Fontainebleau for the Mediterranean port of Fréjus, from where, on a British ship, he sailed to his new kingdom, and on 3 May Louis XVIII made his state entry into Paris. Napoleon's departure provoked no resistance and provided cartoonists, in France and across Europe, with a field day. The Emperor was spared no indignities. One caricature showed him with his former chancellor as they were led to the quayside, Napoleon parodied for the miseries he had piled on his people, Cambacérès mocked for his gluttony and homosexuality.[5] In another, the journey to Elba evoked episodes from Napoleon's past career and the flaws in his character that explained them: pride, ambition, and cowardice (the last of these illustrated by his flight home from the Russian campaign).[6] The Continent, it seemed, could breathe a collective sigh of relief, and from Madrid to Moscow Europeans slept more soundly in their beds, secure in the knowledge that the man they equated with the insatiable pursuit of war was finally out of harm's way. The imperial era, they assured themselves, was over.

The diplomatic niceties, on the other hand, remained to be completed. Napoleon was already on Elba when the political leaders finally signed the Treaty of Paris on 30 May 1814 that restored peace across most of Europe. France was forced to give up the major part of the territory she had conquered, renouncing her claims to land in Holland, Belgium, Switzerland, Italy, and Germany, and to guarantee the free movement of people and goods on the River Rhine. On the other hand, there were to be no reparations; the majority of France's overseas colonies were handed back; and the French were to keep the artworks which Napoleon had collected across Europe for the Louvre. Thanks in large measure to Talleyrand's diplomacy, France was to be included in the new balance of power and—under the restored monarchy—would be treated as a responsible member of the new European order. Britain, true to her traditional foreign-policy interests, insisted that the French should be kept out of the Low Countries, and obtained the strengthening of Holland through a union with Belgium, with the expanded Dutch state to be ruled by the House of Orange. And by securing Malta, the Cape Province, Mauritius, and a couple of Caribbean islands, Britain made sure that she had strategic control of the Mediterranean and the sea routes to the East and West Indies.[7] The Allies also agreed to a federal union of the various independent states in Germany, guaranteed the independence of Switzerland, and resolved some territorial disputes in Italy. Other issues remained unsettled—notably the future shape of Poland and Saxony—and these were deferred for further debate at Vienna, where the powers agreed to reconvene in October. They would still be conferring well into 1815.[8]

Napoleon and War

The fear of Napoleon and of his unquenchable ambition was, of course, well founded. Since 1805 he had launched campaign after campaign against the other powers of Europe and put millions of men into the field in an attempt to control the Continent from Portugal in the west to Russia in the east. But it was not just the scale of his ambition that intimidated others; it was also his skill as a military leader and the loyalty he was able to inspire in his troops. Napoleon had shown himself to be a consummate field commander who was compared by contemporaries to Frederick the Great and to the great generals of classical antiquity. He planned his campaigns carefully, taking note of the lie of the land, taking advice about the weather, and seeking to ensure that in any open battle he held the higher ground and had the larger force at his command. But if he was meticulous in his planning, he refused to be rule-bound. He under-stood the importance of intuition, and did not hesitate to make bold tactical decisions that could turn circumstance to his advantage; indeed, one of his greatest gifts as a general lay in an intuitive ability to read a battle and to adjust his tactics as it raged around him. Not everything could be planned in advance: it was his boast that war was a series of accidents from which it was a commander's duty to extract maximum profit. 'In common parlance it would be called good fortune,' he claimed in conversation with Las Cases, 'yet it is a fortune that is the prerogative of genius.'[9] It was a genius encapsulated in the dazzling succession of victories he had won in his early years as a revolutionary general in Italy, and then as First Consul and Emperor, at Ulm, Austerlitz, and Jena. It was in these years, which culminated at Tilsit in 1807, that he established his reputation as one of the greatest military leaders of all time, the reputation that inspired his soldiers and intoxicated a generation of poets and novelists. 'I feel', wrote Stendhal in 1837, 'a sort of religious sentiment as I write the first sentence of the history of Napoleon, for this was the greatest man to have graced the world since Caesar.'[10]

The rest of Europe had been held in thrall by his strategic mastery of warfare and by his emphasis on fluid movement and rapid strike power. David Chandler notes that 'unlike his eighteenth-century forebears, who rigidly distinguished between manoeuvring and giving battle, adopting different formations for each activity, Napoleon fused marching, fighting and pursuing into one continuous and devastating process'.[11] He also developed his staff system and in 1803, while the Grande Armée was still being assembled at Boulogne, he replaced the divisional structure he inherited with a new system of army corps to give his commanders a greater flexibility in the field. The corps brought units of all three arms—infantry, cavalry, and artillery—under a single administration, each with its own état-major, which allowed for speed of movement and greater autonomy. Each corps consisted of two or three infantry divisions together with artillery (two batteries of six artillery-guns and one of eight), a brigade of light horse, and its supply train. It was relatively simple to assemble on the battlefield, afforded a welcome rapidity of movement, and made it possible to extend over a larger frontage, which in turn facilitated any move to outflank and encircle the enemy. In Jean Tulard's phrase, the corps formed 'an army in miniature' and was symptomatic of Napoleon's skill in military innovation and tactical deployment.[12]

Yet, most of his victorious campaigns were long past by 1814, and neither the army he commanded nor Napoleon's own health and physical resilience were what they had once been. The years from 1805 to 1808 had represented the zenith of his military conquests, and since then his reputation as a field commander had taken something of a battering—against the Archduke Charles at Aspern-Essling in 1809 (the first battle in which he had suffered personal defeat in over a decade), in the Peninsular War (though there the bulk of the fighting had been left to his marshals), in the Russian campaign, at Leipzig, and now on the soil of France itself. Those who pointed to his incisive judgement in the field and who argued that his influence could change the course of a battle still took their inspiration from Austerlitz or Jena—especially Jena, where he had won decisively, and in the process both destroyed the Prussian army and drawn full political advantage from his victory. Later campaigns produced less total victories. Napoleon's enemies had come to learn from past mistakes and had adapted their tactics to mount more effective opposition to his attacks; they increasingly coped with the French corps system on the battlefield and learned to take on the main French field army and win.[13] This both increased their confidence and damaged that of Napoleon's armies, for after the retreat from Moscow in 1812 his soldiers could no longer comfort themselves with the feeling that they were invulnerable. They could not trust that Napoleon would lead them to victory or to save their lives in battle, and this undoubtedly had a significant effect on the army's morale.

Figure 2. *Buonaparte at Rome giving Audience in State Ick.* By Cruikshank, Isaac, 1756–1811, printmaker

The composition of the army, too, had changed following the slaughter of the Russian campaign. The armies Napoleon led to Leipzig in 1813 and in the *Campagne de France* the following year were young armies, composed mainly of conscripts, and were increasingly recruited from the 130 departments of Greater France, with the numbers of foreign troops severely reduced. In part this had to do with the defection of Napoleon's erstwhile allies, but it was also a matter of conscious policy, since from April 1813, the number of foreigners was fixed by decree at 36,000.[14] The army suffered in comparison with its predecessors in other ways, too. Many of the officers had had to be replaced, as many of the eighteen marshals and 370 brigadier generals who had accompanied Napoleon to Moscow had not returned. If they were not lacking in courage, they were short of the battle experience which had characterized the previous generation of officers. Many of the soldiers, too, had no previous experience of war. They were too young, their bodies too unformed, to make resilient troops. Discussing the quality of the new army which Napoleon recruited for Leipzig, Digby Smith explains that

> The strength and physical stamina of the young conscripts, and consequently the quality of their regiments, left much to be desired; they could not march like the veterans, fell easy prey to sickness, and the standard of their training when they left the depots in the spring of 1813 was frighteningly low. The ability of battalions to manoeuvre was poor, and many recruits could not even load their muskets. When the reinforcement drafts marched to the front, carts had to follow to pick up the footsore and the exhausted.[15]

The artillery was excellent—a remarkable feat given the huge scale of the losses incurred in the previous year—but the army now lacked high-quality cavalry, while after the losses of the Russian campaign even the Imperial Guard emerged diminished.[16] By the end of the Empire the troops available to Napoleon could not compare with the best of his earlier campaigns.

Napoleon himself—increasingly overweight, often ill and tired when on campaign, needing longer periods of rest, and showing the first signs of the duodenal cancer that would finally kill him—was not the incisive commander he had been in his younger days. He was slower and more lumbering in his reactions; he forgot to secure his communications; and he failed to delegate sufficiently to others. And when he did rely on his marshals, he often found them wanting. The marshals of 1813 and 1814 did not always show the same military insight as those of his earlier campaigns; too often they had been promoted for their loyalty rather than their talent, and Napoleon has been criticized for failing to bring on others or to develop the talents in those around him.[17] For all Ney's fearlessness in attack, he could not match the speed of movement or tactical mastery that had been shown by Morand or especially Davout at Jena in 1806, the qualities which had helped make Napoleon's armies so formidable in the past.[18] In short, though he would never admit it, he was beginning to make mistakes. But that did not mean that he was no longer trusted by his army, or that the sight of him at the head of his troops did not continue to inspire fear in the ranks of opposing armies. Wellington, who had faced him in the Peninsula and would defeat him at Waterloo, continued to show respect for Napoleon as a military leader long after the war was over, and would famously declare in conversation with the Earl of Stanhope that 'his presence on the field made the difference of forty thousand men'.[19] In 1814, his name had lost nothing of its power to inspire fear or to conjure up images of war stretching into a limitless future, and the leaders of Congress Europe were determined to preclude any possibility of his return to power. By banishing him from mainland Europe to what they saw as an inconsequential island in the Mediterranean they confidently believed that they had removed a major threat to peace, which would allow them to reorder the political map of Europe and build a solid and lasting balance of power.[20]

Escape from Elba

They could not, of course, have foreseen the next stage in the drama as it unfolded. Indeed, the other leaders seem almost to have forgotten Napoleon after he had embarked for Portoferraio, as they turned to the more important diplomatic questions about the terms they would impose on France and the future boundaries of Europe. Elba seemed reassuringly remote, a small island from where Napoleon, now ensconced with his entourage in his official residence at the Palazzina dei Mulini, would cause them little trouble. He was not a prisoner: he was still a head of state, ruling his island empire with a ten-man council of state, and was allowed free access to the outside world (though both the Empress and his young son were expressly forbidden from visiting him on Elba). He had friends and collaborators on the island in the persons of Cambronne, Drouot, and Bertrand, three of his most loyal officers who volunteered to come with him from France. Indeed, life in Portoferraio was punctuated by the comings and goings of friends and associates, not least by members of the Bonaparte clan, and tedium was relieved by a succession of balls and receptions. He was also allowed to maintain a tiny army and navy with which to guarantee the island's defence. But they, like his imperial household, were sadly diminished in size and importance, and they provided rich material for humorists and caricaturists, both in Britain and France, eager to pour scorn on the pretensions of the King of Elba. With his limited resources there was little he could do to offer defensive capability in the event of an attack from outside; and though he could raise a certain amount of extra revenue by imposing local taxes on vineyards, olive groves, and quarries, it was difficult to imagine that this army and navy were more than an extension of his domestic establishment, part of the ceremonial of court life.

But the seasoned observer would have noticed something more, something that was arguably more worrying. Napoleon devoted himself to the tasks of running his island with an astonishing energy and commitment, and, with the help of the loyal officers and soldiers sent out from France in accordance with the terms of the abdication treaty, he set about building and training his tiny forces. He had, it seemed, lost nothing of his concern for detail, none of the working habits he had developed during the years of Empire. As Sir Walter Scott wrote, perspicaciously, a few years later, 'he was like a thoroughbred gamester who, deprived of the means of depositing large stakes, will rather play at small game than leave the table'.[21]

What onlookers perhaps failed to spot, though, in this most impatient of men, was the boredom that soon afflicted him on Elba. He knew a great deal about what was happening on the Continent and he followed the news of the day, while his extended family and his small navy accorded him regular communication with the mainland, both with France and with southern Italy. Napoleon, it should be emphasized, still felt vulnerable to attack during his early months on Elba: he did not trust the Allies to honour their promises, and his worries about money grew as the pension that was due to him from Louis XVIII failed to arrive (a failure that was in flagrant contravention of his treaty obligations).[22] But, more than that, he felt ennui and resentment at his fate, a sense that he still had his destiny to fulfil. He had not lost interest in the politics of the Continent to which he dreamed to return, and he watched out eagerly for any signs of unrest which he might exploit. He noted, for instance, with growing interest and increasing relish the popular ferment in Italy, the anger and disquiet in the ranks of the French army, and the increasing unpopularity of the Bourbons amongst the French population at large. He kept in contact with those of his marshals and former ministers who had served him loyally and had not defected to the King—men like Maret, Davout, and Thibaudeau—through whom he gained intelligence about Parisian opinion and collected news of Bonapartist circles in Paris.[23] And even as his enemies comforted themselves with the thought that he had been rejected by his people, Napoleon planned his next steps with the same extraordinary concern for detail that had characterized his earlier military campaigns.

Everything was prepared in secrecy. He ordered a ship to be made ready, disguised as an English merchantman and loaded with enough supplies to feed his army on a ten-day voyage. Then, on the designated day, he put on dress uniform, complete with the Legion of Honour and the Iron Crown of Italy, and buckled on the sword he had worn at Austerlitz; he attended morning mass in the town church before reviewing the National Guard on the main square. Having satisfied himself that the coast was clear, he ordered his troops to change into battledress. At the appointed hour, cheered by a large crowd of islanders, a small flotilla of boats left harbour, carrying Napoleon, his personal staff, and his army, consisting of around a thousand soldiers—the Guard, the Polish lancers, and his Corsican battalion— along with forty horses and four cannon. His intentions he kept shrouded in mystery, with some observers concluding that he was headed for Italy to join forces with Murat. But his real destination was France, and with a measure of good luck and the assistance of the winds, he was not intercepted by either the French or the British navies during the crossing. Within days of leaving Elba on 26 February he and his tiny army made land at the Gulf of Juan, near the town of Antibes on the south coast of France. There he disembarked his tiny army and set out on that most improbable of missions, to march on Paris and reclaim his throne.[24]

Paris, of course, was thoroughly alarmed by the news of his escape; the Bourbon Restoration had been established for only a few months and the government was aware that it had alienated many of its subjects, not least in the army. Napoleon was seen by the Bourbons as an escaped prisoner, an outlaw to be hunted down, who had surfaced, armed, on the soil of France. The prefects of the departments along the Mediterranean coast received instructions to keep the coast-line under close surveillance, and an order was put out for his capture. A royal decree of 8 March accused Bonaparte of leading an armed insurrection and threatening to plunge France into civil war, and called for him to be arrested for treason and put on trial by a military court.[25] Napoleon, of course, projected a different version of recent history, claiming that in his exile he had listened to the complaints and woes of his people and that he had returned to lead them again. 'I come back among you', he famously proclaimed, 'to resume my rights, which are also yours.'[26] The man who had ruled France as an emperor wrapped in the symbolism of monarchy now presented himself to his people as a son of the Revolution, determined to liberate them from the tyranny of kings, and portraying the Bourbons as traitors who had been placed on the throne at the whim of France's enemies. He transformed his public image and appealed to the troops who had followed him across Europe to abandon Louis XVIII and follow him, once again, to the ends of the earth. He was one of them, a man who had risen on the basis of talent, who knew how to share their joys and their pain, and who was seemingly unconcerned with the luxury of office. As he strolled among his soldiers at the Gulf of Juan, Napoleon had already adopted the persona of the 'little corporal' which would become such an important part of his appeal and of the romantic legend that would continue to inspire future generations of Frenchmen, not least in the oral political culture of village and small-town France.[27]

The improbable story of Napoleon's march northwards, avoiding towns and cities in the first hours, then appearing more openly along the highways and passing through peasant communities, is the stuff of fantasy.[28] As they advanced across the French countryside the band of soldiers encountered little resistance, and if the reception they were given was often guarded, driven by curiosity rather than enthusiasm, they met with little opposition. There was no need for an armed struggle, or for French blood to be shed. National Guard units came out to welcome them, and some of the soldiers sent from their barracks to stop them joined forces with them instead. Along the route he was cheered by well-wishers and was joined by veterans of his previous campaigns. Of course, this was not achieved by chance; if the plan succeeded, it was because it had been prepared in advance, and Napoleon was careful to avoid known pockets of royalism where he would have met with serious resistance. But even he must have felt cheered by the warmth of the welcome that greeted him the further north he rode, by the realization that his charisma still counted for something amongst his former troops. As he marched northwards thousands of his former soldiers came to join him, his little army swelling as it passed through the foothills of the Alps, through Dauphiné, Burgundy, and on towards Paris. At Grenoble he was feted by his supporters in their thousands, in Lyons by city fathers and silk workers alike; indeed, it was when he passed through Lyons that General Macdonald finally realized that he could no longer rely on the loyalty of his troops and bowed to the inevitable.[29] Even men who had sworn loyalty to Louis XVIII a few months earlier—most famously, of course, the unfortunate Marshal Ney, who had sworn to the King that he would bring the Eagle back to Paris in an iron cage— now returned to their Emperor's side, with, in Ney's case, fatal consequences. By the time Napoleon was at Auxerre, his last stop before the capital, his tiny force had been transformed into an army of 14,000 men. Remarkably they had arrived there without encountering any armed resistance: the one scuffle had been at Montereau where the 6th Lancers had seized a vital bridge that crossed the Yonne and the Seine, and even that had been secured without loss of life.[30] The only signs of opposition had come when his troops tried to find food and fodder on neighbouring farms; no preparations had been made, no advance warning given, and in such circumstances no army could have expected to be received with open arms.

The march north was fast turning into a triumphal procession. Yet many of the army officers who had sworn loyalty to Louis XVIII faced a difficult decision, and the Emperor's return elicited unease rather than joy. In his journal Lieutenant Henckens, a Dutch officer in French service, relates how his cavalry regiment responded to the conflict of loyalties which it posed. His commanding officer, Colonel de Talhouet, was of a Norman noble family, and clearly had his opinions and his sense of honour. Talhouet lined up his troops in battle order, called the officers to the front and addressed them, explaining that a new political order had been established and that they would have to respond. He himself, he said, was in poor health and would therefore have to resign, but he urged them to respond as soldiers: 'I am asking you to take your places in the column that will join the Emperor now that he has been proclaimed, and always to maintain the honour of the corps.' But his illness was diplomatic, as he explained to Henckens in private. He was not, he said, a 'chameleon'; and he felt obliged to resign; he would not fight for Napoleon, but he would not fight against him, either. But 'as for the others, he thought that they should follow the mood of the moment'. The author felt that he had no choice but to agree, and he duly joined the troops who rallied to the Emperor. He did so, he tells us, reluctantly. Even when Napoleon addressed them, he notes that 'our enthusiasm was very relative'.[31]

As Napoleon approached Paris, he learned that the King had fled during the night, safeguarding his personal wealth by sending a valet ahead of him carrying the crown jewels and around 4 million francs in gold.[32] Louis's destination had originally been England, but he changed his plan when he was persuaded that it would be politically imprudent, since seeking protection from France's most determined adversary would seriously damage his reputation at home. He therefore headed for Belgium instead. In this way he arrived in Ghent, accompanied by troops from his personal guard, the *Maison Militaire*, but openly scorned by many of his own subjects who did not hesitate to accuse him of cowardice. It was hardly an auspicious start for the Restoration monarchy: the government was left in a state of confusion and Paris was abandoned as the King's army simply melted away, with soldiers deserting and unit after unit defecting to the Emperor. Louis commanded little loyalty among his own troops, and their commanders took the prudent decision to offer no resistance. There was now nothing to stop Napoleon's advance on the capital. He rode on through the night, escorted by a troop of a hundred cavalrymen, and arriving at Fontainebleau at five o'clock on the morning of 20 March. It was a symbolic moment as he dismounted in the courtyard of the palace, eleven months to the day since he had left from the same courtyard on his journey to exile on Elba. By nightfall he was back in

Paris, receiving guests at the Tuileries and already planning the liberal empire that would be the next phase of his imperial project.

The Hundred Days

Despite the best efforts of the Bourbons and their legitimist supporters, political reaction to Napoleon's return was surprisingly muted. If there were pockets of royalism in the south—in the Rhône valley, for instance, in the Gironde or in Corsica—they were limited in scope, and none of them held out for more than a few weeks. More serious was the threat of a renewed outbreak of civil war in the west, in those communities which had risen against the Republic in 1793, where the King sent the Duc de Bourbon to raise troops for a new royalist army; here the next three months would be marked by recurrent violence between royalists and republicans or Bonapartists which the military had to be called in to repress. But these remained isolated risings, relatively contained outbursts of Catholic, royalist, or counter-revolutionary sentiment which ultimately posed little threat to Napoleon. Even many of his supporters would admit that the success of his exploit was little short of miraculous. He had escaped from his island prison with a tiny army and had seized power without spilling a drop of blood. He had done so, too, without the aid of the mass of the population. There had been no popular insurrection, no violent overthrow of the royalist regime; this was a coup that had been achieved primarily with the support of the army, of those soldiers who had felt poorly rewarded by the Restoration monarchy and who looked again to Napoleon to restore what they regarded as their rights.[33] Now all that remained was for him to consolidate his power in France and with the French people, and recreate the institutions which the restoration of the Bourbons had destroyed. But to do that he needed his regime to be recognized by the rest of Europe, and that would have required a colossal loss of nerve by the leaders, still assembled at Vienna, who eleven months before had insisted on his exile. If his flight had represented something of a miracle, it would be as nothing compared to the challenges that lay ahead.

The first part of the challenge proved the easier to accomplish. Napoleon lost no time in burnishing his new image as a man of the people, a democrat in the tradition of 1789 who had been wronged by foreign tyrants and British treason, a man in whom liberals and former revolutionaries could place their trust. He no longer presented himself as a powerful emperor who bestrode a continent, as the man who had dined with kings and commanded respect from the crowned heads of Europe, nor yet as an autocratic ruler who had whittled away popular liberties, imposed conscription, and reinforced the authority of the state. He talked of a liberal empire in which the constitutional rights of the people would be respected. He offered wider voting rights to his people and emphasized his hatred of feudalism and hereditary privilege, banishing those émigré nobles who had flocked back with the Bourbons and expropriating their estates for the benefit of the nation. He shared legislative authority with two chambers, an upper house of hereditary peers whom he nominated, and a lower house of deputies who were to be elected indirectly through a two-tier process. He took steps to win over Catholic opinion by permitting the return of priests from emigration, though he fell short of returning the lands which the Church had lost during the Revolution. And he restored one of the most treasured institutions of his earlier period of power, the Legion of Honour, which did much to strengthen the pride and self-belief of the army, while at the same time he placed military values at the very heart of civil society. In short, though he remained loyal to many of the principles that had guided the governance of the Empire, he offered the French people a different polity and a different image from those which he had fostered during the years of imperial pomp.[34] He gave the impression that he shared the revolutionaries' hatred of noble and clerical privilege. But did he believe it, or was it born of sheer opportunism? He had certainly taken note of its populist potential, remarking that 'Nothing has surprised me more on returning to France than this hatred of priests and the nobility which I find as universal and as violent as it was at the beginning of the Revolution.'[35]

Return to War

Winning over the European leaders assembled at the Congress of Vienna proved a far more daunting challenge. Though they had worked painstakingly throughout the winter on a number of unresolved diplomatic issues—the most intractable of these concerned Poland and Saxony[36]—and though they had frequently shown an irritating lack of resolve and unity, the news of Napoleon's return shocked them to the marrow and may even have given them new vigour and sense of purpose. At first, it is clear, they did not believe what they were hearing; there are reports that the news of Napoleon's supposed escape was greeted with laughter, as though it were a joke, a witty fabrication to leaven the atmosphere.[37] But when it sank in that Napoleon was really free and had returned to mainland Europe, they showed unexpected unity and determination. There could be no compromise with a man they now denigrated as a usurper; they all understood the import of his *coup d'état*, and however little the individual leaders might sympathize with Louis XVIII and his legitimist ambitions, they could not allow the peace which they had so laboriously worked for to be put in jeopardy. The texts of Napoleon's appeals to his people made it clear that he understood the inevitability of war, and he made no secret of his desire to take revenge on those who had humiliated him a year previously, appealing to his former soldiers to join him once more in the pursuit of glory, and trying to inveigle Murat in Naples to join him in a fresh act of war against the new European order. On this occasion the Allies acted quickly: on 13 March they declared him to be an outlaw; and twelve days later they renewed their alliance to overthrow him. There were few dissident voices among them, though again the Tsar would prove to be Napoleon's most implacable foe, and once the British government had agreed to provide subsidies for the war effort, the die was effectively cast. All Napoleon's assurances that he wanted to live at peace with his neighbours were brushed aside as the worthless lies they undoubtedly were, and even as the diplomats were concluding their deliberations in Vienna, the armies of the principal European powers were again assembling for a final confrontation with France.[38] The four Great Powers—Russia, Prussia, Austria, and Britain—each pledged to put 150,000 men in the field and to keep them under arms until Napoleon was no longer in a position to disturb the peace of Europe.[39] Of the four, only Britain was incapable of providing this number, and for that reason was allowed by the other powers to make up her share with subsidies in gold.[40]

Britain did, however, provide the commander for the Allied forces in the person of the Duke of Wellington, who had attracted widespread praise for his successful campaign against the French in the Peninsular War and who in 1814 was transferred into the diplomatic service as British ambassador in Paris. Though he could have stayed on there during the months that followed, contributing to the work of the Congress of Vienna, he opted to return to the military to take command of the British army in the Netherlands with the aim of blocking any French expansion. As he had in Portugal, Wellington commanded what was in essence an expeditionary force with limited numbers of troops, since many of the men who had fought under him in Spain had since been moved to North America to fight in the War of 1812. He was left with relatively young and inexperienced recruits and an army with a high proportion of Dutch and Hanoverian troops under his command. He had to work closely with the other Allied governments, most especially the Prussians, if he was to construct a force capable of resisting Napoleon. Wellington fully understood the size of the task he faced, since the Netherlands was where Napoleon was likely to strike. He had left Vienna with the words of the Tsar ringing in his ears: 'It is for you to save the world again.'[41]

Though constructing the new alliance against Napoleon was complicated by internal dissensions among the Allies and power struggles over who would take ultimate command of their army, they lost no speed in mobilizing their forces. Indeed, even before they had voted Napoleon's outlawry the major powers had begun to plan military action, so that by 12 March Wellington could report that they planned to mount a pincer attack against France using three large corps, and that these were already being assembled. Austria was the leading player at this stage. An Austrian army 150,000 strong was to move north from Italy; a second army, composed of Austrian units and their German allies, would assemble on the upper Rhine; while a third force, under Wellington's command, would group together another Austrian contingent and Prussian, Dutch, and British units stationed in Flanders. Huge forces waited in the wings—including an army of 200,000 Russians that was massing to the east, somewhat to the alarm of the Austrian archduke, who is known to have feared that his supposed ally posed more of a threat to his country's security than any army which Napoleon could muster.[42] Indeed, the numbers of troops on the Allied side so heavily outnumbered Napoleon's army as to make the outcome of the campaign a foregone conclusion. Even if he had won at Waterloo, Napoleon would surely have lost the war, and victory would have provided him with only the briefest of respites. In a drawn-out and bruising campaign there could only be one winner.

Napoleon knew this, too, and it strengthened his resolve to go on the offensive. At first, he had dreamed of scoring a diplomatic triumph by exploiting the contrasting interests of the Allies, playing Austria off against Russia to break the alliance aligned against him. When it became clear that this tactic would not work, he followed his natural instinct to seize the initiative and attack, believing that he could profit from the time it would take the Allies to deploy their forces, that he could divide the armies of his enemies and defeat them one at a time. This was a reasonable strategy since, if the forces he commanded could not match the combined strength of his opponents, they were certainly a match for his enemies individually. He could not raise conscripts as he had done during the Empire, since conscription had been abolished in 1814 and there would be strong political opposition to its reinstatement. But he was not without resources. He had the bulk of Louis XVIII's army at his disposal, and he recalled troops on leave and called for volunteers to bolster his numbers. Although there was no legal route to conscription, he tried to categorize the class of 1815 as discharged soldiers who were therefore obliged to serve.[43] In all he raised around a quarter of a million men, but of these over 100,000 were consigned to the defence of the frontiers and to guarding against royalist insurgency in the interior. His key force for the 1815 campaign, the Armée du Nord, numbered around 124,000 troops and 358 cannon; it was with this army that he headed north and crossed the border on to Belgian territory, launching the campaign that would end at Waterloo.[44] The strength of his army should not be underestimated, nor yet the damage it could wreak. But it could not compare with the huge armies he had assembled for Russia or at Leipzig, and it is impossible to see how it could have reversed the outcome of the wars or destroyed the peace settlement at Vienna. The final battle at Waterloo may indeed have been fiercely contested, and Napoleon's troops were not men to lie down in the face of adversity. But it is hard to disagree with Tim Blanning when he observes that Napoleon's last campaign must be seen for what it was. Far from representing a climactic conclusion to the Napoleonic Wars, it was 'nothing more than a coda marked *diminuendo*'.[45]

3

The Waterloo Campaign

It was not in Napoleon's character to fight a defensive military campaign. In his heyday his career had been characterized by a desire to seize every initiative and to launch blistering attacks on the enemy. In 1815, he was eager to eschew defensive tactics, especially against an adversary like Wellington who had shown throughout the Peninsular War that defence was an area in which he excelled and that he still adhered to the concepts of the strategy of attrition.[1] Wellington planned meticulously, and, though he had never previously faced Napoleon in the field, he certainly did not underestimate him. After all, the Emperor's reputation as both tactician and strategist was unequalled, and Wellington had studied his campaigns with care. He understood that he would have to devise some means of countering Napoleon's operational strengths: the powerful field artillery which he used to pound enemy positions before launching his cavalry and infantry against them; the heavy cavalry which he used to launch shock attacks; and the corps-sized infantry columns which he deployed in close fighting.[2] Wellington knew that he had to find the counter-tactics that would deny Napoleon their operational benefits in battle.

Some things he could confidently assume. It was entirely predictable, for instance, that once Napoleon had assembled his army he would again turn to the attack, hoping that he could take advantage of speed and surprise at a time when the Allies were still negotiating among themselves and assembling their widely dispersed forces. Against him were pitted all the major European powers, which had hastily formed themselves into a seventh coalition and which, taken together, substantially outnumbered the men at his disposal. He realized the importance of launching an incisive initial thrust against them; and his attention focused on Belgium as the most promising point of attack, where he could hope to defeat the Anglo-Dutch and Prussian forces before the Austrians and Russians could join them. As always, Napoleon planned carefully and organized feverishly; this was not a random decision. On 13 May, he was already writing to his minister of war, Davout, to establish a theatre of operations in the north, asking for information on the topography of the region.[3] No detail was overlooked: the breadth of the Scheldt near Mons, the Sambre near Charleroi, and the Meuse near Maastricht; the number of pontoons that would be needed to bridge each of them; the number of field-service wagons that were available in Paris, and the time that it would take to mass them between Avesnes and Laon. Napoleon planned in secret; the Allies at this stage had no idea of the direction he intended to take or the nature of the campaign that he was planning. Until 6 June, when he gave the order that his troops assemble near Beaumont, close to the French border, his army remained dispersed across a front of some 200 miles so as to conceal his real intentions. There is little in the history of these crucial days that would suggest that Napoleon's tactical acumen had in any way diminished.

The Rival Armies

The army which Napoleon assembled for the Waterloo campaign numbered 124,000, among them seasoned veterans from earlier campaigns. But that number was dwarfed by the armies ranged against him. To the north Blücher led an army of Prussians and Saxons, and around Brussels Wellington commanded the British, Germans, and Dutch. Between them they had sufficient firepower to overwhelm Napoleon's troops, and they were only the front line. Further back the Austrians and Bavarians were advancing with an army of around 200,000 commanded by Prince Schwarzenberg, while the Russians, moving west from Poland, threatened to add a further quarter of a million soldiers to the Allied cause.[4] If Napoleon was going to make war against such force he had few choices available to him. His only real chance of success lay in preventing the Allied armies from coming together and picking off his enemies one by one. To this end the 'Armée du Nord', as he explained to Davout, had to be his 'principal army'.[5] Napoleon himself took command.

But it was not only numbers that he lacked in 1815. As we have seen, he was also significantly short of marshals and of the high-quality field commanders he had been able to enlist in the past. If the appointment of Davout to the war ministry was unquestionably made on merit, it deprived him of his ablest commander in the field. And he could no longer turn to his trusted chief of staff, Berthier, killed in mysterious

Figure 3. Sir Thomas Lawrence, *Field Marshal von Blücher*

circumstances when he fell from an upper window in Bamberg; instead he had to rely on the largely untested Soult.[6] Napoleon clearly missed the assurance which Berthier had given him, all the more so since, with Davout office-bound, he had only five of his former marshals available for active service (Brune, Mortier, Ney, Soult, and Suchet), together with Emmanuel Grouchy to whom he had given his marshal's baton only a few days previously. These men would be his chief support in the days that lay ahead; despite their unquestionable courage and long experience of military campaigns, they were a pale shadow of the leadership cadres to whom Napoleon had been able to turn in the past.

The 1815 campaign was always going to be a gamble against extra-ordinary odds, and some would argue, against all military logic. The 124,000 men he led were all that could be spared from other duties and assigned to the war in the north, for his army had other priories, too: to defend French territory from attack from across the Pyrenees, for instance, or along some 600 miles of France's eastern borders. He could not afford to leave these frontiers unprotected, since he knew that the Allies' ultimate aim was to invade France for a second time and to overthrow the imperial regime. But the resources he could devote to defence were wafer-thin. Twenty-three thousand men under General Rapp were to defend Strasbourg and watch over the Rhine, defending France against the might of the Russian advance. General Lecourbe was given a mere 8,400 to guard the Jura against a possible Swiss attack. Brune was given 5,500 troops with which to hold the whole of the south coast. In Lyons, Suchet was expected to push back any Austrian attack with just 23,500 soldiers at his command.[7] These numbers were dwarfed by the riches at the disposal of his enemies, and they illustrate both the weakness of Napoleon's logistical position and the importance which he attached to his campaign in the north. It was to this campaign that he now devoted himself.

His target was the Allied armies that were already assembling in Belgium: Blücher's Prussians to the north-east and Wellington's Anglo-Dutch army, stationed around Brussels. The Allies had considered launching their own pre-emptive strike but had held back, waiting for reinforcements to arrive. Their caution gave Napoleon his chance. He believed he could split the two armies and then attack them in turn, dreaming that in this way he would score a double victory over his opponents and break their morale before moving on the Belgian capital. Given the numerical superiority of the enemy and the inadequacy of his logistical support, this plan might have seemed over-optimistic, but his intelligence reports told him that he had until 1 July before the Allied armies would be prepared for action.[8] Besides, the shortcomings which he detected in the forces that opposed him gave him reason for hope. He consoled himself with the thought that numbers were not everything, and that his army was distinguished by its quality, its patriotic determination, and its self-belief. He still looked to luck and trusted in his star. And among his opponents there were many who remained in awe of him and who approached the upcoming war with a deep apprehension. John Kincaid of the Rifle Brigade was one of those present on the battlefield who expressed grave doubts about the quality of the troops on his own side. 'We were,' he writes, 'take us all in all, a very bad army', placing the blame for this very largely on Britain's allies. 'Our foreign auxiliaries', he suggests brusquely, 'were little better than a raw militia—a body without a soul, or like an inflated pillow that gives to the touch and resumes its shape again when the pressure ceases.'[9]

It is undeniable that the Allies fielded a heterogeneous force of veterans and raw recruits as well as men from a wide range of nations and military cultures, some only newly given independent status as part of the Vienna settlement. The Dutch in particular had a notably young army, hastily assembled by their newly proclaimed king, William I, to serve his fledgling kingdom after it had been freed from French control; while the liberation of Hanover in 1813 gave George III the opportunity to raise new—and, again, largely untested—Hanoverian battalions for the war. Nor was the British army in prime condition. Wellington's own line infantry was composed of many second battalions which had seen little or no active service, and he protested about the lack of seasoned troops from the Peninsular campaign. It was, he felt, a deliberate provocation by Horse Guards:

> It will be admitted that the army is not a very good one; and being composed as it is, I might have expected that the Generals and Staff formed by me in the last war would have been allowed to come to me again: but instead of that, I am overloaded with people I have never seen before; and it appears to be purposely intended to keep those out of my way whom I wished to have.[10]

While Wellington was given to exaggeration in his protests to those in authority, there was, as always, a germ of truth in this outburst. More broadly, the danger of nationalist tensions within the Allied ranks was real enough. The Belgian troops, in particular, were treated with distrust as many of them had until recently been fighting on Napoleon's side and their loyalty could not be taken for granted. Great care was taken to brigade them with Dutch units in the hope that this would dissuade them from future treasonable activity; but the men they fought alongside continued to distrust them, with the consequence that Dutch troops enjoyed an unenviable reputation with other regiments of the army. William Tomkinson, a cavalry officer at Waterloo, relates how, afterwards, the Spanish General Alava gently evaded a question from the Prince of Orange about how Spanish troops might have conducted themselves in the battle with the words, 'Your Highness, I do not think they would have run away, as your Belgians did, before the *first* shot was fired.'[11]

Blücher's army, too, had its problems: serious breaches of discipline during the invasion of France in 1814, a record of looting in Holland and Belgium, and such bad blood between the Prussian troops and their Saxon allies (who had fought on Napoleon's side at Leipzig in 1813) that the Saxons came to blows with Prussian staff officers when they were transferred to Prussian service. This had led to charges of mutiny, to Saxon soldiers facing court martial and execution, and to 14,000 of them being sent home in disgrace.[12] None of this inspired confidence in the army as a unified fighting force. Distrust was further intensified by often acrimonious relations between the various national commanders, not least between the principal actors on the Allied side, Wellington and Blücher. In the early part of the campaign their relationship was soured by a lingering suspicion among the Prussian officers that the British were leaving them to bear the heaviest casualties and were not offering the Prussians the same level of support which they accorded him. The Prussian Count von Gneisenau phrased this uncompromisingly in a letter written later that summer to the nationalist campaigner Ernst Moritz Arndt in which he complained that during the short campaign 'the worst behaviour has come from Wellington who without us would have been smashed to pieces'. For good measure he added that 'the man has rewarded our many services with the most contemptuous ingratitude'.[13] Wellington, Gneisenau believed, was amoral and untrustworthy, and during his earlier service in India had 'so accustomed himself to duplicity that he had at last become such a master of the art as even to outwit the Nabobs themselves'.[14]

Ligny and Quatre Bras

For these reasons Napoleon could persuade himself that a concerted French attack, by men who had been hardened by service in wars fought across Europe, would enable him to repulse the enemy and to spread division in their ranks. He left Paris early on the morning of 12 June and headed in the direction of the Belgian frontier, passing first to Laon, where he met up with Grouchy and the cavalry, then to Avesnes, where he was joined by the Imperial Guard. The other commanders moved their units towards him, and by the evening of the 14th they had assembled at what would be Napoleon's headquarters at Beaumont, ready to strike into Belgium. The entire manoeuvre had taken less than ten days, while the Allies, despite receiving regular intelligence reports about French troop movements, were still spread along the frontier, uncertain of where the French would converge. Napoleon's choice of Maubeuge from which to mount his attack helped to sow further confusion amongst them, since they still had little sense of the route he would follow. If he chose to advance through Charleroi he would encounter the Prussian army; whereas if he took the route through Mons he would be opposed by Dutch troops under the Prince of Orange.[15] To the very last, it seemed, Napoleon held the initiative and his enemies could only wait apprehensively to discover what he would do next. In the event, he advanced on Charleroi in the afternoon of 15 June, capturing the city and driving back the Prussian outposts before launching his invasion of Belgium. He aimed to drive the two Allied armies apart, preventing them from using their numerical superiority to advantage; in response the Allied strategy was to unite as soon as they had a clear idea of Napoleon's intentions. Of the Allies, it was Blücher who moved immediately to engage with Napoleon; Wellington appeared sluggish and indecisive, opening himself once more to the Prussian charge that he was protecting the lives of his own men and leaving them to bear the brunt of the fighting. His army was still dispersed, and it was only on the evening of the 15th that he gave the order to his troops to assemble around the crossroads at Quatre Bras, to the south-east of Brussels, where the Charleroi–Brussels highway crossed the road from Namur to Nivelles, to cut off Napoleon's march on Brussels.

On 16 June the fighting began in earnest in the twin battles of Quatre Bras and Ligny. At Quatre Bras a section of the left wing of the French army commanded by Marshal Ney engaged an Anglo-Allied army under Wellington that included British, Dutch, and Belgian units and troops from Nassau, Hanover, and Brunswick. Napoleon himself was not present; he had moved against the Prussians and he hoped that Ney, by pinning down the Allied army and pushing aside Wellington's resistance, could prevent his enemies from joining forces against him. The Allies were at first outnumbered, and the plan looked as though it might succeed. Ney attacked confidently; but during the day Wellington's force was strengthened as reinforcements arrived, and by late afternoon French attacks were being repulsed, the British defending in lines against French infantry attacks and in squares against their cavalry.[16] In contrast, the reinforcements which Ney had been anxiously expecting never materialized, having been given countermanding orders by Napoleon to join him in battle against the Prussian army at Ligny. By seven in the evening, Wellington had around 30,000 men under his command and could afford to launch a major assault of his own, regaining much of the ground that had been lost, ending the threat of French dominance, but leaving the outcome of the battle inconclusive. Both sides retained their positions in the field; casualties were around 4,000 on the French side and perhaps 4,800 for the Allies.[17] Ney was unable to press home his advantage. He had managed to keep the two armies apart, but neither had been knocked out of the war. Wellington retired tactically to protect Brussels.

Of the two battles fought on 16 June, Ligny was the more serious engagement, and it would provide Napoleon with his final victory. The village of Ligny, some 30 miles south of Brussels, was surrounded by hamlets set in undulating farmland, where the Prussians had managed to dig themselves in before fighting began, and from which Napoleon had to flush them out. He had around 76,000 men under his command and was slightly outnumbered on the day, though, once again, he expected reinforcements which failed to arrive. In both these battles, and again two days later at Waterloo, the French army suffered communications failures which put its success in jeopardy. Against them Blücher lined up a slightly larger force of around 83,000 men, though these included some untried militia units. At the outset Napoleon's aim seemed relatively modest: he sought to drive the Prussians from what he presumed was a rearguard position and hasten their retreat. But when he saw the enemy columns forming he changed his plan and tried to engage them in a decisive battle. As Jacques Logie explains, it was the most classic of manoeuvres as Napoleon 'proposed to launch a frontal attack and then, by a turning movement from the left, crush him between the jaws of his pincers'.[18] It almost worked. Four times the French attacked against a Prussian force that was committed to aggressive defence, breaking out periodically to launch counter-offensives against them, though with limited success. By the evening it was clear that there was only one winner: Napoleon was left in command of the battlefield, and when he sent in the Imperial Guard his attack broke the Prussian centre, forcing them to retreat in some disorder towards Wavre, some 10 miles behind their lines.

Napoleon's victory was incisive, but it had not been gained cheaply. Ligny was a bloody encounter marked by often vicious hand-to-hand fighting, and by the end of the day the French had suffered around 8,500 casualties to the Prussians' 12,000. Blücher himself had fallen from his horse while leading a cavalry charge, suffering concussion and bruising which he treated with an interesting mixture of garlic and schnapps. Although he suffered no long-term damage—he recovered quickly and showed remarkable resilience for a man of 72—some at Prussian headquarters had believed that he was dead.[19] A younger Napoleon might have known how to take fuller advantage of his victory, but on this occasion the Emperor was curiously indecisive. Though he had fresh troops in reserve, he inexplicably failed to follow up the Prussian defeat, with the result that, instead of destroying the enemy army and driving the Prussians out of the campaign, pressing his opponents hard and forcing them to change their battle plans, he allowed them to regroup.[20] On 17 June there would be no fighting as the skies darkened and torrential rainfall made combat unusually difficult, a circumstance that gave the armies time to prepare themselves and offered the generals welcome opportunities for reconnaissance and tactical planning. The next battle was delayed until the following day, when the two sides met again, at Waterloo.

Wellington had already identified the most defensible landmarks in the rolling countryside south of Brussels, and it was here that he chose his ground. On the evening of 17 June he arranged his army along a ridge just to the south of Mont-Saint-Jean, where he planned to take full advantage of the natural defences provided by the landscape. The ridge afforded its defenders the protection of thick hedges to either side of a road, which, in a slight hollow, ran along a substantial part of the 2½ miles that formed the main battlefield. His left flank was protected from cavalry attacks by a landscape of trees, streams, and damp, marshy ground; to the right there were small clumps of trees and patches of brushwood, offering, once again, a degree of cover. Two clusters of farm buildings allowed him to post strong garrisons ahead of the ridge—the farmhouse of La Haie Sainte which lay ahead of his army, and the chateau of Hougoumont which stood off to his right. These were to become two of the British army's strongholds in the fighting of the following day; they obstructed French attacks and became iconic symbols of the British army's dogged resistance. Wellington had chosen his ground well, with a soldier's keen sense of the value of the terrain, as he prepared to fight a defensive battle against an opponent who, he knew, would be unable to resist the temptation to attack and who could achieve his goals only by outright victory.[21]

Waterloo

Napoleon's failure to press home his advantage after Ligny would prove to be very costly. During the thirty-six hours that followed he, like the Allied generals ranged against him, planned his next moves. But we should not exaggerate the quality of intelligence on either side. News of the Prussian defeat at Ligny and of Blücher's withdrawal to Wavre filtered through slowly and imperfectly, and Grouchy, on Napoleon's orders, went in pursuit of the Prussian army without any clear notion of how badly it had been damaged or of how it might respond to defeat. Similarly, Wellington appeared to be as uncertain as anyone about Napoleon's next move; for that reason he felt that it was necessary to allow Napoleon to take the initiative before he committed his own troops further. Besides, British tactics depended on Prussian cooperation, and he had to be sure that he understood his ally's intentions. His plans, as he explained them to Blücher when the two commanders met, famously, on the evening of 17 June at a wayside inn called La Belle Alliance, were therefore still fluid. 'I propose to take up my position at Mont-Saint-Jean,' he informed the Prussian field marshal; 'There I shall await Napoleon to join battle with him if I can count on the support of just one Prussian corps. But if I cannot have support, I shall be obliged to sacrifice Brussels and take up position behind the Scheldt.'[22] When Blücher agreed that he would march west to join Wellington and attack the French on the flank, the die was cast. Wellington was then able to prepare for battle knowing that he could count on receiving Prussian reinforcements, the very outcome which Napoleon had set out to prevent. The manoeuvres of the two armies on the 17th had left Wellington with an important tactical advantage.

Napoleon, typically confident of his own abilities, refused to acknowledge that he had been outmanoeuvred, and insisted on the advantage which the French could gain from the lie of the land. In his opinion the battlefield was too restricted for fluent movement, while the barrier presented by the Forest of Soignes to the rear of the Allied forces imposed more of an impediment than it offered protection. 'If the English army remains there tomorrow,' he declared on the evening of the 17th, 'it is mine.' Though this judgement may seem rash given what happened on the following day, it was not entirely foolish, as Lemonnier-Delafosse, the chief of staff to General Foy, duly observed:

> Never, it is fair to say, has a general [Wellington] displayed less science in his choice of battlefield. I speak not of the disposition of his troops, the deployment of his army was good, without doubt, but placed in front of a forest, Soignes, it was unable to manoeuvre and found itself stuck there like a strong point holding out until capitulation.

To the French observer, indeed, Wellington's choice smacked less of inspiration than of arrogance, since it implied that he thought only in terms of victory, and consequently had no plans for the possibility of a retreat. 'And what a retreat it would have been,' he mused, 'leaving the battlefield, suffering from inevitable disorder which defeat occasions, encumbered with material, the embarrassment of all armies, driven back into the forest.'[23]

British officers saw greater benefit in Wellington's choice of ground, which they had reconnoitred carefully in advance. Sir Augustus Frazer, the commander of the Royal Horse Artillery, described the British position as he adjudged it on the eve of the battle:

> We retired to a position previously selected, and we shall now make a stand; our right towards Braine l'Alleud, our left towards Limalle; headquarters at Waterloo, and Genappe (now in the enemy's possession) in our front. In this position the forest of Soignes you will observe to be in our rear. Four *pavés* run through it. The wood is open and practicable for infantry or cavalry. The trees are high, the roads and the whole wood very dark, and except in the paved part of the road, the ground is very deep.[24]

The wood was not an impenetrable barrier in his view, either to infantry or to horse. Rather he saw it as a position that was defensible against whatever attacks Napoleon threw at it.

Wellington's deployment of his forces might also seem rather imbalanced, with a strong right wing and a strong centre, but with what looked to be a much weaker left. But this disposition had been carefully prepared, and Wellington knew that it was from the left that Blücher would arrive with reinforcements.[25] He placed many of his best forces along the ridge, to the west of the crossroads: they included the formidable Guards Division, which he entrusted to two of his most inspired commanders, Halkett and Maitland. To the right of the main army, defending the village of Braine-l'Alleud, he positioned the infantry of Lord Hill; to his left, the three divisions of Picton's infantry and the cavalry brigades commanded by Vivian and Vandeleur. Uxbridge's cavalry were nowhere to be seen; during the early stages of the battle they were held in reserve, to the rear of the main army.[26]

Napoleon saw no reason to revise his opinion of Wellington's position; indeed, on the morning of the battle he repeated his satisfaction to his men. Nor did he feel it necessary to revise his tactics, for though he had as yet no firm intelligence as to the whereabouts of the Prussian army, he had no reason to suspect that Grouchy would be

held back at Wavre and prevented from providing him with reinforcements. Napoleon's own forces were strung out to the south of
Wellington's position, symmetrically deployed and ready to launch an
attack. He confidently believed that he could defeat Wellington and
turn in triumph on Brussels, capturing one of the Allies' capital cities
after only three days of action. Indeed, the major problem he identified
on the morning of the 18th had nothing to do with his resources or the
enemy's position. It was the drenching rain which persuaded him to
delay his attack for some hours, as he feared that his heavy gun
carriages would sink into the saturated mud of the battlefield. He
therefore waited for several hours for the ground to dry out, before
arranging his army in preparation for an attack, in three discrete
sections, defending his headquarters at La Belle Alliance. To his left
he placed Reille's Second Corps, directed against Hougoumont, to his
right d'Erlon's First Corps, facing towards La Haie Sainte and the main
Allied army under Wellington. The Old Guard he kept, as was his
custom, in reserve.

The Old Guard was the elite of the Napoleonic army, a unit of
seasoned troops which had first been formed under the Consulate,
almost in the manner of the *Maison du Roi* under the Old Regime. Its
loyalty was to the person of Napoleon, and it had become battle-
hardened in his service. The Guard considered themselves to be the
cream of the army: admission was restricted to men who had served in
a number of campaigns, had been wounded, or who had performed
heroic deeds in battle. The Guard had grown progressively larger in
the course of the Napoleonic campaigns to constitute a virtually
autonomous elite force, paid more highly than the rest of the army,
and unwavering in their devotion to the Emperor. As the Guard
expanded, so, too, it was subdivided, with the Old Guard retained as
a reserve, too precious to risk in the initial fighting, and new units
created of the Middle Guard and the Young Guard. These 'New Guard'
regiments were not held back like the Old: they had been formed in
1804 and 1809 to provide additional infantry regiments, and especially a light infantry capacity. In 1815 the Young Guard was briefly

re-formed, but they were assembled in haste. Only the 1st and 3rd Tirailleurs and Voltigeurs were present in the field at Waterloo.[27]

Hougoumont

When Napoleon did attack, at around 11.30 a.m. on 18 June, he unleashed Reille's Second Corps against Hougoumont in a move which he planned partly as a diversionary tactic but was also intended to remove what he saw as a serious impediment to his advance. The chateau and its farm buildings and outhouses were situated in the heart of the battlefield, between the French and the bulk of the Allied army, and they had natural defences in the form of walls and ditches, a garden, and a small wood. Wellington had allotted substantial numbers of men to their defence, including some of his most seasoned troops—men of the Guards Division along with units of Nassauers and Hanoverians—and Napoleon had little alternative but to try to dislodge them. In the event the fighting around the farmhouse tied down far more French firepower during the day than it disrupted the Anglo-Dutch army, as its defences proved formidable, forcing the French to deploy more and more troops in a vain bid to capture it. The battle for Hougoumont continued throughout the day, lasting nearly eight hours, during which fewer than 3,000 Allied troops held off a French force which at its peak numbered some 13,000 men, inflicting considerable casualties on the attackers. British accounts of the action may exaggerate the number of French assaults; some claim six or even seven attacks from the arrival of the first skirmishers at 11.30 a.m. to the final infantry attack at 6 p.m.; whereas the French accounts speak of only three.[28] What is clear from them all, however, is that in the course of the day Hougoumont evolved into what was virtually a separate battle, and, unsurprisingly, it went on to hold a special place in the more romantic British accounts of Waterloo. Especially fondly remembered was the heroic defence of the gates by a clutch of men from the 2nd Foot Guards, who suffered terrible losses as the French finally threatened to burst into the farmyard. Their success in repelling the enemy was to play a vital part in ensuring that Waterloo would end as an Allied victory, and it was a moment that would go on to hold a cherished place in British—and especially Scottish—military lore.

D'Erlon's Assault

At about 1.40 p.m. the main attack was launched, partly in response to the arrival of the first Prussian units on the battlefield. Napoleon did not attempt to outflank Wellington's force on its weaker left side, as prudence might have dictated, but instead chose to mount a frontal attack against the Anglo-Allied centre with the aim of seizing the village of Mont-Saint-Jean and gaining control of the Brussels road which provided Wellington with his principal line of communication and which, if the circumstances demanded it, would offer a means of retreat. To this end he ordered his artillery to bombard the Allied positions while d'Erlon's First Corps of around 16,000 men captured the hamlet of Papelotte from the Allies and attacked La Haie Sainte, seizing its garden and orchard but failing to take control of the farm itself, where the men of the King's German Legion (KGL) clung on desperately. Thereafter fortunes changed rapidly, for as d'Erlon's troops reached the crest of the ridge and drove off a unit of its Dutch-Belgian defenders, they were caught in a rapid counter-attack from Sir Thomas Picton's Fifth Division, first a fusillade, then a fierce bayonet attack, the British cavalry pushing aside d'Erlon's horse before driving the French infantry back down the slope in disarray. But it would prove to be a pyrrhic victory, and a costly one, too. Picton himself was killed, and in the confusion and the elation of their victory the cavalry of Ponsonby's Union Brigade (the Royals, Scots Greys, and Inniskillings) lost discipline and charged too far into enemy lines, cutting down some of the French gunners and capturing two eagles, but failing to regroup, and were trapped.[29] The assault ended with over a third of the British cavalry killed or wounded, while d'Erlon's force had also suffered terrible casualties. By around 3 p.m. this phase of the battle had petered out with both sides exhausted; but once again Wellington could console himself that Napoleon's offensive had been repulsed, and time was passing. More sinister for the French was the sight of more and more Prussian troops assembling on the battlefield, while as yet there was no sign of Grouchy or of the reinforcements on whose arrival Napoleon was relying. His infantry were fully stretched—his only infantry reserve was now the Imperial Guard—and he began to understand that if Grouchy failed to arrive he risked finding himself in desperate straits. A more cautious man would have pulled back at this stage and regrouped, waiting for Grouchy to appear; but Napoleon preferred a more aggressive response, seeking to regain the initiative and restore morale to his battered troops.

Ney's Cavalry Charge

Led by Marshal Ney, the French unleashed a heavy cavalry charge, and did so without the support of the infantry on which the horse normally depended. Napoleon was reluctant to throw the Imperial Guard into the battle, preferring to retain them, as he had so often done in the past, for a final surge that would deliver victory. Still worse from a French viewpoint, the cavalry were left without significant artillery cover; in all, they were supported by only six batteries of horse artillery. Ney's impetuous attack is difficult to justify in military terms. He may have been trying to win the battle by a grand and courageous gesture; or he may have concluded that infantry support was unnecessary. Either way he miscalculated badly, first failing to capture La Haie Sainte, then trying to clear Allied forces from their stronghold on the ridge by means of a massive cavalry attack, supported by sporadic artillery fire from the French Grand Battery below. It was soon apparent that this was a hopelessly ineffective tactic as wave after wave of horsemen charged up the slope only to find themselves facing serried ranks of infantrymen, deployed in squares and bristling with bayonets, who, safely out of range of their sabres, were able to fire their muskets more or less at will at the advancing horses and their riders, then reload and wait for the next incursion. In all, the French threw some eighty squadrons, or 10,000 men, into these futile attacks, and they fought to the death with an indomitable spirit, unable to charge at more than a canter because of the mounds of mud and bodies that stood in their way.[30] When the French cavalry charges ceased, after about two hours, Wellington's squares remained intact and, though both sides suffered heavy casualties, little advantage had been gained.

Ney may have been 'the bravest of the brave', as his Emperor dubbed him, but his impetuousness had cost the French dearly, and by the time the great cavalry battle was over, at around six o'clock, the Prussians were present in force on the battlefield. The French could no longer ignore the threat which they posed, and Lobau's Sixth Corps was sent to hold them back. But Lobau found himself heavily outnumbered by the 30,000 men of Bülow's Fourth Corps who had arrived at Mont-Saint-Jean around 4.30 p.m. and had attacked Napoleon's right wing. The French were first driven back to Plancenoit, and then forced to abandon the village entirely. To counter this Napoleon sent units from his reserve—eight battalions of the Young Guard led by General Duhesme—to recapture the village in the early evening. The battle for Plancenoit was regarded by both sides as critical to the final outcome, since it would give the victor a clear route to Brussels. The village was taken and retaken several times in the course of the day, finally falling to the Prussians when Zieten's First Corps arrived around 7.30 p.m., triggering the final collapse of the French right wing.

The arrival of the Prussians in numbers to the left of the Allied army came as huge relief to Wellington. It allowed him to evacuate part of his own army and reinforce his centre, which threatened to be overrun by Napoleon's reserve, now massed around the inn at La Belle Alliance in preparation for a final grand attack to dislodge the Allied army. Indeed, the part played by the Prussians in the later stages of the battle should not be underestimated. Their army had recovered quickly from defeat at Ligny, had regrouped, and on the morning of 18 June prepared to move on Waterloo. Blücher was committed to defeating

Napoleon and to avenging earlier defeats at his hands, and he stood by the promise he made to Wellington on the previous evening. He was helped in his plans by the dogged inflexibility of Grouchy, the French marshal who had been sent to isolate him, and who showed a curious reluctance to take initiatives even as the news he received from Waterloo changed from hour to hour. Grouchy's instructions were to pursue the Prussians and defeat them, and it is true that he did manage to inflict a defeat on one corps of the Prussian army, under Thielmann, at Wavre. But this effort was largely irrelevant to the main campaign—indeed, when he was brought news that Thielemann faced defeat, Gneisenau brushed aside his request for reinforcements with the observation that 'it matters little if he is crushed at Wavre so long as we gain the victory here'.[31] Grouchy showed little inclination to maintain regular communication with the Emperor, in defiance of Napoleon's express wishes. Or so Napoleon would later maintain, when he went out of his way to blame Grouchy for his army's defeat. Whatever the rights and wrongs of Grouchy's actions, what was critical on the day was that his troops remained unavailable for combat at Waterloo, where their presence was urgently needed. It was Blücher, with three of his four corps intact, who would make the critical intervention, marching through Wavre to Saint-Lambert and engaging in a flank movement that would allow him to throw fresh men into the final stages of the battle.[32] His arrival would make a critical difference.

La Haie Sainte

It was in the fourth phase of the battle that Napoleon's army stood the greatest chance of making a breakthrough and the centre of Wellington's line looked most vulnerable. With Napoleon engaged in overseeing the struggle against the Prussians, Ney struck again. The farm at La Haie Sainte had been defended throughout the day, bravely and resolutely, by around 400 men of the KGL, under Major Georg Baring, reinforced by a further 800 troops, during six hours of fighting. They fought off successive attacks but as evening fell they had run desperately low on ammunition. Though they appealed to Wellington for new supplies, the British were unable to help, in part because the Germans were issued with rifles instead of muskets, and these required a very different kind of shot. And so an exhausted garrison prepared to fight the French one last time in the knowledge that they would surely be overwhelmed. Against musket fire they had little with which to defend themselves other than rifle butts and bayonets. It was a hopeless fight. Ney's men set fire to the thatch on the farm buildings and forced the garrison out into the open, where their escape route was cut and they faced almost certain slaughter. In all, only around forty soldiers of the hundreds who had manned the farmhouse escaped alive, and the KGL's last stand at La Haie Sainte became a symbol of gallantry and intrepid self-sacrifice, a brave if ultimately doomed defiance of the odds.[33] But the loss of the farm had important operational consequences, too, since it left Wellington's army more exposed to a French attack than it had been at any time throughout the day. Ney called for reinforcements, but to no avail. Napoleon's reserves were already engaged against the Prussians, and he still insisted on holding back the Middle and Old Guard for a final assault. It was perhaps a mistake. Ney had the momentum at that moment, when Wellington's centre had been mauled and almost bled dry by repeated French attacks and when some British troops were being driven to desertion. But without reinforcements he could not turn his superiority into a decisive victory. The Allies might be battered, pummelled, some may even have been demoralized, but the defences did not break, and what was perhaps the key moment for Napoleon, the moment when he was presented with the opportunity to destroy Wellington's army, was lost.[34] The French were the unquestioned victors of this fourth phase of the battle. But they had been unable to press home their advantage, and the Allies, critically, were given a breathing space in which to regroup and strengthen their lines. All the time Prussian troops were still arriving, providing them with new strength and fresh limbs for a final confrontation.

Nemesis

If Napoleon was to gain the victory he needed, he had to act quickly before the Prussians had arrived en masse, yet he hesitated, as though unsure of his next move. On the one hand Ney was on the cusp of victory; on the other he feared being surrounded by the advancing Prussian army, his route to Brussels cut, his retreat blocked by the enemy. Should he hold back the fresh troops of his reserve to protect his retreat? Or should he throw caution to the winds and consign them to one final assault on Wellington's positions? In the end, he decided to attack, finally ordering the 5,000 reservists of the Old and Middle Guard into the conflict, the majority of whom he placed under Ney's command. It was 7.30 p.m. and the sun was already sinking as they marched in tight columns up the hillside, those same men that Ney had requested half an hour earlier, when Wellington's centre lay gaping open and the French might have marched right through. But now the French were met by more than thirty of Wellington's cannon, primed with double grapeshot, which ripped through their ranks and heralded the carnage that was to follow. They were marching through open farmland exposed to Wellington's artillery fire even before they reached the top of the ridge. Ney himself had his horse shot from under him, his fifth of a blood-soaked day. Once up on the crest they faced fierce fighting with heavy casualties on both sides, the British infantry firing on the French line as soon as it appeared over the ridge, the French returning fire rather than using fixed bayonets in close combat. The Allies made their first significant breakthrough when a Dutch-Belgian battalion under de Chassé, moving over to strengthen their defences, repulsed the first of the Guards units, the elite 1st/3rd Grenadiers. The 3rd Chasseurs soon followed them down the hillside, beaten off by Wellington's Foot Guards with bayonets fixed, as, one by one, the elite French Guard units, some badly weakened by their earlier encounter with the Prussians, were dislodged and pushed back. Most of the Allied soldiers, exhausted by their efforts, watched them retreat down the mud-drenched slopes, trampling the bodies of their comrades and their horses. But some units smelt more than victory and carried on the pursuit. Among them were men of Adam's brigade, Du Plat's brigade, and Detmers's Netherlands Brigade, who hurled themselves in an ill-disciplined charge down the hillside. In the fading light the French retreat turned into a murderous rout.

At around eight o'clock the unheard-of cry went up among the French troops that 'la Garde recule', as the remainder of the French army came to accept the unpalatable truth that their elite troops had been defeated. The French positions elsewhere on the field unravelled with apparent ease as men who had defended them with such grit and determination throughout the day saw no point in holding out. Hougoumont and La Haie Sainte, over which so much blood had been spilt, were quickly evacuated, the soldiers taking flight where they could, abandoned by their cavalry and left at the mercy of the enemy. The Prussians, too, resumed the attack, retaking Plancenoit and the hamlet of Papelotte from their French defenders in the last hours of the battle. The rout was now total. Of the Emperor's troops, only the four Guard infantry battalions, three of the Old Guard and one of the Middle Guard, offered a solid resistance, albeit in hopeless circumstances. Their squares, though they could muster no more than some 2,000 muskets among them and under concentrated attack from the British cavalry, impressed both friend and foe by holding firm in the midst of the chaos, providing cover for the retreating French army as it made its way south towards Charleroi, and then on to France itself. Just as Ney had discovered earlier in the day, well-primed infantry squares, bristling with bayonets, could deter advancing cavalry, and the exhausted British horse found it easier to pursue French stragglers on the road than engage with the remnants of the Guard. The four squares held until nightfall before they accepted defeat and blended with the other fugitives as they made their way back home. It was a last vain gesture, but in a sense the day belonged to them, too, since they had done much to save the honour of Napoleon's defeated army, defending its eagles and its battle honours to the last. It is for this that they would be remembered, and their praises sung, long into the nineteenth century. As Alessandro Barbero has so neatly phrased it, 'on that June evening the squares of the Old Guard wrote the last chapter in the Napoleonic epic and entered directly into legend'.[35]

It had been a bludgeoning encounter, and the victorious Allies were in no mood to show forgiveness or to allow their adversaries to escape. In the chaos of their retreat French soldiers were shown no mercy, and many were cut down and left to die. There was little compassion, little gallantry towards the vanquished. If British and Dutch soldiers had lost friends and seen colleagues mangled, among the Prussians the desire for vengeance was even greater, vengeance for Jena, for the decimation of their territory in the peace that followed, for all the excesses and humiliations they had suffered at Napoleon's hands during a decade of war and occupation. Their reputation for brutality was well earned in these hours, as they set upon the retreating French, killing with rare abandon, bayoneting the wounded and cutting down stragglers as they sought to make their escape. The battle ended in total victory for the Allied side, a victory which denied Napoleon and his defeated army any hope of recovery, any opportunity to regroup to carry on the conflict. His army had been destroyed, utterly. Over the three days of the campaign, between 15 and 18 June, it had sustained over 67,000 casualties, compared to Wellington's 22,800 and the Prussians' 30,000.[36] Napoleon's only option was to sue for peace, from a position of palpable weakness, and hope that his enemies would show him even a fraction of the generosity they had shown the previous year. As he must have known, it would prove a forlorn hope. His adventure would end on St Helena.

If Waterloo had been a dogged battle, it had produced a number of encounters that would leave lasting images in popular memory across the nineteenth century. For the British public, and above all for the regiments that had fought there, the heroic defence of the farms at Hougoumont and La Haie Sainte continued to be cited as illustrations of supposed national qualities of stoicism and determination in the face of ferocious enemy attack. The memory would be revived during the Crimean War, when the British commander, Lord Raglan, who as a young officer had fought at Wellington's side at Waterloo, was pilloried for ordering the ill-fated charge of the Light Brigade against Russian artillery posts that sent thousands of men to their deaths; the contrast with Wellington's careful planning and execution could not, it seemed, be more stark.[37] His reputation as one of Britain's great military leaders seemed safe. But if his tactical command is not in doubt, or the trust placed in him by all the Allied heads of state and commanders, his strategic handling of the battle is much more open to criticism, as he misread Napoleon's intentions and delayed assembling his army as a consequence. His grasp of strategy, for his critics, had atrophied in the Peninsula, and had advanced little since the time of Frederick the Great. One former army officer and military historian of Waterloo, Gordon Corrigan, goes as far as to suggest that his performance in the field was very average, noting that 'at no stage of the battle did Wellington have to direct manoeuvres of any sophistication, nor was his tactical acumen put to any great test'. Indeed, he concludes that 'there were many other British generals who could have done that just as competently as Wellington'.[38] But all that was forgotten in the afterglow of victory, in the final rout of his adversary.[39]

It was not only the victors who gloried in memories of the battle. In France, too, the dominant memory of Waterloo would be of their soldiers' heroism amidst the carnage, of the squares of the Old Guard fighting to the last man to save their eagles and their honour, a courage that was encapsulated in the *mot de Cambronne*. These images would recur again and again in old soldiers' tales, in military memoirs, in the poetry and novels of successive generations, and they are the subject of the remainder of this book.

4

First Responses to Waterloo

News of the Allied victory travelled rapidly across Europe, borne by couriers and passed on by word of mouth to the various courts and capital cities of a continent fatigued of war. But it still took time: military despatches, like other messages, arrived at the speed of the fastest horse, and in the British case there was the added problem of finding a ship on which to carry the messenger across the Channel to reach London. In the event, news of Wellington's victory—for it was as such that it was announced—reached London three days after the battle, on 21 June. Its bearer was Wellington's young (and only surviving) aide-de-camp, Henry Percy, grandson of the Duke of Northumberland, whose dramatic arrival ended a day of feverish speculation and contradictory rumours in the capital. Percy had fought at Waterloo and had been on the road without a break since the final rout of Napoleon's army. He arrived in a chaise-and-four hotfoot from the Channel, bloodstained and exhausted, and still dressed, it was reported, in the scarlet tunic he had worn at the Duchess of Richmond's ball in Brussels on the eve of Quatre Bras. With him he brought Wellington's Despatch and two captured imperial eagles, and after first reporting to Earl Bathurst at the War Office, he and his companions moved on to St James's Square to seek out the Prince Regent. The victory was announced to an excited crowd, and Percy's chaise swung into the square amid cheering and exultation, preceded by link boys brandishing tapers. For his efforts Percy was rewarded with the rank of lieutenant colonel and elevation to the Order of the Bath.[1] The Waterloo Despatch had been written within twenty-four hours in Wellington's own hand: this gave it a rare authority, so that even its composition came to be regarded as one of the iconic aspects of the battle.[2] The country prepared to join in a national celebration.

The Waterloo Despatch

The Despatch was famously reticent, a factual account rather than the triumphant statement that many had expected. In form it was consistent with the despatches he had sent after each one of his battles on the Peninsula, an official account restricted to outlining the actions for which he had been responsible and reporting on the outcome of the engagement.[3] Wellington acknowledged the valuable assistance of the Prussians in gaining the victory, though he insisted that their role was limited to assistance, and lamented the loss of fellow officers in the cause. The Duke of Brunswick was among the dead; so, too, was Sir Thomas Picton, who 'fell gloriously leading his division to a charge with bayonets, by which one of the most serious attacks made by the enemy on our position was repulsed'. It has been suggested that the words of the Despatch revealed little of Wellington's true feelings, that he was overcome by the sight of carnage that met him when he returned to the battlefield. 'My heart', he wrote in the weeks following the battle, 'is broken by the terrible losses I have sustained of my old friends and companions, and my poor soldiers!' Among the deaths that especially affected him was that of his loyal aide-de-camp, Sir Alexander Gordon, who died from wounds he received as he helped the Duke to rally the Brunswick infantry in the thick of the fighting. To Gordon's brother, the Earl of Aberdeen, Wellington wrote these lines:

> The glory resulting from such actions, so dearly bought, is no consolation to me, and I cannot imagine that it is any to you: but I trust the result has been so decisive, that little doubt remains of our exertions being rewarded by the attainment of our first object; then it is that the glory of the actions in which our friends have fallen may be some consolation to me.[4]

Wellington spoke as a soldier. He made no apology for the losses, expressing only sadness; death he saw as part of the necessary cost of war. As he told Bathurst, the Secretary for War, after the battle, 'such a desperate action could not be fought, and such advantages could not be gained, without great loss; and I am sorry to add that ours has been immense'.[5] But that does not mean that he was unaffected by them. Indeed, we know that he interrupted writing the Despatch when he heard news of General Ponsonby's death and grief overwhelmed him.

For some contemporaries, among them many who had been present on the battlefield, his words seemed too dull, his response too stoical, too lacking in praise and enthusiasm for the sacrifices they had made; they felt that the army deserved more. All that the Duke could manage was the characteristically terse statement that 'the army never, upon any occasion, conducted itself better'. In later life it seems that he expressed regret that he had not been able to be more fulsome; when, as an old man, he was asked if there was anything he could have done better, he is reputed to have replied, 'Yes, I should have given more praise.'[6] But at the time he felt unable to do so. Weariness and sadness for the loss of his companions-in-arms made it impossible for him to exult, though his apparent lack of excitement at the scale of his victory was widely assumed to stem from a cold aloofness that would make him a hard man to like and a somewhat ambivalent national hero.[7] Though his popularity peaked sharply after Waterloo, during a long political career he would never again enjoy such affection.

The Commons heard of the victory on 23 June, when member after member heaped praise on the victorious Wellington and the troops he had led with such distinction against a commander who, as Lord Castlereagh reminded MPs, 'had been called the greatest Captain of his age'. To defeat Napoleon on land was no mean feat, and the Foreign Secretary did not hold back in his appreciation of Wellington's prowess, offering his judgement that 'it was an achievement of such high merit, of such pre-eminent importance, as had never perhaps graced the annals of this or any other country till now'.[8] He talked of the relative youth of the Allied army, their comparative

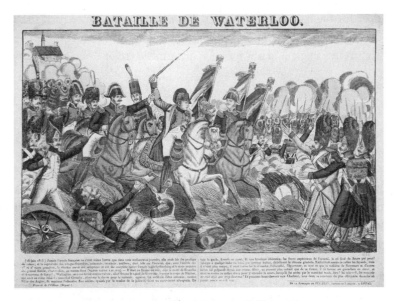

Figure 4. Image d'Épinal, *La Bataille de Waterloo*

inexperience when faced by Napoleon's seasoned soldiers, 'the flower of the French army, brought together from all parts of Europe and concentrated for the purpose of making this first attack'. And though he acknowledged the contribution of the Dutch and the Prussians to the final victory, Waterloo was unequivocally presented as a British battle. Only the English troops, he suggested, came to the battle with the requisite experience of war. The others brought youth and courage:

> Great, however, as that merit was, it was fit that he should remark that with the exception of the English force the army engaged might be called a green army, as those who composed it had, for the most part, never been in action before. The greater part of the force engaged had been newly levied, so that the Duke of Wellington (with the exception of the English army) was at the head of troops almost wholly unaccustomed to war.[9]

Blücher had been strong and steadfast, of course, but it was not he who had secured such a clear-cut victory; Britain was 'indebted' to her allies for the role they had played, for what Castlereagh termed their 'cordial assistance'. But, as he emphasized rather pointedly in the Commons, theirs had always been a secondary role:

> Notwithstanding the intrepidity for which the Prussians had always been distinguished, and with which they would ever fight under a commander so dear to them as Prince Blücher, yet the French had advanced in such masses against them, that his posts had been driven in, and he had been forced to draw back his right wing.

He went on to drive home the point. It was not true that the Prussians had borne the brunt of the French attack, or not, at least, alone. 'The whole of the operations of Buonaparte on that day were not directed against the Prussian army. Two divisions were sent against the English', he insisted, and they had been fought off by a 'small force' of 'ten thousand men'.[10] MPs loved what they were hearing. This was a moment of rare military triumph which would serve to rally the entire nation behind the leadership, one to be savoured rather than shared.

Waterloo in Parliament

Parliament was careful to do nothing to disparage the French, since their strength and valour only made the scale of Wellington's achievement the greater. For nine hours, the British troops and their allies had stood firm against the repeated charges of the enemy, an enemy that was well organized and well prepared and was, said Castlereagh, 'in a high state of organization before the return of Buonaparte to France'. Moreover, the French had had at their disposal 'not only the Imperial Guard but the five most complete corps of the French army, and nearly the whole of its cavalry and artillery'. He went on to praise their courage and discipline in the field and to emphasize how well they had fought, for 'it was but justice to the enemy to say that in the actions which had taken place they had fought with determined courage and well sustained the renown they had acquired in former wars'.[11] All this, of course, merely added gloss to the performance of the British troops and to the splendour of Wellington's achievement as their commander. The soldiers could take satisfaction in what they had done—they were strong, resolute, fearless—but the glory was Wellington's. It was a distinction which Castlereagh did not hesitate to draw:

> The common soldier had only his local duties to perform, but the Duke of Wellington was everywhere in the heat of the action, and everywhere in the presence of danger. Having remained on the defensive for nine hours, the moment at length arrived when he saw there was a prospect of acting on the offensive with success. He then ordered the line to advance. The shock was irresistible—the French could not resist our attacks as we had resisted theirs; their ranks were broken—their first line thrown into disorder on the second; they were compelled to fly in the greatest confusion, and the English and their Allies became masters of at least (as he should suppose) half the artillery of the enemy.

This was not an era that routinely gave credit to the common soldier; but their 'distinguished valour and discipline' at Waterloo were 'highly approved', and this message was to be passed to them by their commanding officers. The officers were to receive the 'thanks of this House'. But the victory, as Parliament learned of it, was Wellington's alone; and it was an unparalleled victory in that 'such splendid trophies of victory had never before been captured under such circumstances'.[12]

By 29 June, when Castlereagh again addressed the House on the subject of Waterloo, the consequences of the battle for Napoleon and his ambitions had become clearer, and the minister was able to claim it not only as a great military triumph but also as a powerful 'moral success'. This time he was more critical of France and the death and disruption which Napoleon had caused, to his own people as to others. Waterloo, he claimed,

> Had made that nation to whom, for the last five-and-twenty years, all the calamities with which Europe had been afflicted were owing, feel the whole extent of the misery and misfortune which its own criminal

ambition had so often inflicted on other countries; and he trusted it had also produced that deep impression upon the heart of every Frenchmen, as it was evident it had upon the apprehensions of the government of France, that they would feel no time was to be lost in repairing, as far as was in their power, the multiplied injuries they had inflicted on mankind.[13]

He was also more explicit about how the battle should be commemorated, and proposed to the Commons that an event as momentous as Waterloo should be marked by the erection of a national monument to the memory of the officers and soldiers who had fallen in the battle, in order 'that they might live in the gratitude of posterity and of an admiring world'. Plans, he said, were already afoot. It was the government's intention 'to erect a pillar, or triumphal arch, some architectural monument in fact, suitable to the magnificence of the nation, and which, of course, would not be confined within the walls of a church'. In particular he recommended that the two most senior officers killed on the battlefield, Thomas Picton and William Ponsonby, should have funeral monuments erected in their memory in the national pantheon of St Paul's.[14] But, significantly, he was less precise when it was suggested that the national monument should be inscribed with the names of the ordinary soldiers who had died. That, he said, 'had better be left for arrangement in the execution of the plan'.[15] It would be a new departure to remember soldiers individually rather than collectively, as divisions or regiments; individual memorials were still for their officers.

The Mood of Recrimination

Parliament was here expressing the relief and gratitude of the nation to those who had finally brought the long years of war to an end. But with relief went recrimination. Waterloo had been costly in human life: losses in Wellington's army were calculated at around 3,500 dead and a further 3,300 missing, all in a single day, and in the mind of the British public there was only one man who should be held responsible. Among London newspapers *The Times* took the lead in exposing the crimes of Napoleon and his henchmen and in demanding that those responsible for what it condemned as a criminal act should be brought to justice. The paper's editorial line was set as early as 28 June, when a pungent leader rejoiced in the downfall of Napoleon and his family and took a certain pleasure in suggesting that the French themselves might take vengeance on a man who had done them and their country so much damage. Rightly, the writer concluded that Napoleon was more at risk from the royalists among his own people than from any foreign government:

> This may be a mere rumour, but it is not improbable that the villain who has entailed on France so many calamities may fall by the hand of some desperate politician—or some exasperated patriot—or possibly by some injured individual whose exhausted patience could no longer repress the strong and just sentiments of personal revenge. Be this as it may, the dynasty, as it was absurdly called, of the vagabonds of Ajaccio is now completely at an end; for the reign of Napoleon II is a greater farce than the second reign of Napoleon I.

The paper went on to rail against the former Jacobins and regicides with whom Napoleon had surrounded himself during the Hundred Days, denouncing them as men of blood, as the 'Queue de Robespierre', and as a 'Rump Parliament' in the tradition of seventeenth-century England, which even now was debating 'the last new oath to be broken and the next new oath to be taken'.[16] *The Times* left its readers in no doubt that it expected them to be held to account for their treason by the returning Louis XVIII.

By this time the Allied armies, among them 'vast armies of Bavarians, Austrians and Russians', were rapidly closing in on the French capital. This led to anxiety in London that the Continental powers would seek to interfere in the French political settlement, something which *The Times* felt could be safely left to the royalist authorities in Paris. Those who had run France during the Hundred Days, serving the returned Emperor, were still in post, and it was a moot point how they would be treated when the Bourbons returned. Louis XVIII had expressly forbidden any of his subjects to take part in Napoleon's government, and those who had done so risked being charged with treason. *The Times* showed little sympathy and focused on the fate that should be reserved for Napoleon and his henchmen, suggesting in unequivocal terms that their crimes merited capital sentences and that they might fittingly be handed over to 'an executive officer named Jack Ketch', less colourfully known as the public hangman.[17] On the 30th it noted with disquiet reports that the man they called 'the Arch-Traitor Buonaparte' had surrendered to the Duke of Wellington, since

> Those who had a due regard to justice and who consequently viewed the life of this monster as forfeited to the offended laws of God and man, regretted that by any artful appeal to English generosity he should have contrived to elude the penalty of his crimes.[18]

These reports, however, were denied, and during the week that followed, the paper showed an increasing impatience at the slow pace of events in Paris, the tone of its editorials becoming even more irascible. London was impatient for news of the expected attack on Paris to restore order and overthrow the government. Bonaparte, they believed, should be treated as a war criminal, and they insisted that no leniency should be shown to those who had served him:

> It is presumed that the rebel Junta, who exercise the functions of government at Paris, finding there is little hope of pardon for themselves, have been joined by the perjured Generals who are in the same dilemma, in an appeal to the rabble of the *faubourgs* to fight it out to the last, and bury their infamous usurpation under the ruins of that splendid capital.[19]

The rebels by this time had become equated with bloodthirsty regicides, and their government was associated with the worst excesses of the Jacobin Terror. By 6 July *The Times* saw no reason to prevaricate, and its judgement was damning:

It is believed that the ephemeral reign of Napoleon II has wholly passed into oblivion, and that the Jacobins issue all their mandates now in the name of the Sovereign People, and form a kind of Committee of Public Safety as they did in the days of Robespierre. It is needless to observe that the time for such insanities is past; but if they prefer going off the stage in the costume of Directors, or Consuls, or Kings of Brentford, or Mayors of Garrat, they may perhaps be indulged. This, however, is a matter to be settled between themselves and the hangman, to whose care, we trust, their exit will be speedily consigned. Certainly, the longer these villains keep their country in agony, the more exemplary and unsparing should be their punishment.[20]

Their speedy and condign punishment, in the eyes of many in the British establishment, was not only what justice demanded; it was a necessary precondition for France's reintegration into the community of nations.

The Times was not alone in its desire for vengeance. For caricaturists, too, both in Britain and across Europe, Napoleon was now more a criminal than a foreign leader defeated in war, and their images of him became coloured by hatred and contempt. He had always been presented in England as a diminutive figure, but now his small size acquired added significance, reflecting the decline which he, and with him France, had suffered. He no longer posed a threat to British interests, as the peace settlement that followed Waterloo both reduced the territory of France and increased that of her nearest rivals.[21] He was also stripped of any remaining traces of imperial grandeur, becoming instead a simple postulant dependent on the mercy and goodwill of the Court of St James. Already after Leipzig George Cruickshank, who in 1806 had presented Napoleon as the 'Great French Gingerbread Baker', returned to that theme with a cartoon which he pithily entitled 'Broken Gingerbread'.[22] Now the images became more brutal, the sense of a destiny destroyed more incisively driven home. British cartoonists emphasized the irony of his situation, especially after he had surrendered to Wellington and elected to make himself Britain's prisoner. In July 1815 Thomas Rowlandson drew him as a harlequin imprisoned in a small cage on a cart being pulled by two donkeys, under the caption *A Rare Acquisition for the Royal Menagerie*. The man who had dominated Europe had been reduced to a figure of fun, left with no role in life other than to amuse the King of England in his leisure hours.[23] And Cruickshank pointed out how much difference a month had made in another famous cartoon, *Buonaparte on the 17th of June, Buonaparte on the 17th of July—1815*. By July, Napoleon has been brought to England, but John Bull declines to allow him to land; and when Napoleon asks pleadingly for asylum, he is received with a stony stare. In the background loom landmarks of his future travels in the form of Port Jackson and the island of St Helena.[24]

Napoleon after Waterloo

If these caricatures tell us something of the state of public opinion in England in the weeks following Waterloo, they also point to the desperate position in which Napoleon and France now found themselves. Napoleon, after all, had chosen to surrender to the British for good reason, in that, among his enemies, he imagined Wellington to be the most correct, the most honourable, and the most likely to treat him generously. He certainly had no reason to trust the Bourbons, or to look to royalists in France for any vestige of leniency: for them he was a traitor to his king, a revolutionary, the friend of regicides, and many were simply waiting for their opportunity to have him put on trial and hanged. The mood in France was anything but conciliatory, and here, too, cartoonists brutally lampooned the man who, it was felt, had led them to disaster at Waterloo. In the weeks following his defeat on 18 June the same themes recur in cartoon after cartoon printed in Paris, inspired, of course, by the return of Louis XVIII and the anti-Napoleonic atmosphere in the French capital. He is portrayed as a coward, habitually abandoning his troops and running from the battlefield. For one artist he is the schoolboy with his drum, beating the retreat in the face of the enemy, personified by Wellington.[25] In another, entitled *Bonaparte's Sacrifice*, he is seen riding away from the battle on a gleaming steed, deep in conversation with Death, who is sitting behind him; the battlefield in the background is presented as a scene of frightful carnage.[26] Others emphasize his humiliation, his indifference to losses, or suggest that he had signed a pact with the devil. In *Le Diable l'emporte* he is shown clutching on to the shoulders of a devil, the colour of fire, with the tail of a monstrous snake, which is bearing him off to Hell. It represents, declares the artist, nothing less than 'the dearest wish of France'.[27] In the aftermath of his defeat French jibes and denunciations were at least as hurtful as those of his enemies.

In war, of course, the winner takes all, and in the nationalist atmosphere enveloping Europe the victorious Allies had every intention of driving home their advantage. They may not yet have used the phrase 'war guilt', but it was clear that by escaping from Elba and rekindling the embers of war across the Continent Napoleon had made himself, in the eyes of his enemies, an aggressor, a warmonger, and for many a criminal. In 1814 the Allies had been generous in their treatment of Napoleon, but this time they would be less forgiving. France would not be spared either the humiliation of military occupation or the weight of heavy reparations: she was required to pay some 700 million francs to the coalition powers. Prussia had not forgotten the huge financial demands that had been made of her after Napoleon's victory at Jena, and in 1815 there was a general feeling that France should be made to pay for her transgressions, that she should be shorn of territory and forced to return the art treasures and historic spoils she had been allowed to keep at Vienna the previous year. The army of occupation that was imposed on France was there in part to ensure that the new government honoured its war debts. But it was also intended as a graphic reminder to the French people that this was a war that they had lost.[28] Besides, the very presence of Allied troops on French soil gave the Allies extra diplomatic leverage in the post-war world.[29] It was not something that they would easily give up; the lesson of the Hundred Days was too recent in the memory of all Europe.

The Allied powers were determined to impress on France that she must abide by her international obligations, for—whatever Napoleon may have believed when he returned from Elba—this was a war which they had no intention of reopening, a struggle which they could not allow Napoleon to win. And they would not have done so even if the Battle of Waterloo itself had been lost. For the Allied forces that were massing against Napoleon in June 1815 were not confined to Belgium, nor were the armies circling France limited to the Anglo-Dutch and Prussian armies of Wellington and Blücher, those that were actively involved in the fighting at Waterloo. There was no thought of compromise: all were agreed that Napoleon must be defeated and removed from office at any cost.[30] Indeed, other Allied forces were preparing to attack in the event of a Napoleonic victory at Waterloo, with the Austrians and Russians assembling massive armies in preparation for war in July. An Austro-Piedmontese army of some 80,000 men, an Austro-German army of around 180,000, and a Russian army of 150,000 were all massing to move against the French in the event of a Napoleonic victory. In that sense, though Waterloo was the instrument that led directly to Napoleon's overthrow, it was not in itself critical to the outcome of the war. The odds that faced the French in 1815 were overwhelming. If not at Waterloo, the defeat would have happened elsewhere.

This raises a number of questions about Wellington's motives in giving battle at Waterloo. Why, if Napoleon's defeat was already assured, did he risk the lives of so many of his men? And why did he unleash his last murderous assault on a beaten army? Was it so important to destroy the French army? Was it, indeed, so important that the victory should be seen to be British? In a recent study Huw Davies suggests that Wellington's motives were primarily diplomatic. The battle, he argues, was fought less to end the war than to prepare for the peace that would follow; in that sense Waterloo was as much a political victory as a military one. Wellington could not afford to allow his Continental allies, not least Prussia, to share in his victory, since to do so would risk unravelling the delicate peace terms drawn up at Vienna in 1814. Britain's position in the post-war world depended on imperial conquests and control of the seas; but to exercise it Britain also needed to maintain a balance of power on the Continent, which meant that Prussia must be held in check and that France, the France of Louis XVIII, must be allowed to rise again as a great European power. For Britain, argues Davies, this meant 'establishing political dominance over her allies', which was exactly what Wellington's victory delivered. In its essentials the Congress System was saved.[31]

Reaction in Paris

The manner in which the outcome of the battle was announced in Paris was very different from the triumphant scenes across the Channel. There were no public celebrations, no fireworks, no lanterns to light up the streets of the capital. Rather it was a moment when the country's leaders—ministers, generals, and deputies alike—had to take urgent stock of a situation that held the threat of civil war and might destroy France's status as a Great Power in European politics. The early news reaching Paris was confused, and the tone of the first reports was often hysterical. Had the army really been routed? Was French military might so totally destroyed? Reports circulated in the capital that Soult had rallied 2,000 men of the Guard at Rocroi, that Grouchy had defeated Blücher, and that an army of 60,000 was protecting France's northern frontier. Even the generals who had fought at Waterloo offered different accounts of the battle: whereas Drouot cited reassuring figures about France's military situation, claiming that the troops were ready to fight on, Ney flatly contradicted him, insisting that the French people must face the truth that their army had been effectively destroyed as a fighting force.[32] What were the people of Paris, or even the members of the Chamber of Deputies, to believe? Immediately after the battle Napoleon himself rushed back to Paris, apparently with the aim of continuing the war and of raising more troops for yet another campaign. He seemed determined to persuade the Chamber of Deputies and the Chamber of Peers that the fight was not over, and that to succumb to the Bourbons for a second time, or to throw themselves on the mercy of the Allies, would be an ignominious defeat for which France would surely pay a heavy political price. It was better by far to carry on the struggle, to defend Paris and take the war to the enemy. Waterloo had been a disaster, he acknowledged, but it was a disaster from which the army could recover to win another day.

As Napoleon presented it, he had not suffered an overwhelming defeat. His soldiers had crushed the Prussians at Fleurus in the previous days and had gone on to take six British standards at Waterloo, before, as evening fell and with victory beckoning, they had been sabotaged by the spread of malicious rumours. He had come to Paris, he said, to confer with his ministers on ways of building up the army once more to provide it with the men and the supplies needed for a renewed campaign. Assuming the language of the Revolution, he even called for a new *levée en masse* to defeat France's enemies. But his was almost a lone voice. His ministers were more realistic, understanding only too well that France would not enjoy peace while Napoleon remained in command. France had no appetite for more slaughter, and on the following day he was forced to change tack, admitting in a declaration issued from the Élysée that circumstances had indeed altered and offering to abdicate in favour of his young son. 'I offer myself', he declared to the French people, 'as a sacrifice to the hatred of France's enemies.' He added that he hoped they had been sincere in their declarations that their anger was vented against him alone. 'My political life is over,' he said; 'and I proclaim my son Emperor of the French with the title of Napoleon II.'[33]

But this compromise found little support. It was now clear to everyone that the Allies would not stand for any outcome that left the Empire intact, and the deputies were not going to argue. It was they who took the final decision to sue for peace, they who insisted that the Hundred Days, and with it the imperial adventure, were finally over. The Emperor discovered that he had lost the sympathy of the two chambers, which were now seriously questioning whether any benefit could be gained by further resistance. They accepted that

France had now exhausted its military potential and that any further negotiation would be from a position of weakness. There was no appetite for further conflict or aggression and no desire to indulge Napoleon's dreams, even among those marshals who had rallied to him with such optimism in the Hundred Days. Indeed, the most that the deputies would contemplate was to vote the means by which the country might defend itself against further attack. The Chamber there-fore adopted a resolution that defined very precisely the conditions that might justify a future war:

> The French nation renounces for ever all wars of conquest, all wars that are offensive and driven by ambition. It will take up arms only to defend its territory, to avenge affronts to its dignity where it could not obtain reparation through negotiation, or to defend an ally that has been unjustly attacked.[34]

The deputies realized that they emerged from the Waterloo campaign weakened and isolated. It was, in the view of one deputy, unthinkable that they would be granted the generous terms that Talleyrand had negotiated at Vienna. And so, he argued, they had no choice; there was only one way out of the precarious situation in which they found themselves, with enemy armies marching towards Paris. 'It is to commit the Emperor, in the name of the safety of the state, in the sacred name of a country that is suffering, to declare his abdication.'[35] Solemnly this message was conveyed to Napoleon, a message that showed he no longer enjoyed their confidence or support.

There was no jubilation in this moment, no expression of joy at Napoleon's passing. The atmosphere in the Chamber of Deputies was sombre, as men who had given long years of service to the Emperor recognized the significance of the moment in history they were living through. There was little recrimination either. Macdonald, Napoleon's former marshal who would now be nominated as provisional chief of the armed forces, emphasized the regard he still felt for Napoleon and recalled the 'sentiments that he must inspire in his current misfortune'.

In the negotiations that were about to open, he reminded the deputies, 'the representatives of the nation will not forget to defend the interests of the man who over long years has presided over the destiny of the country'.[36] The deputies could not but be moved by the intervention of Regnault de Saint-Jean-d'Angély, speaking now as a simple citizen, but a man who over a long political career had served the Directory, the Consulate, and the Empire, who expressed his feelings on taking leave of Napoleon. They were ambivalent feelings, tinged with sadness, contradictory feelings which he felt the nation should share:

> Perhaps now is the moment to reveal to you what took place inside his office. Yesterday, gentlemen, when I approached him, I told him that nothing could equal the loyalty I had sworn to him, but that, because of the confidence he had placed in me, I had to tell him that he was no longer able to defend the independence and the rights of the nation; I repeated to him that as a minister I would give my life to defend him and protect his throne; but that, as a representative of the people, aware of the obligations that office implies, I owed it to my country to tell him frankly what the security of the state demanded.[37]

But if all sounded measured and serene in the Chamber of Deputies, outside in the streets there was commotion and panic as people reacted to the scraps of news they could glean about the Allied advance. By 28 June the *Bulletin des armées* was publishing what it called 'alarming' details of the enemy's progress, with the virtual destruction of the Army of the Moselle, with the remnants of the French army pushed back across the Île-de-France towards Creil and Senlis, and with Paris itself under siege.[38] It soon became apparent that the French army was in no shape to resist. Discipline was breaking down. Napoleon's army was ravaged by high rates of desertion as it crossed back into France, and deserters were flooding into Paris in defiance of military orders.[39] By the end of June royalist uprisings were breaking out in the West and the country faced a risk of civil war. Waterloo left a legacy of political disorder as well as causing serious damage to the economy, and that legacy would prove corrosive in the years that followed.

Could there have been a different outcome? Could Napoleon have imposed his will by simply dismissing the Chamber of Deputies and assuming absolute power? Had he done so, would the French public have stood idly by? Napoleon asked himself these questions repeatedly during his exile on St Helena, but they were ruminations which even Emmanuel de Las Cases, who faithfully recorded his thoughts for posterity, was unwilling to entertain. No, he told the Emperor, the Legislature would not have allowed itself to be dissolved voluntarily; it would have protested; there would have been uproar. He goes on to explain the strength of opinion that had marshalled against him, and insists that abdication not only saved France but also secured Napoleon's own reputation for posterity:

> The dissent that had broken out would have been echoed across the nation. And then the enemy would have arrived. Your Majesty would have been forced to give in, accused by all of Europe, accused by foreigners but also by ourselves, cursed by everyone across the world and appearing as nothing more than an adventurer and a man of violence. Instead of that, Your Majesty has emerged from the drama with your reputation intact and will remain the hero of a cause which will live for ever in the hearts of all who believe in the cause of peoples... Your Majesty may have lost your power, it is true, but you have immeasurably increased your glory![40]

Las Cases knew how to flatter Napoleon and gain his cooperation, and it is significant that his reply appeared to achieve its purpose and to reassure the Emperor, at least for the moment. By emphasizing the will of the people and the vilification that he would risk from the French public, Las Cases appealed to Napoleon's own view of his relationship to the people and to public opinion.[41] It was his way of discouraging Napoleon's more extreme fantasies.

French commentators and memoir-writers repeatedly emphasized the part played by fortune at Waterloo: Wellington's good luck in making contact with the Prussians, which allowed him to gain the reinforcements he needed just as his own men were tiring in the field;

Napoleon's ill fortune that Grouchy's force failed to arrive on the battlefield when it was so sorely needed. Wellington admitted that the battle had been closely fought, while Napoleon talked of being finally deserted by the lucky star which, he insisted, had smiled on his career and on his armies. But though there is no doubt that the French fought gallantly at Waterloo and inflicted painful casualties in their turn, this argument can be taken too far. On the purely operational front, Napoleon was himself at fault for failing to make clear his intentions to Grouchy, who was left confused, passive, and lacking in initiative perhaps, but technically in the right. He simply abided firmly –his critics would say intransigently, stubbornly, blindly—by the instructions he had received, even after common sense might have suggested that he should search out the French army and join battle. But there is a wider strategic question, too. Did the French have a feasible endgame at Waterloo? The Emperor was, of course, fighting for his political survival, in the hope, no doubt, that a victory would persuade the exhausted Allies to abandon the Bourbons once and for all. He was prepared to promise that he would cease his aggressive policies and stop invading neighbouring territories; France would live within the frontiers that had been recognized at Vienna. And he could demonstrate that he had a degree of authority with the French people, an ability to police the territory and stamp out opposition, which the Allies needed and which the Bourbons clearly lacked. 'In the best-case scenario for the French,' writes Caleb Carr, 'Napoleon would have won that battle and the Allies would have been forced to make peace with the restored Bonapartist regime.'[42] France and its neighbours would thereafter live together in peace and harmony.

But was this ever a credible scenario? The new coalition was formed in record time in 1815 precisely because the other crowned heads of Europe saw Napoleon's return as a barrier to the return of peace across the Continent. Prussia could not forget the humiliation of Jena, Austria the dissolution of the Holy Roman Empire, Russia the invasion by the Grande Armée, or Britain the challenge to her primacy in the colonies and at sea. None of the Great Powers could afford to sink back into another quarter-century of war; and none felt able to live at peace with Bonaparte still at large. Some in France may have allowed themselves to be lulled into false security, dreaming once more of empire and glory when they heard of Napoleon's landing at Fréjus, but it was a dream that was constructed on aggression and conquest and it placed the rest of the Continent at jeopardy. Napoleon's very presence on European soil was now deemed to pose a threat to their security.

The Second Restoration

Many, like Talleyrand, understood this only too well, though he understood, too, the limitations of the Bourbons and the dangers of trying to justify the Second Restoration solely on the basis of legitim-ism. The foremost diplomat of the Congress of Vienna a few months earlier, Talleyrand tried to alert Louis XVIII to the situation in which the country found itself, but with limited success. In a memorandum to the King in the days immediately following Waterloo, Talleyrand explained that while the cause of legitimism might appeal to the more conservative of the Allies, it would certainly cost popular support at home. 'The spirit of the times in which we live', he wrote, 'demands that in great civilized states supreme power shall only be exercised with the consent of bodies drawn from the heart of the society that it governs.'[43] He knew that the Allies would turn again to Louis XVIII, but less through any enthusiasm for the Bourbon succession than through a lack of realistic alternatives. He had made it clear that he himself was open to any viable solution, other, of course, than Napoleon.

For France to conduct a successful diplomacy in the aftermath of the Hundred Days it was clear that she would have to make political as well as territorial concessions and that Napoleon was necessarily the first victim. On 27 June the French government, in the person of Macdonald, made its first contact with Wellington as commander-in-chief of the British army, asking for talks and claiming that the French now wanted to be ruled by a system of constitutional mon-archy. Macdonald offered no defence of the existing political regime, and chose instead to appeal to Britain's own constitutional traditions. He urged Wellington to defend the rights of the French people in defeat, reminding him that in his past conquests he had always defended the rights of invaded nations, the rights of human beings. And, he went on, France now wanted to live at peace with Britain; there was no reason for any lingering distrust. Napoleon's former marshal could not have phrased his loyalties more bluntly:

> The French nation wants to live under a monarch. It also wishes this monarch to rule in accordance with the law.
>
> The Republic has opened our eyes to all that is fateful about an excess of liberty, the Empire to what is fateful about an excess of power. Our ambition, and it is unalterable, is to distance ourselves from both these excesses and enjoy independence, order and peace in Europe.
>
> The eyes of all of France are fixed on the British constitution; we do not seek greater freedoms than in England, and we will not consent to have fewer.[44]

Under France's new constitution he guaranteed that there would be a clear separation of powers on the English model—'separated', he emphasized to Wellington, 'but not divided', and enjoying a harmonious relationship one with the other.

For Frenchmen looking back on Waterloo later in the century, this was the nub of the problem: that the battle had led not just to the end of the Napoleonic Wars, to the peace that so many craved, but to an unconditional surrender that placed in jeopardy all the gains they had made from the era of the Revolution and Empire. The year 1815 witnessed a political as well as a military defeat, which led most immediately to the loss of the relatively generous terms which Talleyrand's clever diplomacy had achieved for France at Vienna. Now the Allies stripped France of all the territorial gains made during the previous twenty-five years, restoring the borders that had been in place in 1789, and holding out the promise of an era of mediocrity in foreign affairs. It also resulted in the restoration of the Bourbons, imposed on a largely indifferent France in response to the Allies' own interests. In short, 1815 was about regime change, an insistence by the other powers that France should abandon the institutions—and for many the political ideals—for which the people had sacrificed so much and accept the imposition of a restored monarchy. The Second Treaty of Paris soon became a hated symbol of France's humiliation, and those who signed it could expect little thanks. 'After what I've consented to,' remarked the Duc de Richelieu, Louis XVIII's foreign minister, 'I deserve to go to the scaffold.'[45]

Though Napoleon would undoubtedly have agreed that the treaty provisions were dishonourable, it is interesting that he did not think them especially harsh. Indeed he could not understand why the Allies had not driven home their advantage, and why the British in particular had not imposed a victor's peace on the French. 'What sort of peace is it', he asked rhetorically, 'that England has signed', in circumstances where Castlereagh held all the cards and 'had the continent at his disposal'?

> What great advantage, what just compensations, has he acquired for his country? The peace he has made is the sort of peace he would have made if he had been beaten. I could scarcely have treated him worse, the poor wretch, if it had been I who had proved victorious!

Napoleon believed that Britain had been presented with a historic opportunity to change the balance of power permanently, and that Castlereagh had chosen to ignore it. He continued:

> Thousands of years will pass before England is given a second opportunity equal to this opportunity to establish her prosperity and greatness. Was it ignorance, was it corruption, that induced Castlereagh to take the line he did? Nobly, so he imagined, did he distribute the spoils of victory to the sovereigns of the Continent, while reserving nothing for his own country.[46]

But Napoleon's view was not widely shared. If he chose to see the terms as generous, the majority of his countrymen did not. Republicans and Bonapartists were as one in seeing the terms as a humiliation.

With the second coming of the Bourbons, France was forced to accept that the years of political experimentation were over, and that her revolutionary and imperial dreams had to be consigned—at least temporarily—to history. Louis XVIII realized that for at least some of his subjects his return was unwelcome and that within the army there were dissident groups who had shown no loyalty to the restored monarchy and on whose support he could not count in the future. This time the Bourbons would prove less conciliatory and readier to give free rein to their natural supporters among the nobility and the Catholic clergy, among whom there were many who opposed any form of compromise, baying for the blood of those whom they regarded as traitors to their king. In his proclamation from Cambrai on 12 July 1815 Louis had promised an amnesty, but he specifically excepted those guilty of leading or instigating what he termed the 'plot that had been hatched against royal authority'. No time was lost: two days later a royal ordinance was issued outlawing fifty-seven individuals whom it declared guilty of having abandoned the King before 23 March 1815—in other words, in the days before Louis had fled the country after Napoleon's return.[47] Trials and executions followed. Labédoyère was shot on 19 August; the Faucher brothers in September; and finally, and for many most tragically, Michel Ney on 7 December.[48] These men had betrayed their king and deserved to be excepted from the amnesty, a point that was hurriedly made by the Duc de Richelieu in the Chamber of Peers following Ney's execution. For Richelieu, his was 'a great example' that had had to be set. But for those who had remained loyal to Napoleon it was a travesty of justice, a vengeful and intensely political act against a man who for them epitomized the courage of the army and the spirit of the Empire. A rare hero to emerge from Waterloo, Ney would always retain their respect and affection; he would always be, in his Emperor's words, 'the bravest of the brave'.

5

Military Memoirs and Communicative Memory

What many of those who had not been present on the battlefield yearned for most in the years that followed was a sense of the reality of the battle, a feel for what it had been like to be there. This was what led whole families in London and other English cities to turn out to watch military parades on commons or town squares or to spend weekends at Chatham enthusing over the naval vessels at anchor along the Medway. In their personal lives they were fulfilling what was for them a sentimental need, to fill a void in their experience and to share in a moment that had entered the history of their nation. Wars create that need, and none less than wars that had lasted a generation and had cut men off from their families, had separated soldiers from civilians, and which left them in the post-war world with memories that were necessarily partial and incomplete. Men who had not been engaged in the fighting, who had been excused service or were too old to serve, felt a need to share the experience of those who had gone to war. And for wives and mothers the need to share something of the experience of their loved ones was just as compelling. What had their husbands felt or their sons gone through in the challenging, dangerous, and unnatural environment of war? It was above all the experience of the individual—the soldier at Jena, the sailor at Trafalgar, the patriot at Leipzig—that fascinated many of them most. This is what made sense to civilians who had never seen or smelt battle, and they searched in soldiers' writings for what

Catriona Kennedy has called 'the intermingling of the everyday and the extraordinary, domestic affairs and international events'.[1]

So much of the official history of Waterloo seemed unreal, far removed from what their loved ones could have known or felt. They craved to hear ordinary voices, the voices that communicated to them the fear, the pride, the honour and compassion of the individual at war. Samuel Hynes draws a clear distinction between history and autobiography and the individual narrative of war: for, he insists, war narratives fall into neither category but hold a position somewhere in between. Historians, he says,

> tell the big stories, of campaigns and battles, of the great victories and the disastrous defeats; synthesising the reports and the statistics, drawing their conclusions about strategy and tactics, assigning credit and blame, turning war's chaos into order. The men who were there tell a different story, one that is often quite ahistorical, even anti-historical. Their narratives are indifferent to the exact location of events in time (they rarely put dates to their actions) or in space (either they never knew exactly where they were or they had forgotten the names). But that seems right for the soldiers' tales they tell; exact dates and precise geography would turn personal experiences into battles, into the accounts that appear in newspapers and history books; unlocated narrative keeps it in the individual's realm. Nor do they have much to say about strategy, or about other battles, fought on other fields. They aren't even interested in victory or defeat, except as it affects them personally; survival is their happy ending.[2]

Though Hynes is writing about twentieth-century wars, his point is every bit as relevant for the Napoleonic era. What civilians most wanted to hear after Waterloo was the testimony of individuals, the voices of those who had been there.

It did not really matter if these voices were fictional, provided that they were realistic, credible, the voices of men akin to those they knew in their own communities or—only too frequently—whom they tended in their later years, still suffering from the scars which the war had left, in their homes, in hospitals or asylums. Émile Erckmann and Alexandre Chatrian, most famously, built on the success of their fictional story of Joseph, a conscript of 1813, by following him to

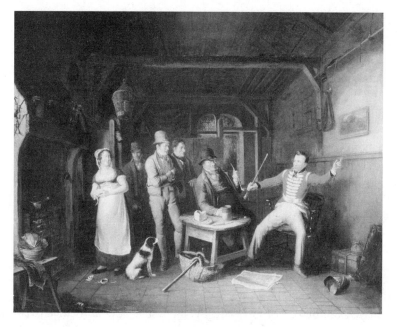

Figure 5. John Cawse, *A Soldier Relating his Exploits in a Tavern*

Waterloo, where he describes death and carnage that he can never have seen. The novel, indeed, admits what few memoirs confessed to—the fact that no serving soldier was in a position to know some of the things they consigned to paper. Discussing the effect of the Prussians' arrival on Napoleon's powers of resistance, the fictional character of Joseph is honest enough to admit to his readers that he is parroting ideas he has heard and that the thoughts he expressed were not his own or those of men like him:

> You must know that these ideas did not occur to us simple soldiers, but to our officers and generals; as for us, we knew nothing; we were there like victims who do not suspect that their hour is near.

His admission did little to undermine his readers' faith, however; it simply added an extra layer of verisimilitude and portrayed the soldier as they wanted to see him, as a simple victim of the great and powerful for whom the lives of common soldiers had little value. He returns to his narrative, assuring his readers that they will find exactly what they are looking for in the pages that follow. 'Now I am going to tell you the rest of the battle as I saw it myself, that every one may know as much about it as I do.'[3]

Waterloo continued to have a personal resonance in the countries whose soldiers had fought there long after the sounds of battle had stilled. In Britain, indeed, that resonance may even have increased with the passage of the years as the numbers of those who had been awarded the Waterloo Medal shrank to the point where only a few survivors were left. What else can explain the runaway box office success, in 1892, of Conan Doyle's one-act play *A Straggler of '15* when it was brought to the London stage? The play was Doyle's first; it lasted a mere 45 minutes; and it was in dramatic terms little more than a vehicle for one of the great stage actors of the day, Henry Irving, who played the hero, Corporal Gregory Brewster, now an octogenarian and one of the last surviving veterans of Waterloo. The play told a simple story, of a man who had saved others on the battlefield by his courage in driving a tumbril laden with powder through a burning hedge to safety. But the man who appears on stage is far removed from the military hero he had been, in the uniform of the 3rd Guards that appears in a painting on the wall; he is shown to be (and here I quote the stage directions) 'gaunt, bent and doddering, with white hair and wizened face', his memory gone, his energy ravaged by time.[4] He has not been kindly treated in the intervening years, and now, with his memory in tatters, he can no more forget Waterloo than he can grasp what is going on in the room around him. The play ends with his death as he slumps into a chair on stage, and the final words—'I think that the 3rd Guards have a full muster now'—spoken by a sergeant from his regiment, do not just bring down the curtain on the play.[5] They also silence a voice which, the audience could easily allow itself to believe, provided a direct link with the past, part of the communicative memory of Waterloo which they were so eager to access.

Unsurprisingly, in each of the participant nations, the thirst was for a different sort of story. Britain produced the greatest number of accounts, in part because of the level of public interest in the battle, but in part, too, because those who had participated in a great victory felt that they had something to communicate, a part of the nation's history they wished to claim for their own. They wanted to tell their story as they remembered it, often embellishing it with the kind of literary flourishes which they felt their readers would expect. Some were natural soldiers, men who had volunteered for the army to escape drudgery at home and who refused to admit to any regrets or second thoughts—men like Edward Costello, who had left his life as an apprentice cabinetmaker in Dublin to join the army and who, many years after the Wars were over, wrote his *Adventures of a Soldier* in a mood of almost jubilant self-justification, tracing his life, with all its dangers, through the battles of the Peninsula to a final sortie, as a member of Picton's Fifth Division, in the Waterloo campaign.[6] Mood, emotion, and personal reminiscence were at a premium as he attempted to open up his world to his readers and paint a picture of the memorable scene that greeted him and his comrades when they crossed the Channel and passed the gates of Brussels on the road to Waterloo.

> It was the 16th—a beautiful summer morning—the sun slowly rising above the horizon and peeping though the trees, while our men were as merry as crickets, laughing and joking with each other, and at times pondered in their minds what all this fuss, as they called it, could be about; for even the old soldiers could not believe the enemy were so near.

Calm and serenity dominate the scene he is describing, a calm that would be rudely disturbed in the hours that followed, but it is that calm, the beauty of the morning light, the peaceful mood of the Belgian countryside, that he dwells upon. 'I could not help noticing,' he writes, 'while we remained here, the birds in full chorus straining their little throats as if to arouse the spirits of the men to fresh vigour for the bloody conflict they were about to engage in.'[7]

The eerie silence of a summer morning, the haunting beauty of birdsong, these were the intimate details that added a personal touch to a memoir, something the reader could not find in the official histories or published accounts of the battle. They were also descriptions of a landscape that would soon be immutably transformed, of a glorious summer day—as in August 1914—that was about to be shattered by war. Within a day even the elements had unleashed all their fury. William Tomkinson recalls the evening of 17 June, by which time all trace of serenity had vanished and the fields were turning into a swamp. 'During our retreat from Quatre Bras,' he writes, 'we had been exposed to the heaviest rain I was ever out in, and in consequence not a dry thread remained throughout the army.' They had chosen a field of clover to rest in as it seemed likely to be drier than standing wheat or fallow; but 'with the horses moving about to get their backs to the rain, and the men walking to feed them and light fires, the clover soon disappeared, and the whole space occupied by the 16th became one complete puddle'. It was, he added, 'knee-deep at daylight'.[8] But Tomkinson appreciated the landscape and appraised the weather differently from his civilian readers: as he looked down towards Hougoumont and La Haie Sainte, he assessed the full implications of the weather and the terrain for the fighting that lay ahead:

> The whole field was covered with the finest wheat, the soil was strong and luxuriant; consequently, from the rain that had fallen, was deep, heavy for the transport and moving of artillery, and difficult for the quick operation of cavalry. The heavy ground was in favour of our cavalry from the superiority of horse, and likewise, in any charge down the face of the position, we had the advantage of moving downhill, and yet we felt the inconvenience in returning uphill with distressed horses after a charge. The difficulty of returning up the hill with distressed horses occasioned so great a loss in the charges made by the heavy brigades.[9]

This assessment may, of course, have been made with all the benefits of hindsight; it was not until years later that Tomkinson's memoirs were published. But it does not really matter. For their reader they conjured up the immediacy of the moment as Lieutenant-Colonel William Tomkinson surveyed the scene that lay before him on the morning of Waterloo. And it was the sense of sharing that moment which made these memoirs such enthralling reading.

Of course, readers wanted action, too, moments of courage and danger narrated by those who had lived through them, personal accounts that would bring the battlefield to life and burst through the official prose about operational decisions and casualty rates. This was the reason why they treasured personal letters from the Waterloo campaign, which, in often faltering prose, sought to reassure anxious parents and tell them of the near-death experiences they had lived through.[10] Captain Wildman, though he was saddened by the injury to Lord Uxbridge, who was wounded by one of the last shots of the battle and had to have his leg amputated, called Waterloo 'the proudest, happiest day I ever knew'.[11] Memoirs, some written long years after the event, were more polished affairs, the best of them written with a degree of literary artifice that served to win over their readers. One of the most popular was the *Journal of the Waterloo Campaign* of General Alexander Cavalié Mercer, which provided graphic details of the fighting and of the terrible casualties that were sustained as blocks of troops battered each other relentlessly. Here he describes the impact of the advancing French infantry and the horrors of the slaughter that followed:

> The rapidity and precision of the fire was quite appalling. Every shot almost took effect, and I certainly expected that we should all be annihilated. Our horses and limbers, being a little retired down the slope, had hitherto been somewhat under cover from the direct fire in front; but this plunged right amongst them, knocking them down by airs and creating horrible confusion. The drivers could hardly extricate themselves from one dead horse ere another fell, or perhaps themselves.

Confusion, indeed, is one of the recurrent themes of Mercer's narrative, a confusion that adds realism and conviction to his account. 'What was passing to the right and left of us,' he says, 'I know no more about than the man in the moon...The smoke confined our vision to a very small compass, so that my battle was restricted to the two squares and my own battery; and, as long as we maintained our ground, I thought it a matter of course that others did, too.'[12]

With literacy at a higher level than in past wars, there would be an unprecedented number of memoirs written by non-commissioned officers and private soldiers, men whose sacrifice in war had seldom been commemorated or held up as exemplary in a previous age. Costello's was among them: a memoir that was unashamedly written to celebrate the bravery and devotion of ordinary soldiers, men who had in all likelihood been abandoned to poverty in the bleak aftermath of war. Suffering constituted a real part of their story, suffering and stoicism in the face of material deprivation and often harsh discipline; and some of them were not afraid to suggest the need for social change and recognition for those who had obeyed rather than given orders in battle. Examples abound from the Peninsula as well as from Waterloo, with the publication of such wildly popular memoirs as George Gleig's *The Subaltern* and John Kincaid's *Adventures in the Rifle Brigade*, both published by 1830.[13] Waterloo figured strongly in these soldier narratives, unsurprisingly given the brutality of the battle and the heavy casualties that were suffered. One such, the *Journal of a Soldier of the Seventy-First or Glasgow Regiment*, published in 1819 and going through several editions, was much admired and would become a sort of paradigm for the British soldier memoir of the Romantic age, occupying, in Neil Ramsay's words, 'a canonical position' in the historical literature on the Napoleonic Wars.[14] In part, doubtless, this was due to the simple patriotism it expressed, the story of a boy who had left his family in traumatic circumstances to join the army, which goes on to trace his adventures and battles in South America and the Peninsula as well as at Waterloo. The anonymous author, identified only as Thomas, did not hide the pain and suffering of army life, and this may help to explain the popularity of the book, which supposedly sold over 3,000 copies in its first two editions. John Howell, in a preface to the third edition, writes that Thomas's work exposed the day-to-day experience of ordinary soldiers and thereby helped to counteract 'the pernicious influence of the generally received maxim that there is something particularly honourable in the profession of arms—that it is more glorious to be employed as an instrument of terror and destruction than in promoting the arts that gladden the life of man'.[15]

It would be wrong to exaggerate, however, the element of democratization or to imply that the accounts of other ranks were now the dominant register for military memoirs. In the years following Waterloo it is officers' accounts that still dominate the genre, and their values are reflected in the emphasis placed on gallantry and chivalry, on dancing and entertainment and the social round of the officers' mess. One of the principal themes of Waterloo memoirs, indeed, is the Duchess of Richmond's ball, held in Brussels in the days preceding the battle and attended by the Duke of Wellington and by the cream of the British officer class. It was remarked upon how elegant the ball was, how chivalrously the officers behaved to the ladies present, how Wellington himself left the ball to pass directly to Waterloo to prepare himself for battle.[16] Brussels had become a favoured destination for the British in 1814, with aristocratic families queuing up to leave their London homes to resume the tradition of Continental travel they had had to abandon during the war. Many of them chose to settle, at least temporarily, in Brussels. In part, this was due to their relative poverty: rents were known to be cheap in the city, and other English families had already settled there, making it a congenial place in which to conduct their now familiar social round. In part, too, it may have reflected feelings of friendship towards the newly restored House of Orange. Napoleon's escape from Elba and the news that his army was heading towards Brussels undoubtedly sowed some alarm among these expatriates, but their lifestyle remained unaffected. Indeed, with the arrival of Wellington's army, they were joined by others, the wives of army officers who preferred to live in the shelter of a capital city than share the ardours of life on the battlefield. They settled in easily: the aristocracy provided both the majority of the expatriate community in the city and the officer class of the army, so that in June 1815 any division that might have existed between civil and military society became effortlessly blurred.[17]

On the eve of the battle the ladies who attended the ball were rubbing shoulders, often literally, with the Duke and his officers, hearing their boasts and sharing their anxieties as they prepared for war once again. They were present when news arrived of Napoleon's movements; present, too, when their young consorts hastily left the ballroom in a clatter of swords. And some among them, feeling that they, too, were present as history was being made, shared the same literary ambition as the officers, wishing to consign their experiences to paper, to write memoirs that would inform posterity of the part they had played, if not in war, then at the very least on the brink of it. For Brussels was not exempt from the effects of warfare. It was in Brussels that many of the Allied troops were quartered on the eve of the battle; and it was to Brussels that cartloads of wounded soldiers came looking for medical treatment when the fighting was over. In the days following the battle, the wounded, the groaning, and dying seemed to be piled up everywhere, and the women of Brussels, English gentlewomen among them, were soon mobilized to help make bandages and care for the sick. They also produced several of the best-known romantic narratives that were written about Waterloo, and certainly the only ones by women—among them *Waterloo Days* by Charlotte Eaton and Fanny Burney's *Waterloo Journal*. Eaton and Burney were both civilians, of course, and neither was present on the battle-field, but they claimed that their 'proximity' to the action gave them the status of witnesses.[18] Eaton specifically mentioned her presence in Brussels as giving authenticity to her account and as distinguishing it from the writings of the many scribblers who had arrived after the battle as a sort of pilgrimage to the scene of great events. She was, she insisted, 'on the spot when these glorious events took place'.[19]

German accounts of the battle share in the joy of victory and, quite naturally, claim much of the credit for it themselves. In their reports and correspondence German officers often expressed a strong sense of their own identity, as Prussians, Hanoverians, or Nassauers, and they took an obvious pride in the courage they showed in the face of enemy fire. Among those German troops integrated into Wellington's army emotions were rather more mixed. On the one hand, recalled Captain Carl Jacobi of the 1st Hanoverian Brigade, they had huge respect for the Duke whom they regarded as a highly capable commander: when on 19 April Wellington had inspected his brigade near Mons, Jacobi remarks that 'everyone was filled with joy and confidence upon beholding the highly respected leader, and his appearance inspired and confirmed our trust in his generalship which foretold victory'. But when, a week later, the Hanoverian Brigades were stripped of their independent status and assigned to various divisions of the British army, he does not hide his resentment. They would no longer appear on the battlefield as Hanoverians; their identity had been 'eliminated with the stroke of a pen', and in matters of provisioning, discipline, and the order of battle they were under the command of English officers. This, he believes, had serious consequences for his men:

> To us at least it was a severe blow to our morale. The English generals were totally unfamiliar with the traditions of the Hanoverians; they were therefore unable to appreciate their good dispositions and to connect to the German soldiers' nature. In their eyes, everything was imperfect, even open to criticism that did not conform to English concerns and institutions. There was no camaraderie among the Allied troops, not even among the officers. The ignorance of the other's language, on both sides, the major difference in pay and the resulting great difference in life styles prevented any closer companionship. Our compatriots in the King's German Legion did not even associate with us; the fifteen-year-old ensign with the red sash proudly looked down upon the older Hanoverian officer. In the course of the campaign these disparities often became unbearably more pronounced, and it redounds to the troops' honour that they did not waver in their dedication and loyalty.[20]

Regimental history and past triumphs were as important to Hanoverian soldiers as they were to their British counterparts, and it is clear that their loss was a matter of deep regret.

Figure 6. David Wilkie, *Chelsea Pensioners Reading the Gazette after the Battle of Waterloo*

In German accounts Waterloo is always presented as an Allied operation, and its outcome as an Allied victory. The timely arrival of Blücher is seen as the key moment in the battle, just as the contributions made by von Bülow's corps and the advanced guard under von Zieten are also judged to have been of the first importance in securing Napoleon's defeat. Some, indeed, were openly critical of Wellington's tactics which they saw as doomed to failure if no help arrived. Sergeant Johann Doring, of the Orange-Nassau Regiment, described the battle in which they were engaged as one of turmoil, confusion, and disorder as the French moved against them with increasing ferocity:

> Without interruption, we loaded and fired into the enemy's ranks; no use in aiming at a particular target. As the enemy was forcefully pushing forward, getting more reinforcements all the time, we could hardly have withstood his thrusts much longer. Wellington, moreover, had pulled many regiments towards his faltering centre.[21]

It was at this moment that the Prussians arrived, and then the fighting acquired new intensity. A lieutenant in the King's German Legion

(KGL), Ernst Meier, recalls the level of destruction as 'the enemy projectiles struck all over the battlefield and from all directions... everywhere men and horses were mangled', before a 'desperate affair' developed with French cuirassiers attacking them from both flanks.[22] The battle, in the eyes of these Germans fighting in the British army, was won because of the arrival of the Prussians with the fresh troops they brought to the field. Doring is in no doubt that without them Waterloo would have been lost. The victory, he insists, 'was primarily owed to the Prussians because our army could hardly have held out any longer'.[23] In similar vein, Wilhelm Schutte, writing about the sufferings of his Brunswickers, describes the piles of bodies left on the battlefield as daylight faded and as French resistance finally collapsed. 'In truth,' he told his parents, 'much the same might have happened to us if the Prussians had not come to help us.'[24]

Even Carl von Müffling, the most read of the Prussian diarists and a commander who had worked closely with the Duke on the battlefield, allows himself to question the strength of the British force at Waterloo and to ask whether on its own it could really have held off the French. In Müffling's view, Wellington had left his right flank exposed and would have struggled to contain a determined French attack on Hougoumont, which 'I deemed untenable in a serious assault by the enemy'.[25] Yet Napoleon missed his chance. The author clearly has the utmost respect for Wellington's tactical acumen, but he is also convinced that the Prussian contribution to the final outcome was of the first significance; in the afternoon, after around 3 p.m., 'the Duke's situation became critical, unless the succour of the Prussian army arrived soon'.[26] Again, when Wellington ordered his infantry into the attack, what strikes Müffling is not its strength but its inherent weakness. 'This advance of such weak battalions, with the great gaps between, appeared hazardous,' he writes; 'the Duke, however, would not order them to stop, as the English cavalry formed a second line, ready to support the infantry should the French still be in a position to attack it.' Müffling respected the Duke's decision, though he knew that he was taking a gamble, assuming that Napoleon's army would be unable to launch a counter-attack of its own. But he also, as a Prussian, perceived a political motive for Wellington's gambit, a desire to avoid handing the Prussians any propaganda advantage:

> The Duke, with his practised eye, perceived that the French army was no longer dangerous: he was equally aware, indeed, that with his infantry so diminished he could achieve nothing more of importance; but if he stood still, and resigned the pursuit to the Prussian army alone, it might appear, in the eyes of Europe, as if the English army had defended themselves bravely indeed, but that the Prussians alone decided and won the battle.[27]

In other words, his decision was a political one: Wellington was thinking less of winning the immediate battle with Napoleon than of ensuring his place in history at Blücher's expense.

This was, of course, an archetypically Prussian response, and one which found few echoes in British memoirs of the battle which fed a public eager for tales of British heroism and accounts of Wellington's consummate military skill. For British soldiers the Prussians would seem to have been of secondary interest, an army with whom they acted in concert only rarely and which they associated above all with marauding and plundering, practices which their own officers tried to discourage. After the battle was over the two armies stayed largely apart until the fall of Paris some three weeks later.[28] Yet all, on the Allied side, had a victory to celebrate, one which they could glory in. What of Napoleon's officers and men? Waterloo does not stand out among French engagements as encouraging a proliferation of war memoirs: far more ink was spilt on earlier campaigns, on the successive French invasions of Germany, for instance, or on the Russian campaign of 1812. But French officers did not shy away from talking about Waterloo, or from discussing Napoleon's final defeat. In all, Jean Tulard has counted some thirty-five memoirs published in French, the vast majority of them written by Frenchmen, which discuss the experience of the battle.[29] Waterloo was in no sense a taboo subject after the war was over.

It was not just that the readership was there for military memoirs in post-Napoleonic France; it was also that the men who had fought in his wars felt the need to write, to relate their experiences, and to share them with others. On the French side alone, more than five hundred volumes of memoirs on the Napoleonic years were published during the first half of the nineteenth century, in many cases written by ordinary Frenchmen—soldiers and civilians, administrators and ministers, eyewitnesses to great events, men and occasionally women who had played their part as minor actors on the national stage in the turbulent years of the Revolution and Empire and who now felt impelled to commit their memories to paper.[30] Wider literacy levels had democratized the memorial process, and memoir-writing was no longer the closed preserve of the rich or aristocratic, as had been the case in the Old Regime. The opportunities for publication were expanded too, though not in any simple linear way; during much of the nineteenth century censorship was still enforced, and so much depended on the regime in place, its fears and electoral strategies. The Restoration years were especially intimidating in this regard as the Bourbons had no interest in reminding their subjects of the military glories of the previous era. But after 1830 and more particularly after 1851 official attitudes changed; there was renewed interest in the wars and in the experiences of those who had fought in them, and publishers actively sought out manuscripts. And at moments when France again faced the threat of war with Prussia or the new German Empire—whether in 1870 or in the years running up to 1914—there was once again a keen demand for the memoirs of those from a previous generation who had taken up arms to follow their Emperor across the gaping swathes of German Central Europe. Once again readers wanted to share their experiences, to find out what war was really like. And once again old soldiers were prompted to summon up their memories, presenting to a new generation a vision of war that might inspire them to further sacrifice.[31]

Many of these memoirs were heavily impregnated with patriotic sentiment. They told individual stories, which began when the men were conscripted or entered service and ended with their last campaign, offering personally tailored accounts of the great historical canvases of the day. They described actions in which the authors had been involved, they told of their feelings and their fears, and they described the combat that they had seen around them. They added personal details that were absent from more general, broadbrush accounts and which gave their accounts a persuasive semblance of truth. But the further the author was in time from the events he described, the more he inevitably lent on his memory—quite often the failing memory of an old man looking back nostalgically on the feats of his youth—as well as on such extraneous elements as the accounts he had read elsewhere, the histories that had been published in the interim, the memoirs of other officers, or the accepted views and myths that had built up around the events in the intervening years. Sometimes the language in which events and landscapes are described is transposed, too, from other texts, to take its place in personal memoirs as the author's own, often graphic, impression.[32]

The principal protagonists in the battle, Blücher, Wellington, and especially Napoleon, seldom stray from the fixed stereotypes that could be found in the public prints of the day: they were no longer seen as individuals with their share of human frailties, rather they were *personages*, figures from history whose character was part of common knowledge. They were portrayed very largely as the readers expected them to be portrayed, which, again, became a source of reassurance, an added source of authority for the veracity of the author's account. And yet the very way in which memoirs were written and their narratives shaped shows that they were seldom able to resist the temptations of literary embellishment. The first half of the nineteenth century was a highly romantic period in which writers had difficulty escaping the tropes and literary fashions of the day. In this the writers of memoirs were no different from others as they struggled to make their accounts accessible to a nineteenth-century readership. Many of the memoirs, including those of army officers, fall into one or two dominant literary modes—the sentimental novel and the novel of the picaresque—genres to which accounts of army life lent themselves very easily.[33] That is not to deprecate them; but it does mean that the temptation to romanticize experience or to mould the storyline to fit the literary conceit was always present. In the 1820s and 1830s, insists Damien Zanone, 'history, novels and memoirs were very closely related, with the risk that they could easily become confused'.[34] Novels and memoirs had more in common than most authors of memoirs were wont to admit. Both must be seen as fictions.

The contrast between victory and defeat is never starker than in military memoirs, and Waterloo was a battle where victory was absolute and where there were no degrees of success and failure. The elation of victory, the desperation of the retreating army, the adrenalin burst of the pursuing troops, or the sudden realization that their cause was lost—all find expression in the memoir accounts. There is also the question of proportionality. For many of the British participants in the battle, this was the greatest moment of their military careers, a moment to be savoured and relished. So they linger over the battle, taking time to present something of the landscape, the topography, and the strategic positions which they had occupied. French accounts of the battle are far fewer in number, and they tend also to be rather terse. Captain Coignet, so loquacious about his experiences in earlier campaigns, has little to add to the standard accounts of the battle, pausing only to praise Ney for 'performing miracles of courage and daring'; Waterloo had been a disaster and he wanted nothing more than to get back to France and to cultivate the small vineyard he had bought for his old age.[35] The French knew that Waterloo had been an unmitigated disaster for their army as well as for Napoleon—in the memoirs of General Radet, for instance, the battle is referred to unhesitatingly as 'the terrible catastrophe of Waterloo'[36]—and they showed little appetite for discussing it in detail. It ended the careers of many of them, men with a lifetime of soldiering behind them, who now had to wait only a few weeks before being dismissed or placed on half-pay, their years of active service cut short. For them, too, the battle marked a brutal caesura, the end of a way of life which, in spite of its hazards and hardships, had provided them with status, respect, a circle of friendships, and a sense of worth. Few left joyously; few expressed relief. In Natalie Petiteau's words, 'glory, the nation, the flag and the memory of Napoleon became the points of reference for these men who had been so marked by their years in the Grande Armée and who showed such lasting affection for the man who had dispensed this glory amongst them'.[37] Their memory of Waterloo would always be tinged with nostalgia.

What left an indelible mark on so many French soldiers at Waterloo was not the actual fighting, or the quest for glory, or the genius of Napoleon, but the totality of their defeat and the unaccustomed experience of suffering an uncontrollable rout. Lieutenant Martin of the 45th Line was one who found himself caught up in the flight of his men and who remembered graphically what it felt like when the morale of an army is suddenly lost and a body of soldiers becomes engulfed in total panic. His description captures the moment when the fleeing army passed the one fulcrum of resistance, the squares of the Old Guard:

> Panic had seized the entire army. There was nothing more than a con-fused mass of infantry soldiers, cavalry and guns that rushed, all mixed together, across the plain like an unstoppable torrent, through the Prus-sian squadrons that charged them and the English battalions that des-cended from their plateau with cries of victory. Alone, several squares of the Guard, held back by Napoleon at the foot of La Belle Alliance, remained immobile as rocks in a raging sea. The crowds of fugitives passed between the squares and soon only the enemy surrounded them.[38]

The rout was as sudden as it was unexpected, a response to the Prussian arrival on the field and the troops' sense of being left unsup-ported; they turned and fled when they were taken by surprise as they approached the crest and found themselves ambushed by Prussian fire. Ney may have appealed to the men to stand firm—indeed, a number of eyewitnesses confirm this—but they were suddenly shell-shocked and demoralized, having lost all passion for the fight. It is a difficult condition for a soldier to describe, though a sergeant-major of the 93rd Line, Lerréguy de Civrieux, did make a heroic effort to record the moment for posterity. The entire army, he said, 'was struck by a sudden demoralization' and had only one desire, to escape from that scene of carnage:

> Cries of 'sauve qui peut', 'à la trahison' were heard; the rout became general. All discipline disappeared; the regiments fell into an inexpressible disorder, forming disordered masses of men that were ploughed in all senses by the enemy's cannon.

But even amidst the rout he recalls the one moment of heroism that illuminated the panic, Ney's indomitable courage in the face of disaster:

> Two or three times, Marshal Ney, dismounted, without servants, appeared to us, sword in hand, bareheaded, marching with difficulty, embarrassed by his big boots in this slippery ground, soaked from the day before. His brilliant voice succeeded in rallying a handful of soldiers; but what could this illustrious and unhappy warrior achieve against so many enemies and in this chaos! Vainly, he searched for death.[39]

Through their focus on the last stand of the Old Guard, the defence of the eagles, or Ney's valour in the midst of disaster, these soldier-writers were establishing a template for later French accounts of the battle. Waterloo might be an unmitigated disaster for France, and it was an undeniable defeat for the army. But it had its moments of glory, too. It was a *heroic* defeat.

Defeats can also lead to bickering and recrimination as the survivors try to exculpate themselves from blame for the catastrophe or look around for possible explanations and for suitable scapegoats. How could Napoleon's great army, with its French flair and tradition of honour and glory, have been so thoroughly routed unless human error had been responsible? Marbot, who had fought brilliantly at Genappe on 17 June and was promoted on the spot to the rank of brigadier general—a promotion that would never be confirmed on account of the collapse of the Empire—was one who could not accept his army's defeat. Pulling back with his regiment to Valenciennes, then on to Paris and the Loire, he offered what is perhaps the most damning indictment of French organization and operations at Waterloo. 'We were made to manoeuvre like pumpkins', he wrote with evident disgust on 26 June, before explaining how everything had gone calamitously wrong. He himself had been left out on the right flank throughout almost the entire day, with his regiment, three artillery pieces, and a battalion of light infantry in support. He was supposedly guarding the point where Grouchy would arrive and join up with his unit; but, of course, it was not Grouchy who appeared, but the Prussians, with the disastrous consequences which we know. From that moment, says Marbot, they were doomed to defeat, and his verdict positively drips with the frustration he felt.

> Just think of the way in which we had been laid out! We had been pushed back, and the enemy was right away on our rear. We could have remedied the problem but no one gave the necessary orders. Our top generals were in Paris making bad speeches. The lesser ones lost their heads, with disastrous consequences.

Marbot blames everyone, almost, it seems, indiscriminately. The whole army was at fault, for if the officers lacked both quality and tactical sense, the soldiers lacked loyalty and deserted in droves, heading for the frontier and back into France. They did so, moreover, with total impunity, since no one intervened to stop them; the officers were handing out leave to their men even as they themselves were piling into carriages to take them back to Paris. It was a recipe for chaos and disintegration which, said Marbot, could only be resolved by political will, if the Chamber of Deputies intervened and introduced measures of the greatest severity. Indeed, a full week after Waterloo he is one of the few still arguing that France must fight on, whatever the cost in human life. They could still get 50,000 men under arms, he claims, but at a heavy price: 'for that it would take the death penalty for any man who left his post and for any officer who gave permission to quit'.[40] Marbot may have been no liberal, but this was a last desperate throw of the dice, a counsel of despair.

Among those French generals who had contributed to the Waterloo campaign, the man who came most under attack was, of course, Marshal Grouchy, who was blamed by many—including by Napoleon himself in the *Mémorial de Sainte-Hélène*—for failing to take any initiative or countermand the Emperor's own orders once it had become evident that his troops were far more urgently needed on the battlefield than they were in following up the Prussian retreat after Ligny. In the years that followed, Grouchy was at pains to defend his reputation and to justify his decisions for posterity; at pains, too, to respond to the accusations and sniping of other of Napoleon's former lieutenants, each manoeuvring for position and advantage. Having fled to America in 1815, he published his memoirs in five volumes; and for much of the rest of his life he carried on refuting the charges levelled against him by others with regard to his conduct at Waterloo. His life in exile in Philadelphia seems to have been largely consumed with attempts to clear his name. Thus we find him in 1815 denouncing Gourgaud's account of the battle, and in 1820 that of Napoleon himself; and there were a number of others in between.[41] After he had been given permission to return to France in 1820, the flood of accusations and recriminations continued unabated. In 1829, for instance, he took issue with what he regarded as cheap point-scoring in the memoirs of the Duc de Rovigo, who, as Anne-Jean-Marie-René Savary, had served both as a general in the army and as Napoleon's chief of police.[42] Savary had, he claims, destroyed his reputation, blaming him for military disasters for which he bore no responsibility and misattributing the causes of the final rout at Waterloo. As an officer of long standing who had begun his service under the Revolution, who had taken part in twenty-two campaigns and sustained fifteen wounds in the service of his country, he saw no reason to take such abuse from a man like Savary, whom he regarded with evident contempt, dismissing him as a self-serving placeman and an uncritical publicist for Napoleon. But his remarks, like others before, had clearly hurt Grouchy, and he was determined not to leave these charges unanswered.[43] In 1840, indeed, at the age of 74, he still had not given up hope of redemption, publishing a series of texts from 1815 which, he believed, would refute yet another batch of what he insisted were 'calumnies'.[44] Grouchy would never get the satisfaction he sought. A quarter of a century on, his battle of Waterloo was still not over.

6

Wellington and British Memory of Waterloo

The victorious Allies responded very differently to Waterloo. Only Britain made it into a centrepiece of national memory and commemoration, as press and public rushed to acclaim the significance of the battle and to squeeze every ounce of glory from it. In the narrative they created of the battle, the British turned Waterloo into one of the great military turning-points of modern history and presented it as a victory for British arms, British resolve, and a specifically British national character. The better army, the better general, the better cause had conquered, and they left Great Britain in a dominant position both in European diplomacy and in the construction of a world empire. Within days of the announcement of the victory, on 29 June, *The Times* phrased this uncompromisingly: 'Nothing in ancient or modern history', it thundered, 'equals the effect of the victory at Waterloo.'[1] In similar vein, the Poet Laureate Robert Southey suggested that only twice in the history of the world had there been such an important battle: when the Greeks defeated the Persians at Plataea in 479 BC and when Charles Martel had turned back the Muslims at Tours in 742.[2] The painter and writer Benjamin Robert Haydon also extolled the importance of the victory, and of Napoleon's defeat. He kept a diary, which would become one of the more famous autobiographical works of the early nineteenth century; in 1818 he would write, on the anniversary of the battle, that 'Wellington will truly be considered by posterity as the saviour of the world's intellect, for the age would have been brought back to ignorance and barbarism had the Demon succeeded in his despotic system. Great and Glorious Man, my heart beats when I think of him'. But he also recognized Wellington's principal failing in the eyes of the public when he went on: 'I only fear that he has not a sympathetic heart, and he is not capable of feeling the sensations he excites in others.'[3] Contemporaries were ready to acknowledge that the Duke was a great military leader who could inspire those who served under him; one recent assessment concludes that 'his personal traits of leadership, courage, perseverance, loyalty and charisma on the battlefield produced a European commander whose success was eclipsed only by that of Napoleon'.[4] But there the admiration stopped. Though Wellington could incite passion in his admirers, to the public at large he could seem cold, aristocratic, and aloof.

Sir Walter Scott, with a keen eye for the potent mix of patriotism and gore, rushed, in 1815, to publish his own poem on the battle, *The Field of Waterloo*, where he likened the cutting down of Britain's heroes

Figure 7. Apsley House, engraving of 1810

in battle to the harvesting of wheat on nearby farms. It was a desolate image, one that identified Waterloo less with heroism than with carnage:

> Heroes before each fatal sweep
> Fell thick as ripened grain;
> And ere the darkening of the day
> Piled high as autumn shocks there lay
> The ghastly harvest of the fray
> The corpses of the slain.[5]

Scott's image played a significant part in shaping the representations of the battlefield that were passed down to future generations. As a deep-dyed conservative, he feared Napoleon but went on to write a life of him which painted him as a man of huge early promise, a flawed genius.[6] On the other hand, he saw Wellington as a true national hero, and his appraisal of Waterloo reflects this. It is possible that he took Wellington's own impressions of the battle at face value, since he made a point of meeting him shortly after he returned to England. Scott later admitted that 'he had never felt awed or abashed except in the presence of one man'—and that man was the Duke.[7]

Contemporary Accounts

Early narratives of Waterloo fell on eager ears, a public—especially but not only in Britain—that was enthralled by the battle and had a seemingly inexhaustible appetite for colour and detail. Among the first to be published were the accounts of travellers who had visited the battlefield and who in varying degrees described the countryside, recounted tales of courage and daring, and hinted at the horror of a field where so many thousands had died. In 1815 and 1816 the British public was assailed with titles promising a private and intimate encounter with the battle and its heroes. Charles Campbell's *The Traveller's Complete Guide through Belgium, Holland and Germany* (1815) set the tone for these military travelogues, assigning a discrete section to a detailed description of the battlefield that left little to the imagination.

He talked of shattered wheels and horses' bones protruding from the mud in such quantities that the road from Waterloo to Brussels 'resembled one long, uninterrupted charnel house'.[8] John Booth, again in 1815, wrote an account of the *Battle of Waterloo* that offered, as he promised his readers, 'circumstantial details of the memorable event'.[9] Eyewitness accounts showered down on London's bookshops. John Scott's *Paris Revisited in 1815* gave a long description of the battle-field, as well as of the city of Brussels, still heavily militarized after the battle.[10] James Simpson published his *A Visit to Flanders in July, 1815: Being chiefly an account of the field of Waterloo*.[11] All emphasized the emotional toll which their visit placed on the visitor. 'The great cause of excitement', wrote John Scott, 'lies in his being on the point of converting into a visible reality what had previously existed in his mind as a shadowy, uncertain, but awful fancy.'[12]

Soon afterwards the first works claiming to present an authoritative history of the battle followed: most notably, for the London market, such accounts as Captain Arthur Gore's *An Historical Account of the Battle of Waterloo*, illustrated with plates showing key sites on the battlefield,[13] and Christopher Kelly's *Full and Circumstantial Account of the Memorable Battle of Waterloo*, which also contained engravings and gave 'biographical sketches of the most distinguished Waterloo her-oes'.[14] An exhilarated public was soon awash with accounts of the battle, some of them works of fiction and the poetic imagination, others solid attempts to piece together the evidence and present a coherent narrative. There is no doubting their popularity with the book-buying public. The first edition of William Siborne's *The Waterloo Campaign*—on the title page the author described himself as a 'Captain, half-pay, unattached, constructor of the Waterloo Model'—sold out 'within a very few days' and was greeted with 'very flattering enco-miums', or so the author claimed.[15] Primary materials on the history of the battle would soon be available, too, and nineteenth-century historians were able to access Wellington's *Despatches* and the influen-tial collection of *Waterloo Letters* addressed to Siborne and published by his son.[16] In the months following the battle the template for subsequent accounts of Waterloo had already been created, and if French, German, and Dutch works suggested some changes of emphasis, they did not greatly alter the vision of how the battle was planned and executed.[17] It breaks down fairly readily into a succession of discrete phases, each critical to the final outcome.[18]

Figure 8. Wellington Arch about 1870, with the Wellington statue still *in situ*

Britain, of course, had every reason to put its victory to political use. The British state that went into the Napoleonic Wars was anything but united: indeed, the nature of British identity was still fiercely argued over, with the Scots, Irish, and, to a more limited extent, the Welsh questioning their place in the supposedly United Kingdom.[19] The Scottish Highlands, in particular, were seen as a place where treason still lurked; and the people of Ireland were even more distrusted after Wolfe Tone's rebellion in 1798 threatened to turn the island into the bridgehead for a French invasion. This political context had a considerable effect on both the recruitment of the army and the later representation of the battle. With the passage of time Waterloo was increasingly represented as a British rather than an Allied victory.

The Scottish Dimension

Scotland played a more than proportionate part in the militarization of Britain for these wars; in 1813 John Cookson calculates that Scots held about one-quarter of all military commissions, and we know that a generation later, in 1830, over half of the army's NCOs were born in either Scotland or Ireland.[20] The two countries were almost routinely over-represented in the strength of the British army—a measure that had been deliberately adopted to appease the Scottish Highlands and encourage loyalty to the Crown after the rebellion of 1745 and its brutal suppression by Cumberland's troops, memories of which still festered. At Waterloo, Scottish regiments played a prominent role, though perhaps not quite as prominent as Scottish military lore might suggest. Of the thirty-nine British regiments present on the battlefield, only eight were Scottish, with the Scots making up rather less than one-fifth of the soldiers engaged in the action. But in key engagements—notably the cavalry charge against d'Erlon's infantry and the action around Hougoumont—they suffered heavy losses, and battle honours won at Waterloo went on to play a significant part in their regimental traditions. In the 1820s and 1830s, in particular, the image of the Highland soldier, resplendent in his clan tartan, would become a stereotype of British military identity. It was, of course, little more than a colourful piece of antiquarianism, part of a nineteenth-century 'invention of Scotland' which transformed the rugged Highlander into an icon of the nation.[21] But this did not prevent it from being taken up with enthusiasm by such lobbying groups as the Highland Society of London, who used it in repeated campaigns in the two centuries after Waterloo to prevent the amalgamation of Scottish regiments and the loss of their traditions.[22] Paintings like Richard Ansell's *Fight for the Standard* and Lady Butler's *Charge of the Scots Greys* may not be among the greatest works of art of the nineteenth century, but they provided some of the most enduring images of the battle; and at their heart is the iconic figure of the kilted Highlander.[23]

The British government, anxious to forestall insurrection in the Highlands, was keen to emphasize the bravery of the Highland regiments and to underline the value of the Scots' contribution to Britain's victory, not least their part in the seizure of one of the Napoleonic eagles captured in the battle. Contemporary accounts of Waterloo, especially those written by Scots, take special pride in their distinctiveness. In part this reflects the fact that Scottish soldiers were more distinct, with 70 per cent of Scottish line infantry concentrated in only ten regiments, whereas Irish troops and those from the English counties were spread more widely.[24] But there was more to it than that. James Simpson, the Edinburgh advocate who wrote an account of his visit to Waterloo in 1815, took pride in distinguishing the role played by his countrymen from that of other soldiers. In Antwerp, he claimed, the Highlander was received with a respect and an affection that no Englishman could hope to equal. 'A gentleman whom I saw had seen the wounded arrive. He himself had been recognised and spoken to by a poor wounded Highlander, which absolutely gave him a kind of consideration in the crowd. He felt prouder at that moment than if a prince had smiled upon him.'[25]

The Politics of Commemoration

Englishmen might take pride in their army's victory, but not all were overjoyed by Napoleon's defeat. The country divided on party-political lines, with the Tories wallowing in patriotism while many Whigs regarded the Europe that emerged from Waterloo with distaste, and many on the radical side of politics regretted the restoration of the Bourbons and the reinstatement of royal autocracy and religious intolerance. 'Is Earth more free', asked Byron, as a consequence? He replied in the negative, urging his fellow countrymen to 'prove before ye praise'.[26] But issues closer to home now focused the minds of men on the left of British politics. They feared that new technology would reduce employment in the textile trades, demanded a minimum wage to counter depressed living standards, and sympathized with the Luddites and machine-breakers of industrial England. They feared technology even more when depression struck the spinning mills and weaving sheds, as happened twice in the years immediately following Waterloo, in 1817 and 1819, spreading unrest through the industrial towns of the Midlands and the North West.[27] Radical orators like Henry Hunt and Samuel Bamford saw Waterloo not just as the victory of the British over the French, but as a class victory, too, a triumph for the Tory establishment that would keep the landowning classes in power for years to come. Radicals concentrated increasingly on the suffrage issue, the reform of an electoral system that denied the vote to most of the population and virtually all those living in the new industrial cities. By the end of the decade British opinion was bitterly divided, and the passing unity which Waterloo had brought had already dissipated.

But that was for the future, at least in 1815. In the immediate aftermath of the battle, radical dissent was all but silenced in a great wave of patriotic celebration to welcome a victory that few had expected. London seemed to explode with joy, its citizens effusive in their praise for the country's fighting spirit and united in relief at the defeat of Napoleon. People who had been tired and battered by long years of war did not hide their delight at the downfall of the 'Ogre' and were only too pleased to hail Waterloo as a very British triumph. The press and the public persisted long into the nineteenth century in the belief that Waterloo epitomized the supposed national virtues of endurance and tenacity, and deliberately played down the part that Prussia or any other nation had played in Napoleon's final downfall. This reflected the chauvinistic spirit of the moment; but it was also bred by self-interest, from a desire to secure personal reputations, and most notably, of course, Wellington's own. For though the Duke had been careful to acknowledge the Prussians in his Despatch, that was virtually the last time he mentioned them; and, as Peter Hofschröer has shown, he helped to ensure that the official model of the battle-field, designed for Parliament in the 1830s by William Siborne, reflected his interpretation of the battle.[28] By then Blücher's Prussian divisions are nowhere to be seen.

Figure 9. Waterloo Chamber, Windsor Castle

The immediate public reaction to news of the battle was a display of exaltation—sheer joy that the war was over, relief that a victory had been gained which many had never dared to expect. Waterloo was greeted so passionately because it finally—for a second time in as many years—brought years of fighting to an end, allowed service families to be reunited, and finished what had seemed an interminable litany of carnage. It was a moment which the Establishment, especially the Prince Regent, were determined to milk for advantage as they sought to gain kudos and popularity from the mood of euphoria. The future George IV had already thrown himself into organizing public celebrations in 1814 with a review of 12,000 troops in Hyde Park and a ball for 1,700 people in Wellington's honour at Burlington House, and he himself had revelled in the triumphalism of the moment.[29] A second victory in 1815 encouraged a further outburst of celebration, one that focused specifically, and unusually, on the contribution of the army. The numerous statues to fallen heroes that had been admitted during the Wars to the national pantheons of Westminster Abbey and St Paul's bear eloquent testimony to the central place of the navy in Britain's traditional celebrations of war. Indeed, even in 1815 it was unclear whether Wellington was Britain's real hero, or Waterloo the true zenith of the country's military fortunes. Trafalgar would continue to have pride of place in the national pantheon, and it was on Horatio Nelson, the 'immortal' Nelson', that the nation's praises continued to be showered to a degree that some thought 'quasi-idolatrous'.[30]

The public jubilation was fuelled by the state. Both Houses of Parliament passed a vote of thanks for the outcome, and subscriptions were opened to help the victims of the war, the wounded servicemen who returned from the Continent and the bereaved families of those killed in action. A Waterloo Fund was established, which by 1819 had dispensed around £192,000 to wounded servicemen and their dependents.[31] Over 600 new churches were built—to be known as 'Waterloo churches' and authorized under the Church Building Act of 1818—to provide Anglican worship in areas of the country where need was identified and to thank God for his intervention against the Usurper.[32]

In London alone there were thirty-eight.[33] And across the land cler-gymen joined in the patriotic claim that this war had been fought in the cause of God and of all humanity.[34] They insisted that they wanted the deaths of their brave soldiers to serve some purpose, and therefore clung to the belief that the cause in which they had fought had been just. The British, as the Revd Henry Cotes assured the members of the Westminster Waterloo Association, had been fighting a battle for good against evil, and it was God's battle, too. The French in their wickedness had been the instruments of God, 'who in his omniscience deriveth good from evil, hath permitted for more than twenty years anarchy and misrule in France, together with the extinction of the very forms and shadows of religion'.[35] The Church, at least in its Anglican variant, was on the victors' side; in Scotland such sermons were just as enthusiastically delivered from Presbyterian pulpits.

Parliament hosted banquets in honour of Waterloo and organized public celebrations across the land. It ordered that a medal be struck—

Figure 10. J. M. W. Turner, *The Field of Waterloo*

the Waterloo Medal—to be awarded to every soldier who had served in the battle: it was the first time in British military history that such a gesture had been made, and of course it set an important precedent. On one side the medal showed two figures on horseback riding into battle, quite recognizably Wellington and Blücher; on the other an allegorical scene in which Peace and Justice were seen victorious following Napoleon's defeat.[36] Prize money was distributed to those who had fought at Waterloo, the sums ranging from £2. 11s. 4d. for privates and drummers to a handsome £61,000 for the Duke.[37] This was, of course, hugely popular with those troops who had served at Waterloo, but less so among the veterans of the Peninsula, who felt slighted and undervalued. Many senior officers were also critical of what they saw as the indiscriminate issue of campaign medals: distributing them to every officer and private of a regiment, according to Colonel Luard, 'defeats the object by destroying the distinction'.[38] Wellington himself, newly promoted to the rank of field marshal, was proclaimed a national hero, and riches followed. The government purchased a country estate for its victorious general at Stratford Saye in Hampshire, though Wellington seldom stayed there, preferring to remain in London at Apsley House, the town residence across from Hyde Park Corner which he bought in 1817. Stratford Saye has been described as a modest estate, though it is modest only in comparison with Blenheim Palace, the Oxfordshire estate that had been voted to Marlborough following his victories in the War of the Spanish Succession.[39] Wellington used it sparingly, an occasional rural retreat from the political world of London. His favourite horse, Copenhagen, on which he had fought at Waterloo, was buried there with full military honours on his death in 1836.[40]

Waterloo in Art

Waterloo would be an inspiration for artists, too. Almost immediately the British Institution, founded to promote works by contemporary artists, offered a prize of £1,000 for a work presenting an allegory of the victory; though, in truth, the battle was already providing a high level of inspiration to the artistic community. Painters competed with one another to record the victory and to heap praise upon the victor, making the battle a rich source for the depiction of military masculinity but also presenting it as the fulcrum from which emerged peace, tranquillity, and imperial prosperity. The most famous English representation of the battlefield is probably Turner's oil painting of *The Field of Waterloo*, a work that defied convention by introducing women and children alongside the dead and wounded soldiers and which emphasized the vulnerability of the troops by allowing the domestic and military realms to merge. Philip Shaw sees this as an emotive demonstration of the damage caused by war, and not just to the soldiers who fought in it. The women who are depicted are no less damaged than the men, even though their lives have been spared, with the consequence that 'the comfort that femininity offers to the dying man is placed in the context of the greater wound suffered by the family and thus, by extension, the nation'.[41] Almost as iconic is David Wilkie's painting of veterans of Waterloo, old soldiers conversing and finding solace in one another's company, which told another story of the consequences of war. *Chelsea Pensioners Reading the Gazette of the Battle of Waterloo* was presented at the Royal Academy in 1822, where it caused a sensation. It depicts the scene when word first reached London of the outcome of the battle, and it shows a miscellaneous crowd of old soldiers and shabbily dressed workers outside an inn close to Chelsea Hospital. The painting is careful to depict veterans from successive wars and from all the nations of the United Kingdom, united in an outpouring of British patriotism. 'The horseman shown bringing the news of the victory is from a Welsh regiment', writes Linda Colley, while 'the soldiers gathering around him include Scotsmen, Englishmen, an Irishman and even a black military bandsman'.[42] The message was clear: Waterloo had brought unity to the Islands and had helped to forge a single British nation. It was a powerful message; whether or not it was true mattered little.

Figure 11. Lady Butler, *The Charge of the Scots Greys at Waterloo*

The Prince Regent's ill-disguised attempt to present himself as a military hero and to claim credit for the victory meant that there were rich commissions for artists to compete for. The most lucrative was bestowed on Sir Thomas Lawrence, whom the Prince Regent engaged to paint all the major figures—sovereigns, politicians, and generals—who had contributed to Napoleon's downfall, including Wellington, naturally, but also Tsar Alexander I, Pope Pius VII, the Prussian and Russian generals Blücher and Platov, and the Austrian diplomat Metternich. Lawrence added the portraits of other British officers from Waterloo, among them Picton and Anglesey, in the 1830s, and the paintings, many of them full-length portraits, were hung in a specially created Waterloo Chamber in Windsor Castle. This is aptly described by Holger Hoock as a 'painted pantheon' to match the statuary of Westminster Abbey or St Paul's. The chamber, sumptuous and magnificent, is lined with Lawrence's portraits, with that of the Duke in the place of honour.[43] Again, the identification is made of Waterloo as a specifically British victory, as it is in one of David Wilkie's later paintings, his *Portrait of the Duke, representing his Grace writing to the King of France on the Night before the Battle of Waterloo*. Here the focus is on Wellington, alone on the eve of the battle, committing his thoughts to paper, and portrayed, as he himself wished it, as the 'sole progenitor of Waterloo'.[44]

For those for whom painting was too static a medium, or who were intrigued by moving images and the potential of technology, the vogue for historical panoramas that had developed in the last years of the eighteenth century offered a novel alternative. The panorama gave the visitor the illusion of being present in the city or at the historical event that was featured, a dramatic effect that was produced by the intermingling of light and dark in the restricted space of a rotunda. Battle scenes translated easily into the panoramic form, as the visitor found himself in the midst of the noise and the smells and the dangers of the battlefield, surrounded by violence, sabre blows, cavalry charges, and piles of the dead and wounded. Waterloo was a favourite subject for the entrepreneurs who set up panoramas in London and the provinces, a subject that could claim to combine education and historical imagination with the thrill of danger and personal involvement. The inventor of the panorama, Robert Barker, made his fortune from displaying *The Battle of Waterloo* at his Leicester Square rotunda in 1816, his customers paying a shilling to share the excitement of the victory and to follow Wellington's imperious gaze across the battlefield. Other panoramas followed, regenerating their displays to take account of the latest technology and mounting touring exhibitions of provincial cities.[45] They offered those without the money or opportunity to visit the battlefield an alternative to the circus melodramas that formed part of London's popular entertainment at the time. These were held in circus rings, where they built on the equestrian displays that had been popular in the second half of the eighteenth century. In the 1820s circus melodramas about the Napoleonic Wars enjoyed an exceptional vogue, incorporating colourful battle scenes, of course, but also presenting domestic scenes from the lives of the heroes. In J. H. Amherst's 'grand military melodrama' of Waterloo, performed in London in 1824, each act ended with a tableau of a battle scene, starting with the Bridge at Marchienne and Quatre Bras and building up to Ligny and the final triumph at Mont-Saint-Jean.[46] It was a

Figure 12. William Salter, *Waterloo Banquet, 1836*

spectacle for the masses, a mixture of drama and patriotism, theatre and spectacle.

Napoleon would become one of the most popular subjects for displays and exhibitions in post-1815 London as the capital's museums vied with one another to attract audiences. Almost as soon as the battle was over, the preserved body of Napoleon's horse, Marengo, was put on show to the public in the newly opened Waterloo Rooms on Pall Mall, and a Waterloo Museum was opened nearby, displaying a giant painting of the battle along with military mementoes. The carriage in which Napoleon rode to battle also made its way to London in the baggage train of the army and was given an honoured place in the London Museum in Piccadilly, where it was viewed by an estimated 10,000 people a day. It was later transferred to a so-called 'shrine of Napoleon' at Madame Tussaud's in Baker Street, one of the most successful and enduring enterprises to exploit the new passion for waxworks.[47] But wax representations alone could not win mass audiences; and Madame Tussaud, believing that her exhibitions should be seen as part of the historical record and anxious to create displays approaching the authenticity of a museum, added historical artefacts to her waxwork models. In the Napoleon rooms—one of her most famous exhibits—the effect was stunning, as they contained not only a wax model of the Emperor but also various parts of his body, rescued for posterity after his death. Pamela Pilbeam notes how 'his real tooth and hair lay close to his waxen image, which was dressed, slept or rode in the emperor's own possessions'. The illusion of authenticity was such that 'a visitor could feel much closer to Napoleon in Baker Street' than if he stood before his tomb at Les Invalides in Paris.[48]

Monuments and Memorials

The design of national monuments presented a more difficult problem. In the early nineteenth century it was not yet customary to recognize the contributions of the rank and file. National memorials were reserved for commanders or marked exceptional bravery by individual officers, while at local level officers and even some men from the ranks might be remembered on plaques in their parish churches. But there public commemoration stopped. There was no tradition of publicly funded memorials to military and naval figures; before the 1790s the majority of the funeral monuments celebrating their lives, even those erected in public places like Westminster Abbey or York Minster, were the result of private initiatives.[49] Their messages were private, too, as much testimonies to their families as to the cause of their country. Indeed, it was only during the French Revolutionary and Napoleonic Wars, with the emergence of St Paul's as a military pantheon and the commissioning of monuments by public subscription or by order of Parliament, that we can begin to see them as part of a wider official commemoration. The number of military monuments rose dramatically in these years: between 1794 and 1823, thirty-six monuments to military leaders and political figures were commissioned, all sanctioned by the King and funded by Parliament.[50] For Britain this can be seen as nothing less than a revolution in military memorialization.

The victory over Napoleon provided the authorities with a particular challenge. How, in the aftermath of the battle, could the memory of Waterloo best be translated into stone and plaster? What memorial would be eloquent enough to encapsulate the magnitude of the battle or its significance in the defeat of Napoleon? There were surprisingly few precedents to draw on. Where memorials had been erected, to General Wolfe, for instance, or Admiral Vernon, the theme had generally been triumphalist, the victory of Christian virtue over barbarism.[51] There was a concern in 1815 to be politically and socially inclusive, to suggest that this was a people's victory, the victory of all the British people and of the troops who had represented them on the battlefield. One MP even proposed that a monument be built listing the names of all the soldiers who had died at Waterloo, and though the idea was rejected, the very fact that it was discussed shows the huge symbolic importance that was attached to the battle.[52] In the event Parliament voted a sum of £310,000, a sum far in excess of any previously granted for a British monument to heroism, with the commission to construct two memorials—the one to commemorate Trafalgar, the other Waterloo—which would reflect the huge debt of gratitude felt by the British people.[53] Architects and sculptors were understandably excited by the competition, and the public responded with interest and enthusiasm, at least in the first years of peace. After 1817–18 levels of popular enthusiasm perceptibly waned.

Designs for a national monument to Waterloo were duly submitted, but little was actually built.[54] There were rival schemes for a nineteenth-century reconstruction of the Parthenon on Primrose Hill and for what its architect termed an 'ornamental tower' in Regent's Park, but neither got beyond the planning stage. Only in Edinburgh was William Playfair's 'Monument to the Napoleonic Wars' actually built, or at least started, on the Calton Hill, looking down over Princes Street from the east. Here, as in London, Playfair set out to construct a new Parthenon, befitting the cultural and artistic pretensions of the new 'Athens of the North'. But it would remain an unfinished ruin, since the money ran out in 1828, long before the building was completed; and what had been planned as a glorious monument to Britain's military heroes lay abandoned and unloved, attracting derision from local people.

Around the country funds were collected and monuments were erected by public subscription to acclaim the battle and its heroes. Building generally began in the years immediately after the battle, but often, as in Edinburgh, funds ran out before the monument could be completed and its construction was interrupted or abandoned. Thus the monuments to Wellington in Somerset and Dublin, both begun in 1817, were not finished until 1854 and 1861 respectively, by which time they had become posthumous memorials to his long career in public life. Wellington did, however, enjoy one last public honour when he was granted a state funeral in 1852, attended by an array of political leaders and foreign dignitaries. France was represented by her ambassador to London, Alexander Walewski, who was, with ironic symbolism, Napoleon's son by his Polish mistress, the countess Marie Walewska.[55]

It is perhaps no accident that a number of the memorials to Wellington and Waterloo were placed in areas of Celtic Britain whose loyalty to the Crown was less assured and where a memorial perhaps had greater political significance. Scotland alone built two monuments to Waterloo, one at Ancram in the Borders, the other at New Abbey near Dumfries; here the foundation stone was laid within three months of the battle, in October 1815, a plaque recording 'the valour of British, Belgian and Prussian soldiers who gained the victory of Waterloo'.[56] In Ireland, too, there were overtly political reasons for ensuring that the victory remained solidly ingrained in public memory.

In London, while no national monument was instituted to the battle, there were various attempts to commemorate Waterloo in works of art and public sculpture. The nude Achilles statue that was the product of a subscription by the 'ladies of Great Britain' risked becoming a national laughing-stock when it was unveiled in 1822; though the idea for the statue, based on the theme of one of the horse-tamers in the statue on the Monte Cavallo in Rome, was serious enough. Benjamin Haydon commented approvingly that it was to be made of the bronze guns taken from the enemy during the battle, 12 and 9 pounders, left strewn on the battlefield. He added that in his view there could be no better use for surplus army supplies than the celebration of Britain's military heroes.[57] But it was never adopted as a national monument. Similarly, the Waterloo Vase proved too heavy to be housed in a new Waterloo Gallery, and that idea had to be abandoned. Nash's grandiose project for the Marble Arch, presented in 1825, was to be decorated with scenes from the life of Nelson and reliefs of the Battle of Waterloo; but again, by the time the arch was inaugurated in 1833, the project had been handed to another architect and the design greatly simplified.[58] Nearly twenty years had passed since Waterloo, and levels of public interest had fallen away.

The more utilitarian idea of renaming bridges and highways after the battle proved far more enduring. In London the new Strand Bridge, which was opened by the Prince Regent in 1817, was named Waterloo Bridge in a ceremony made famous in a painting by Constable.[59] It was not alone, and the idea of associating Waterloo with modern feats of engineering had wide appeal. In North Wales, for instance, Thomas Telford's new iron bridge, a single-span structure over the River Avon near Betws-y-Coed which was under construction in 1815, was also named in honour of the battle. On the outer ribs of the bridge bold signs declared to the world that 'this arch was constructed in the same year the Battle of Waterloo was fought', while the stonework was patriotically decorated with the emblems of the four nations that constituted the British Isles: a rose, a thistle, a leek, and a shamrock. As a symbol of the nation's patriotic pride and confidence in the future, it could scarcely be bettered.[60]

The Name of Waterloo

After 1815 a fashion developed for naming streets, suburbs, and even whole towns after the battle and its victor, with the consequence that the name of Waterloo became familiar across the country and in many parts of the British Empire. England saw at least two towns named after the battle—Waterloo-with-Seaforth to the north of Liverpool and Waterlooville in Hampshire—while a large number of factories, textile mills, and industrial suburbs, which sprouted luxuriantly in the North and Midlands during the early part of the nineteenth century, took their identity from the battle. There are townships named after Waterloo in both Scotland and Wales, in Perthshire and near Pembroke Dock respectively. And since this was also the period when much of the Empire was being opened up and colonized, it was perhaps only natural that the battle and its general should be celebrated in towns and cities across the globe. In Canada, Waterloo (Ontario) would grow into a major university town; the capital of New Zealand is Wellington on the North Island; while peaks called Mount Wellington dominate two other cities in Australasia, Auckland and Hobart. And these are just a few instances. Settlers to the United States also carried the name of the battlefield with them to the New World, with the consequence that no fewer than fourteen American states have towns named Waterloo.[61] Nor should it be forgotten that in Quebec the name of Waterloo carried a particular political resonance in a province where French settlers had been under British rule for only half a century. The victors did not hold back, commemorating Wellington's victories in the Peninsula on a series of penny and halfpenny tokens and renaming the village of Cantons-de-l'Est, founded by loyalists in 1793, in honour of Waterloo.[62]

It is perhaps in the names of the streets and squares of Britain and its Empire that the memory of Waterloo lived on most tangibly, the thoroughfares which were criss-crossed daily by thousands of passersby on their way home or to work. Timing played a part in this, of course, since the Regency period was one of great urban renewal, with elegant new city landscapes being planned and new streets constructed in London and in many provincial cities, producing a crop of naming opportunities at a moment when civic leaders were keen to commemorate the greatest victory in the country's recent history. In London the name of Waterloo Place was reserved for one of the most prestigious pieces of city renewal, the extension of Regent Street linking Piccadilly to Pall Mall and the Prince Regent's mansion on Carlton House Terrace. Other cities followed London's example. In Edinburgh, the end of the war was the cue for an ambitious scheme of urban renewal with the opening up of the New Town and the extension of Princes Street to the east. This last was a major exercise in civil engineering, requiring 'a larger expenditure in seven years than was needed in laying out the essentials of Craig's New Town in the course of a quarter of a century'.[63] It goes almost without saying that the streets it produced were named Waterloo Place and Waterloo Bridge. Many towns also named streets after the Duke, though few went as far as Ashton-under-Lyne in what is today the Greater Manchester borough of Tameside. Nineteenth-century Ashton spawned a suburb called Waterloo, opened up for development in the immediate post-war years, and the spirit of the battle lay heavy on the town. Not only does it have a Wellington Street—Wellington is commemorated in the names of nearly fifty thoroughfares in present-day Greater Manchester—but it also boasts streets named after Uxbridge, Picton, Anglesey, Brunswick, and Blücher, and (in a rare moment of generosity towards a defeated enemy) a Ney Street as well.[64] The people of Ashton would have had great difficulty in avoiding a daily reminder of the battle and of their country's heroes.

Battlefield Tourism

For many in post-war Britain it was not sufficient to exult in victory by visiting a memorial or looking up at a column. They wanted to visit Waterloo; to see the place where the world had been changed—as they believed—by British arms. A few chanced to be on the spot in Brussels as tourists or travellers as the battle was being fought a few miles away, and took advantage of their good fortune to write about the atmosphere in the city or to describe the looting of the victors: two such visitors were Fanny Burney and Charlotte Eaton.[65] Other tourists crossed the Channel and made the journey to Waterloo to see for themselves, rather as Britons had flocked back to France after the Peace of Amiens to assure themselves that Paris was still standing after the excesses of the Terror. Guidebooks acquainted the visitor with the topography of the battlefield and recommended the best vantage points from which to follow the Duke's campaign or share the vista from Napoleon's tower, the very spot from which he had surveyed the battle.[66] John Scott's *Paris Revisited in 1815, by way of Brussels*, for instance, combined tourist information with descriptions of the battle and choice anecdotes about their heroes. Scott leads his reader through the suburbs of Brussels and out on to the battlefield, warning him of the emotional pitfalls ahead. 'The great cause of excitement', he counsels, 'lies in his being on the point of converting into a visible reality what had previously existed in his mind as a shadowy, uncertain but awful fancy', the imagining of a place where such 'prodigious actions' had taken place. Yet the visitor's first sight of the battlefield is so unexceptional, so surprisingly ordinary. 'I was', he wrote, 'struck by the plain of Waterloo. No display, I think, of carnage, violence and devastation could have had so pathetic an effect as the quiet orderly look of its fields, brightened by the sunshine, but thickly strewed with little heaps of upturned earth, which no sunshine could brighten.'[67] A battlefield has its dark side, and it was this dark side which many of the tourists had come to see. One anonymous 'gentleman', cited in one of the best-sellers of the months immediately following the battle (Booth's six-volume *Battle of Waterloo*) made no effort to conceal the horror of some of the scenes he had witnessed, reporting with seeming unconcern the screams of the dying and the painful sight of local peasants dragging dead bodies on fish hooks.[68] The frisson of horror was not to be lightly glossed over; it was presented as an integral part of the experience of war.

For visitors from Britain, as from the other combatant nations, the battlefield was a place with strong emotional ties, where over 50,000 soldiers had lost their lives. As they looked more closely, they could see clearly the telltale signs of that destruction. Scott goes on, pointing up the contrasts he observes all around him:

On a closer inspection, the ravages of the battle were very apparent, but neither the battered walls, splintered doors and torn roofs of the farm houses of La Haie Sainte, astounding as they certainly were, nor even the miserably scorched relics of what must have been the beautiful Hougoumont, with its wild orchard, its parterred flower garden, its gently dignified chateau, and its humble offices, now confounded and overthrown by a visitation which, from its traces, seemed to have included every possible sort of destruction—not all these harsh features of the contest had, to my mind at least, so direct and irresistible an appeal, as the earthy hillocks which tripped the step on crossing a hedgerow, clearing a fence, or winding along among the grass that overhung a secluded pathway.[69]

The destruction was not all, of course, material. There were the decaying bodies of men and horses, and the smell of death was all around. 'Bodies were extended here by the side of the waggon ruts,' Scott wrote, 'only covered with the loose gravel; a man's head showed itself to terrify away the look from one of these heaps.'[70] The emotion of seeing the battlefield could soon turn to revulsion.

Some of those who made the journey from England had family reasons to be there; they were seeing the landscape where their loved ones had fought, or fallen, visiting what was for them a precious chance to grieve. Others were driven by pride or emotion: they claimed to feel an upsurge of sentiment, a sense of the tragedy of the moment, of the terrible carnage that had ensued. But there were also confessed souvenir hunters, men and women who came back home from the Waterloo battlefield with their own trophies of war: ripped-off buttons, pieces of cloth from tunics, objects that provided them with the sense that they had been there, on the field where history had been made. Not all went in a spirit of solemnity, or even reverence. For some the trip to Waterloo was simply a day out, a novel leisure activity with a ghoulish twist thrown in. Within weeks of the battle a group of young men calling themselves the Brentford Boys had arrived in Belgium; in the words of Susan Pearce, 'two of them took a finger each from a dead Frenchman's half-burned hand to be taken home bottled in spirits'.[71] Material remains from the battlefield—or what purported to be so—soon found their way into the hands of dealers and itinerant pedlars, and the arrival of tourist parties from Britain provided them with the opportunity they were waiting for. Scott, again, faithfully records the scene. 'Miserable paralytics, aged men and women bent double, and dirty ragged children gathered about you here, clamorously importunate that you should buy from them eagles, buttons, serjeants' books of companies, grapeshot, and other refuse of battle.'[72] These were the civilian trophies of war, which would go on to decorate the studies and mantelpieces of Victorian England, providing a material link with Waterloo and with the men who had never returned.

Wellington: A Contested Hero

Wellington had never been a consensual figure, and he went on to have a political career in the post-1815 world which, for some, made him appear narrowly sectarian. For Tories he would remain a hero whom they could claim as their own, and they continued to adulate him and to celebrate his achievements on the battlefield long after his military career was over. And, as reported in *Blackwood's Edinburgh Magazine* twenty years later in 1835, they continued to hold anniversary dinners, where toasts were drunk to the great Duke and speeches made honouring Waterloo, the battle 'that is to more than one nation, and to many millions of beings, the anniversary of freedom and of independence'.[73] The orator was happy to claim this as a partisan celebration, a party occasion. Wellington was their hero, but their enthusiasm was not universally shared, and the same article was uncompromising in its attack on the Whigs, whom they still saw, in the image of Charles James Fox, as poor patriots and unrepentant apologists for France. Even the Britishness of the victory was reduced to a party-political issue as the Whigs sought to demean and slander the Tory leader:

> Of all days in the year most hateful to the Whigs is the 18th of June. True, they believe, that but for the arrival of the Prussians the French would

have been victorious; that, but for that 'untoward event', as Wellington had not provided for a retreat, his army would have been driven into the wood of Soignes, the wood set on fire, and all of them burnt to a cinder. That he in fact lost the Battle of Waterloo is certain; and then what great general ever before had the folly to fight in solid squares? There was nothing in the march to Paris. What was it in comparison with Napoleon's on his escape from Elba? And think of the Duke's conduct in the affair of Ney! He had not the heart to save 'the life of the Bravest of the Brave'—he saw in him but the double-dyed traitor![74]

Twenty years on, there was still no general consensus; the celebration of Waterloo and the regard in which Wellington was held had become the stuff of political point-scoring.

Britain in 1815 was politically and socially divided, and it would be still more so after the war was over and thousands of troops faced demobilization and unemployment and were condemned to spend the rest of their lives in poverty. Society did little to care for them or to help them to reintegrate into civilian life, and resentments flared. Former soldiers were among the demonstrators who assembled from all over the industrial North West at St Peter's Fields in Manchester in 1819 to hear one of the leading radical orators of the day, Henry Hunt, advocate parliamentary reform in a city which, despite its rapidly expanding size and industrial importance, still had no representation in the Commons; and they were brutally dispersed by the forces of order, acting on the instructions of the city's magistrates. In all, eighteen demonstrators lost their lives that afternoon, and over 600 others, men and women, sustained injuries, though not all were victims of the yeomanry. St Peter's Fields had been transformed into a scene of carnage which the radicals compared to a battlefield, and which, with a certain propagandist genius, the radical press instantly dubbed 'Peterloo'.

The national unity that had been created in June 1815 around a military victory over the French had been exposed as shallow and brittle, and for many of the radicals it was Tory conservative politicians like Wellington who were their real enemy in a society divided by interest and class. Michael Bush has examined the files of the victims at Peterloo and shows how, of those who died at or near to the scene, seven received sabre cuts, a further three were struck by police truncheons, four were trampled by cavalry horses, and one was crushed to death in a cellar. The other three victims died elsewhere: two men were shot by the army during the evening, in New Cross, well away from St Peter's Fields, and the final victim was a Special Constable—and Waterloo veteran—who was set on by a crowd seeking to avenge the earlier killings.[75] Bush shows, too, that blame for the massacre cannot be placed solely on the heads of the sixty part-time soldiers of the Manchester and Salford Yeomanry who policed the demonstration. They were supported by around 400 Special Constables and by other regular and volunteer troops who were in the vicinity: 340 cavalry from the 15th Hussars and 420 members of the Cheshire Yeomanry cavalry.[76] The use of excessive violence cannot therefore be blamed on amateurs. The attack seemed cruel and deliberate, and it soured any positive associations that the memory of Waterloo might have held for working people in much of industrial Britain. It certainly goes far to explain the suddenness with which the sense of national unity that was evoked by the first news of the victory evaporated within a few short years.

There were some in Britain, of course, who went further, admitting to the lingering admiration they still felt for Napoleon and for the exciting, extravagant dream he had so very nearly realized. Throughout the Napoleonic Wars they had continued to lobby for peace and for some accommodation with the Emperor. Among them were Whigs close to Charles James Fox, who had led the faction until his death in 1806; and thereafter, small groups led by Lord Holland in the Lords and Samuel Whitbread in the Commons. Outside Parliament the self-styled 'Napoleonists' were heavily concentrated in London, prominent among them radical poets and writers like Byron, Godwin, Hazlitt, and Leigh Hunt. For them and their friends Napoleon's defeat at Waterloo came as a crushing blow, 'throwing them', in Hazlitt's words, 'into the pit'. This was the time when Byron first seriously considered suicide, and when Hazlitt was 'staggering under the blow of Waterloo'. Byron, indeed, opted to go into exile in 1816, travelling in a replica of the Emperor's carriage.[77] As the painter Haydon wrote of him in the terrible days following the news of Wellington's victory, 'it is not to be believed how the destruction of Napoleon affected him: he seemed prostrated in mind and body: he walked about unwashed, hardly sober by day, and always intoxicated by night'. For many radicals, like Jeremy Bentham, Waterloo appeared as a threat, undermining the possibility of achieving the parliamentary reforms which, he felt, were necessary to restore freedom to Britain. As he remarked bitterly in 1817, 'the plains, or heights, or whatever they are, of Waterloo will one day be pointed to by the historian as the grave, not only of French but of English liberties'.[78] Henry Brougham came to terms with this disappointment by leaving London society and withdrawing to the country. Whitbread, overcome by despair, committed suicide. Four members of Godwin's immediate circle would follow his example in the following year.[79]

The significance of Waterloo was always linked in the popular imagination with the breadth of Napoleon's imperial vision and his indomitable ambition. For his admirers these were not negative qualities, and many who had lived in fear of him remained awestruck by what he had achieved. Writers produced biographies of him in the very first years after his death, not least among them Walter Scott himself.[80] But the most poignant evidence of Britain's fascination for its recent tormentor came in 1819 with the publication of a work by the Oxford theologian and future bishop of Dublin Richard Whately, with the somewhat alluring title *Historical Doubts Relative to Napoleon Bonaparte*.[81] The publication, little more than a pamphlet, was an instant success, going through fourteen editions before the 1860s, during which time the author carefully amended the text with each new edition, adding further evidence to suggest that the Napoleon known to history might have been a complete fabrication. He was not suggesting that Napoleon had not been a real person, of course, or that he had not lived; rather that the stories told about him were inventions, each more fantastical than the last, since no one man could possibly have done all the remarkable things that were attributed to him. He wrote as a philosopher, not a polemicist: his concern was to question the truth of accepted narratives, to demonstrate the gulf that often existed between an event that was witnessed and its subsequent reporting, particularly in the press, which, he claimed, had a vested interest in exaggeration and dramatization. Napoleon, he believed, had too often been presented as a miracle-worker, but where was the proof? At Waterloo, he argued, the soldiers were undoubtedly present on the battlefield, but what could they tell of Napoleon's role? 'I defy any one of them to come forward and declare, on his own knowledge, what was the cause in which he fought, under whose commands the opposing generals acted, and whether the person who issued these commands did really perform the mighty achievements we are told of.'[82] The great deeds that are attributed to him are so absurd that they defy the laws of probability, and they were massaged to serve Britain's own myth of its military invincibility. He concludes with this challenge to his readers:

> It may all be very true; but I would only ask, if a story had been fabricated for the express purpose of amusing the English, could it have been contrived more ingeniously? It would do admirably for an epic poem, and indeed bears a considerable resemblance to the Iliad and the Aeneid, in which Achilles and the Greeks, Aeneas and the Trojans (the ancestors of the Romans) are so studiously held up to admiration. Bonaparte's exploits seem magnified in order to enhance the glory of his conquerors— just as Hector is allowed to triumph during the absence of Achilles, merely to give additional splendour to his overthrow by the arm of that invincible hero. Would not this circumstance alone render a history rather suspicious in the eyes of an acute critic—even if it were not filled with such gross improbabilities—and induce him to suspend his judgement till very satisfactory evidence (far stronger than can be found in this case) should be produced?[83]

In wartime Britain may have feared Napoleon and the threat of invasion that he represented. But amidst the demonization and the public expressions of contempt for a usurper there was also an undeniable fascination for Bonaparte, a fascination which only increased after 1815.

Waterloo and the British Army

Among British army officers, the Napoleonic Wars, and Waterloo in particular, would continue to exert a fascination in the decades that followed which stood in the way of reform. This was especially the case with officer-training and military education, where the very success of Wellington's army tended to become an excuse for sticking with the well-tried systems of the past and for opposing any moves towards greater professionalization of the officer class. Unlike the French army of the Revolution and Empire, unlike the Prussian army with its well-developed General Staff, the British seemed unwilling to change the traditional structures and traditions of officer-training that had served them so well in the past, or to put a premium on greater professionalism in the leadership of the armed forces in peace and war. It was still assumed that wealth and influence made for good officers, and the purchase system was not abandoned until 1871. Indeed, throughout much of the century conservative military opinion continued to repeat Wellington's view that 'the British officer should be a gentleman first and an officer second', and it was only in the second half of the century, as a result of the reverses of the Crimean War, that this was rescinded. It had long been necessary, as war had changed in character, had become more technically complex, since the Age of Napoleon. Yet, for as long as the purchase system remained unchallenged, it was impossible to introduce any truly professional criteria for advancement in the British army.[84]

Wellington's power and reputation within the army was part of the problem. He did not contemplate adopting anything like the Prussian system, where a chief of staff exercised considerable independent authority; and this greatly reduced the importance attached to the work of the Royal Military College at Sandhurst. The professor of military science there had few qualms about telling a Select

Committee in 1855 that 'military education is but little valued by the greater part of the high military authorities', adding that 'they consider, after all, whether a man is professionally educated or not, it will make not the slightest difference with regard to his qualities as an officer'.[85] The changes, when they did come, were in the direction of introducing greater practical training and physical exercise, including less repetitive learning in the curriculum, and encouraging young officers to form their own opinions, a development where a succession of teachers and theorists made their contribution. Guided by men like Hamley and Henderson, the Staff College reformed its curriculum, more closely geared to the problems a young officer might encounter in war. In military history classes students were asked to solve problems rather than recite facts. But this does not mean that Waterloo was forgotten, or that Wellington's tactics on that day did not continue to inspire. Even in the 1890s Henderson was still asking his students to deal with problems that had their roots in the Waterloo campaign, and surviving Staff College papers of these years reflect this obsession. 'The Waterloo Campaign: Discuss Wellington's dispositions up to the time he left Brussels on 16 June 1815', one student was asked. Another was told to 'Write Napoleon's order for attack of the original position at Waterloo with reasons, assuming that the flanks cannot be turned'.[86] On the eve of a new century, and with the risk of war again growing, these were questions that simply would not go away.

7

France, Waterloo, and the Napoleonic Legend

If Britain had every reason to celebrate a memorable victory in 1815, France had to come to terms with a crushing defeat, and this posed a challenge of a very different kind. Victories are, of course, much easier to commemorate, as the most cursory glance at the exhibits in any of the world's military museums or national art galleries will confirm. Artists record the deeds of victorious armies, portraitists paint their conquering generals, and proud governments strike medals to celebrate their moments of triumph. In contrast, defeats often pass unrecorded and unlamented. Those who lose in war are often forlorn figures, left—as Napoleon laconically remarked after Waterloo—to shoulder the blame for catastrophe. Yet Napoleon and those who remained loyal to his memory were not content to dismiss the battle in this way, convincing themselves that, but for a cruel stroke of luck, the day would surely have been his. 'The English thought the battle lost throughout the day,' Napoleon wrote on St Helena, 'and they are agreed that it would have been won but for Grouchy's error.'[1] He never doubted that he had been a conqueror until the bitter end, and he believed that he would win the battle for public opinion. 'While history may be temporarily made by the victors,' wrote Reinhart Koselleck, 'it never allows itself to be ruled for long.'[2] Napoleon kept faith that he would be exonerated by posterity.

A Culture of Defeat

Waterloo was far from being the only defeat that this generation of Frenchmen had had to bear. The generation that fought in Belgium in 1815 had suffered a series of crippling reverses in the final stages of the Napoleonic Wars: in Russia in 1812, at Leipzig in 1813, and in 1814 in the *Campagne de France*, which had ended in Napoleon's first abdication. What, one might reasonably ask, was there for the French to celebrate about a war that had ended in invasion and surrender on two separate occasions, had decimated France's overseas empire, especially in the Caribbean, and left the British Empire in a virtually unassailable position for most of the nineteenth century?[3] While Britain and Prussia could celebrate a victory that provided their deliverance from Napoleon—and in Prussia's case revenge for the humiliation at Jena—France was left to lick her wounds and dream of what might have been; and after nearly a quarter-century of war and the loss of several million lives, Frenchmen were entitled to ask what had been achieved by Napoleon's thirst for glory and empire. It did not take the sight of what Jacques Hantraye graphically terms 'the Cossacks on the Champs-Élysées' to bring it home to ordinary people that this was a war that had ended in disaster.[4] As France started to rebuild her trade and industry after 1815—to say nothing of her political ambition and public morale—the scale of her defeat and the extent of what had been lost was clear to all. Hundreds of thousands of soldiers returned to civilian life broken, wounded, and without hope of employment. The question was not whether these wars would be remembered in nine-teenth-century France, but how.

This culture of defeat goes far to explain the extreme factionalism of the decades that followed. For many who had supported the Revolution two decades earlier it was their army that had been defeated, their cause that was lost in 1815; and any distinction that might once have existed between the nation-in-arms of the early 1790s and the con-script army of the Consulate and Empire became quickly blurred.

Figure 13. Memorial to General Cambronne, Nantes

Some of the same men had, of course, served in both, though few of them would survive until 1815. But for those who did, and for the generations that followed, the distinction between Revolution and Empire was largely lost, as the revolutionary *demi-brigades* and the regiments of Napoleon's Grande Armée came to merge seamlessly into a single nostalgic haze. Napoleon himself assisted this process during the Hundred Days, when he went out of his way to emphasize his revolutionary credentials, presenting himself to the army as one of their own, as the 'little corporal' who shared their sufferings and who had, like them, risen from the ranks on merit. The Napoleon to whose standard the troops rallied in 1815 and whom they followed at Waterloo appeared to share their egalitarian instincts and presented himself as a man of the people. After his years of imperial pomp this was perhaps his most brilliant propaganda coup, guaranteeing that he would retain the lasting loyalty of the men he commanded.[5]

For the politicians and army officers who had steered Napoleonic France and had shared the imperial dream of a new, modernized polity, it was the defeat of their life's work which seemed most crushing. Defeat was not limited to a few prominent individuals, though some—like Michel Ney—paid the supreme price for their loyalty to Napoleon, while others, most notably those deputies who had been regicides in 1792, were forced to drag out their remaining years in exile.[6] But these men represented only the tip of a huge iceberg, the large number of army officers and public administrators whose service to the Emperor ensured that they were distrusted by the returning Bourbons and who saw promising careers abruptly terminated. France's defeat affected, and blighted, a whole generation who had made their careers under the Revolution and Empire. The army was perhaps the worst affected in the immediate aftermath of defeat. It had to be scaled down for economic reasons and to adjust to the needs of peacetime: that was predictable, and was widely accepted. But the savagery with which it was cut, and the preference that was given to returning royalists whose only service in the wars—if they had served at all—had been to the armies of France's enemies, spread anger and disillusionment among the Napoleonic officer class. They would prove an important source of dissent which would pose a danger to the Bourbon cause.

Defeat left nineteenth-century France a country bitterly divided against itself, a nation that might be sure of its national identity and proud of its collective culture, but which was politically fractured, unable to unite behind any regime, and continually prone to violence and revolution. Not all Frenchmen had followed Napoleon, and for the minority of royalists and émigrés who had been irreconcilable in their opposition to the Empire, the totality of France's defeat could be a cause of rejoicing. Most showed some discretion, conscious that they could not be seen to mock the millions who had died. But rejoice they did, safe in the knowledge that they enjoyed the support of the

Figure 14. Gérôme,
L'aigle blessé, 1904

restored monarchy. In many areas, and in the South especially, the politics of the years from 1815 were dominated by outbreaks of White Terror, with royalists and Catholic fundamentalists taking their revenge on those who had served the cause of the Revolution and Empire.[7] There is little to suggest that they felt defeated. Indeed, there was an element of subjectivity about the whole idea of defeat which ensured that it held different meanings for the various political constituencies within the nation.

Many in the army felt abandoned by the Bourbons, cast out of active service on *demi-solde,* their sacrifice unappreciated, their injuries a lasting blight, and their chance of finding employment permanently diminished. The regime carried out its purges insensitively, casting out experienced officers who had served their country well to make way for noble officers and royalist placemen. Between 10,000 and 12,000 officers were retired on half-pay, whilst the civilian population was swollen by over 300,000 soldiers for whom the regime had no further use. The elite of the Imperial Guard, whose commitment to Napoleon raised particular suspicion in Bourbon eyes, found themselves dispersed across provincial garrisons, their unquestionable prowess ignored or disregarded by a regime to which they felt little loyalty. And, by his insistence on certain symbolic reforms in the structure of the army, reforms that raised the spectre of a return to the Old Regime, Louis XVIII was unnecessarily insensitive to the views of the army. In 1814 and 1815, for instance, he insisted that the King's Household be reconstituted along traditional lines to form a privileged elite within the army, creating, as the British historian Munro Price notes, not only 'the whole panoply of Gardes du Corps, Cent-Suisses, Gardes de la Porte du Roi, Mousquetaires gris and Mousquetaires noirs' reminiscent of the old order, but even five regiments of Swiss Guards, the same troops that had left such an indelible mark on revolutionary Paris when they opened fire on a crowd of demonstrators in 1792 while defending the Tuileries.[8] It is difficult to think of measures that would be more certain to arouse hatred and bitterness both among the citizenry of Paris and in the ranks of the Napoleonic army.

Nostalgia and Conspiracy

The frustrations of the years that followed 1815 led many former soldiers to look back on the war with unashamed nostalgia. That is not to say that the hardship and suffering of the campaigns were forgotten, as the ample evidence from memoirs and letters from the Russian campaign makes clear. Men had faced exhaustion and starvation and had been reduced to hacking slabs of meat from their dead horses if they were to survive. They had witnessed many acts of savagery and barbarism. They had lost friends and comrades and seen men lying horribly mutilated on the battlefield, their bodies left for crows and dogs to strip. War had not been fun. But amidst the horror there had been moments of warmth and companionship to treasure, and tales of adventure which lived with them for the rest of their lives. They had seen foreign lands, had met exotic peoples, and admired European capital cities as they could never have hoped to do in civilian life.[9] And they had been present at events on the world stage, events that had made history. These memories, too, stayed with them, and for many of the survivors it was these that came to dominate their recollections and to colour their judgement on the Napoleonic years long after they had returned to civilian life.[10]

Besides, the years of the Restoration proved a terrible anticlimax, and some reacted against it. If the 1820s were a period of unemployment and retrenchment for many, and were characterized politically by the conservative values of monarchism and Catholicism, they were also, for thousands of Napoleonic veterans, years when it was still possible to dream. The growth of *charbonnerie* and secret societies was particularly strong among army veterans and those of Bonapartist sympathies, and the severity of the government repression that was directed against anyone agitating for a return to the Empire only served to strengthen their resolve. The 1820s were punctuated by plots and conspiracies which, after the assassination of the Duc de Berri in Paris, made royalists fearful. Political conspiracies, real and imagined, were rarely out of the headlines, as meetings and conversations involving Napoleon's former troops were watched, listened to, and reported on by an army of police spies. Most notable, perhaps, was the conspiracy of the Four Sergeants of La Rochelle in 1822, whose youth and idealism played to the Romantic imagination; the seeming inevitability of their condemnation and execution only helped ensure that they lived on in popular memory and inspired a new generation of conspirators.[11] And when, following the 1830 Revolution and the coming to power of Louis-Philippe, it became safe for the opponents of legitimism to raise their voices publicly once more, the cult of Napoleon would enter mainstream French politics and result in a powerful and recurrent tradition of strong personal government. It is a tradition that has traces of populism and of democratic centralism

Figure 15. *A Rare Acquisition to the Royal Menagerie : a Present from Waterloo by Marshalls Wellington & Blucher.* By Thomas Rowlandson, 1756–1827, printmaker

and it has had resonances ever since, from Louis Napoleon to General Boulanger in the nineteenth century, and from Philippe Pétain to Charles de Gaulle in the twentieth. For a wide section of the French population—largely concentrated in small towns and rural departments—the lure of Napoleonic glory continued to be seductive.[12] In 1823 French intervention in Spain created a heightened patriotic fever, attracting further support among the popular classes and helping to rekindle memories of the Empire.[13]

The memory of Napoleon would be evoked with almost predictable regularity across the nineteenth century. Some continued to refuse to believe that he had been defeated at Waterloo and preferred to place the responsibility for Napoleon's defeat on others, blaming the lack of leadership or the cowardice of his marshals and the lack of political will amongst the deputies back in Paris. In a pamphlet published in 1835 in reply to what he took to be an attack on Napoleon's memory, Lucien Bonaparte argued that all had not been lost on the morning

137

after the battle, and that when he had left his army to hurry back to Paris Napoleon had not been running away or thinking of his own safety; he had been offering a lead to his countrymen, showing them the most effective way of carrying on the struggle to defend Paris against the Allies. And who, implied Lucien, is to say that he was wrong? Could his strategy not have worked? 'If the chambers had responded to his heroic confidence; if they had called for a *levée en masse*; if they had pressed themselves around the person of their head of state; then let us ask the most audacious of our enemies ... would they have dared to march on Paris?'[14] The possibility of a different outcome after Waterloo, the construction of a history of counterfactuals, was a recurrent theme among those nostalgic for Empire; and it would continue to sustain the Napoleonic myth in future decades, not least, of course, after the *coup d'état* of 1851 that overthrew the Second Republic and brought another Bonaparte to the imperial throne. There were significant continuities between these two imperial moments. Louis Napoleon played relentlessly on his popular roots, on the direct bonds which linked him to the people. There were personal bonds, too. Support for him remained strong among the families of those who had served the first Napoleon, the descendants of Murat, Ney, and Cambacérès whose personal devotion to the Emperor remained unshaken.[15]

Republicans and Bonapartists united in their opposition to the reactionary politics of the Bourbons, symbolized for many by the revival of the old landed aristocracy and by the punitive missions of the Catholic Church. But it is in the imagery of public commemoration after the Revolution of 1830 that the blurring of Revolution and Empire is most clear. The July Monarchy was eager to exploit any associations with the recent past at a time when the Napoleonic legend was at its most powerful. Louis-Philippe deliberately sought to cultivate the Bonapartist vote, and it is no accident that the panels of the Arc de Triomphe in Paris—surely the most enduring monument to Napoleon's Grande Armée—were sculpted in these years. The four panels commemorate the glory and sacrifice of French troops across the twenty years of the Revolution and Empire. Three of them celebrate Napoleon's army—a winged Victory representing Napoleon's triumphs; the heroic resistance of the French people in the *Campagne de France*; and the signing of the peace treaty that brought the final peace. The fourth is François Rude's *Le Départ des volontaires en 1792*, which contributes to the military legend of the Revolution, emphasizing the voluntary character of recruitment, the joy on the faces of the young, and their burning patriotism and devotion to the cause of the French Republic. And yet this revolutionary prelude cannot disguise the central purpose of the arch: it was a monument to the genius of Napoleon Bonaparte, to his conquests, his leadership, and his victories.[16] Waterloo, significantly, does not figure. The medallions sculpted on the Arch record all the battles of the Revolution and Empire, from Valmy in 1792 to Napoleon's last victory, at Ligny. Then there was silence. It was not the purpose of the Arch to draw attention to the Emperor's final defeat.

The July Monarchy was unapologetic in using Napoleon's reputation in a bid to maximize popular support, and Louis-Philippe took care to map out his reign with periodic reminders of the Napoleonic glory with which he sought to identify.[17] Four Napoleonic marshals flanked the new king at his coronation ceremony in 1831; the Vendôme Column was erected to Napoleon's memory in the centre of Paris in 1834; the Arc de Triomphe was inaugurated in 1836; whilst in 1840 the Emperor's body was returned from St Helena to the Invalides, where it would lie in state, as he himself had wished, 'by the banks of the Seine, in the midst of the people he loved'. The Revolution of 1848 brought little relief, as Louis Napoleon capitalized on his links to the Great Napoleon to seize political power. And under the Second Empire the government openly encouraged the growth of nostalgia for the Napoleonic age, the new emperor going so far as to reward every surviving veteran of his great-uncle's armies with the *Médaille de Sainte-Hélène* in 1857 (and there were more than 400,000 survivors).[18] The reign ended, of course, in national disaster with the collapse of the French army in the Franco-Prussian War—a defeat

which Frenchmen regarded as humiliating and which only demonstrated what many already knew to be true: how much the country's
army, and with it, France's imperial ambition, had fallen since the
glorious days of Austerlitz and Jena. Everyone, it seemed, had an
interest in keeping the memory of the Napoleonic Wars alive. In
that memory Waterloo was not forgotten. Rather it was cast in the
role of the heroic defeat that added a romantic poignancy to their
Emperor's life and triumphs.

Public Art and Memorialization

The battle was, however, strikingly absent from France's memorial
landscape. In the capital there is no street bearing the name of a battle
that left over 30,000 Frenchmen dead or wounded, though reminders
of Napoleon's victories are liberally scattered around the city, in the
names of streets and bridges and railway terminals from Rue d'Ulm
and the Pont d'Iéna to the railway station that would serve central and
south-west France, the Gare d'Austerlitz. The broad boulevards of the
Second Empire that stretch out from the Étoile commemorate battles
like Wagram and Friedland, while the artery running west to Neuilly is
named after the Grande Armée itself. At Napoleon's tomb in Les
Invalides, which would become a site of pilgrimage for many in the
nineteenth century, Waterloo again passes unnoticed. None of this
need surprise us, for these are official sites of memory, planned and
financed by the state, and no state is interested in recalling its military
disasters. Even the battlefield of Waterloo went unmarked until the
early years of the twentieth century, by which time France was the
only one of the principal combatant nations not to have erected some
kind of memorial to its dead. Indeed, it was not until 1904 that the
French finally commissioned a monument, and even then they demonstrated some unease and ambiguity. The statue of the 'Wounded
Eagle' which was erected on the initiative of a private society, the
Sabretache,[19] was intended to honour the sacrifice of France's soldiers
in 1815 and not, it was made clear, to commemorate the battle.[20] At the

inauguration ceremony, attended by leading military and political figures, the painter Édouard Detaille explained the intentions of the promoters. The Eagle, he said, was a memorial to the courage of the soldiers of the First Republic and Empire, soldiers who had fought bravely 'for liberty and glory, enshrined in the idea of the motherland', before being 'fired by enthusiasm for the Emperor'.[21] It was a simple patriotic message on which, in the years of ill will between the French republic and its army which followed the scandal of the Dreyfus Affair, the politicians of the Third Republic and France's military leaders could hope to agree.

Indeed, in as far as Waterloo leaves a trace on French memorial sculpture, it is less to commemorate the battle as such than to evoke its legend, especially the courage of the Old Guard and the famous *mot de Cambronne*, that 'the Guard dies and does not surrender'.[22] In many ways Cambronne was an unlikely Napoleonic hero, since, despite his previous loyalty to the Emperor, he later went over to the side of the Bourbons and he almost certainly never uttered the words he is supposed to have shouted to encourage his men.[23] But his myth lived on, his words being taken as the very epitome of French courage, so that it is he, and not the battle, that would be commemorated by a statue in a French public square. In 1842, just two years after the return of Napoleon's remains to be buried at the Invalides, the city of Nantes issued a call for a public subscription to commission a statue in honour of one of its most glorious sons. Again there was no specific mention of Waterloo; the words were carefully chosen to emphasize courage and glory and to straddle both Revolution and Empire:

> The city of Nantes is proud to have given birth to one of the purest glories of the former army, Cambronne, soldier of 92, general of 1815, who fell on the field of battle at the head of that *Guard which dies and does not surrender*.[24]

Cambronne was indeed a brave soldier who had fought throughout the Revolutionary and Napoleonic Wars, from his baptism of fire at Jemappes to the last embers of the Empire; he survived Waterloo—it was part of the legend that he 'fell on the field of battle'—whereupon he was imprisoned for his apparent loyalty to Napoleon and put on trial before a military court in 1816. After being acquitted, he then rallied to the monarchy, and rehabilitation and honours followed. Cambronne married the British nurse who had tended him after the battle, before leaving the army in 1823 and retiring to his native Nantes with the title of viscount, bestowed on him by Louis XVIII.[25] He died in 1842, after which the city took the decision to honour him by erecting a statue.

Waterloo in Literature

Not all those who had served in Napoleon's last campaigns were harmed by their experience, and many of the officers, in particular, would go on to have rewarding careers after the war was over. As Stéphane Calvet has demonstrated in his study of the Charente, their years in uniform could form a socially-acceptable transition period in their lives, and they very often resumed the lifestyle and social status that they had enjoyed before they enlisted. Young noblemen, especially, were able to slip easily back into a privileged lifestyle on their farm or chateau; it was rural poor, especially farm workers and rural labourers, who had the greatest difficulty in reinsertion. For many of them, 1815 could seem like a 'final rendez-vous' before they were thrown to the four winds.[26] Relatively few, as we have seen, left written records of the battle, but those who did, or who simply told their stories in bars and at street markets, were guaranteed an eager audience. They told stories that others wanted to hear, providing later generations with a link to their Napoleonic past and novelists and poets with a sense of the grandeur and pathos of the imperial adventure. Conscious of the importance of what they were saying and eager to convey their sense of pride and adventure, their stories rarely disappointed.[27] And at the heart of many of their stories was Napoleon.

Even Walter Scott—British and patriotic to the core but, like many of his countrymen, fascinated by the events he had lived through—was dazzled by the person of the Emperor and by the extent of his military ambition, though it was an ambition which Scott saw as the fatal flaw that led to his downfall. 'He might have played the part of Washington', he wrote in his *Life of Napoleon Buonaparte*, but 'he preferred that of Cromwell'.[28] Scott's work was widely read in France, although Bonapartists were unimpressed by what they saw as his dismissive judgement on the Emperor. They agreed with Napoleon's former companion on St Helena, Gaspard Gourgaud, when he condemned Scott for showing the partiality of a British writer, insisting that Napoleon had been motivated less by personal ambition than by a commitment to France and its people.[29] Through such writings a new generation would come to share the experiences of their elders. For the Napoleonic faithful, the fact that the imperial adventure had ended in failure—and in Napoleon's own abdication, a political failure to add to the military defeat—was as nothing when compared to the magnificence of his imperial dreams. Indeed, his final defeat may even have added pathos and poignancy to Napoleon's legend, an element of Shakespearian tragedy that helped to illuminate his very existence. It was a battle which those who continued to adulate him could so easily convert into a 'glorious defeat'.

It was as a 'glorious defeat' that Waterloo would be remembered in France, a battle enshrouded in fog and mist yet illuminated by acts of outstanding courage in the pursuit of victory, which would be remembered long after the sun had gone down on the *morne plaine* and its 70,000 dead. It was epitomized by two moments of valour and sacrifice: the heroic defence by the final square of the Old Guard; and the famous, if apocryphal, words of Cambronne. These images would live long into the nineteenth century and would ensure that Waterloo gained a uniquely romantic place among Napoleon's battles, a place that would be immortalized by a generation of poets and novelists. For Balzac, Stendhal, Mérimée, Paul-Louis Courier, Maurice Barrès, and, most memorably, Victor Hugo—the last of these the son of a Napoleonic general—were all dazzled by the figure of the Emperor, and through their writings a new generation came to experience the thrill of battle and the call of glory. Waterloo is almost universally presented as a tragedy, to be talked of with a tinge of sadness as they wrote of the decline and fall of the last of the eighteenth century's Great Men. In the process they contributed powerfully to Napoleon's myth.[30]

Hugo's haunting poem on Waterloo, published in *Les Châtiments* in 1853, made the battlefield into a nineteenth-century *lieu de mémoire* that was a tribute to French gallantry as much as to unquenchable ambition, a place of sadness and tragedy where dreams of heroism lay shattered; and it is as such that it would be remembered and commemorated across much of mainland Europe. The poem went far to romanticize the battle, to gloss over the savagery and butchery, and retain only the passion and the glory. It was the moment, wrote Hugo, when victory had finally deserted Napoleon, a moment of tears and melancholy. Hugo also offered up a paean of praise to Napoleon's soldiers: for him 'these last soldiers of the last war were great; they had conquered the whole earth, chased out twenty kings, crossed the Alps and the Rhine'. This was not a battle limited to tales of suffering and misery, images of human flesh and dying horses; and there is no hint of reproach to the Emperor for either bad judgement or overvaulting ambition. In *Les Misérables* in 1861 Hugo made his own view clear, and it is one that was widely shared:

> His plan of battle was, by the confession of all, a masterpiece. To go straight to the centre of the Allies' line, to make a breach in the enemy, to cut them in two, to drive the British half back on Hal, and the Prussian half on Tongres, to make two shattered fragments of Wellington and Blücher, to carry Mont Saint-Jean, to seize Brussels, to hurl the German into the Rhine and the Englishman into the sea. All this was contained in that battle, according to Napoleon. Afterwards people would see.[31]

For Hugo fate had played its hand at Waterloo—fate and God. 'Was it possible that Napoleon should have won that battle?' he asked rhetorically. 'We answer No.' And why? 'Because of Wellington? Because of Blücher? No. Because of God.'[32] His remained a romanticized image of a world France had lost, but it was a world to which many Frenchmen still aspired and a vision they would retain in their dreams and their prayers long after Napoleon's death on St Helena.[33] For them Waterloo was more than an opportunity missed, a battle lost; it was a moment of supreme tragedy. Military romanticism saw war as an art, with Napoleon, in John Lynn's words, 'its outstanding artist'.[34]

The identification of Napoleon with glory on the battlefield, and of Waterloo with the ultimate fading of that glory, would be one of the leitmotifs of French Romantic literature, its novels as well as its poetry. At times, as with Henri Beyle (the novelist Stendhal), life and inspiration were relentlessly interwoven. The young man who had so admired Napoleon's military feats himself went on to embrace the life of an army officer, only to find failure and to conclude that he was not cut out for the life of pure action he so craved in his writings. As Gita May observes, though this was undoubtedly a source of huge disappointment to him, he never allowed it to dominate his consciousness or to involve his whole being. 'His rapid disenchantment with army life and his decision to resign his commission', she writes, 'clearly testify to early loss of interest in the hero myth which had played such a vital part in his youthful dreams and fantasies.' Yet, she adds, his fascination with Napoleon was not so easily dispelled. 'He continued to be spellbound by Bonaparte and by the combination of psychological and sociological factors that had gone into shaping this extraordinary being.'[35] Spellbound and, one would suppose, rather overawed by the Emperor, if we judge by the sentiments he expressed in *Les Temps héroïques de Napoléon* in 1837. 'I feel', he wrote, 'a sort of religious sentiment as I write the first sentence of the history of Napoleon, for this was the greatest man to have graced the world since Caesar.'[36] Defeat at Waterloo, quite clearly, had done nothing to dent Napoleon's reputation in the eyes of the young writer.

Napoleon's presence lowers over several of Stendhal's novels, too, from *Le Rouge et le Noir* to *La Chartreuse de Parme*, and his lifelong involvement with the Napoleonic myth is an important part of his creative power. In this myth Waterloo plays a significant part—it is the battle over which he lingers longest and which, together with the early campaigns in Italy, exerts the greatest fascination over him. But, unlike Victor Hugo, Stendhal makes no effort to describe the heroic actions on the battlefield; rather he focuses on the exhilaration which men felt as the moment of the battle approached, and on the character of his hero, Fabrice, as events unfurl and he is able to forget past miseries.[37] Sounds and smells, noise and adrenalin are everywhere, exalting the young man to ever-greater efforts and pervading the atmosphere of the entire battlefield. Old soldiers and veterans of Napoleon's campaigns pepper the pages of Stendhal's novels, often saddened and sometimes alienated by the lives to which they were condemned once the war was over. Lucien Leuwen is one who dreams of a glorious past that is already fast receding into memory as he contemplates a France in which 'I shall become a pillar of the soldiers' café in the sad garrison of a small, ill-paved town; for my pleasure in the evening I will have a few games of billiards and bottles of beer'. Leuwen had seen too many old soldiers and too many broken lives. But still he manages to end on a less gloomy note. 'I shall feel exhilarated', he writes with more than a flicker of humour, 'when I am presented to Napoleon in the next world.'[38]

Napoleon's Reputation

Waterloo may have ended Napoleon's regime and destroyed any possibility of a return to power, but it did not destroy his reputation as a military commander. He had his critics, of course; indeed, ever since the Russian campaign there had been an increasingly loud chorus of critical voices, suggesting that he had taken unwonted risks, that he had lost his grip on reality, that his ambition had seduced him into pursuing impossible dreams. And after Waterloo, again, some of his soldiers criticized his overconfidence, even his naïvety, for trusting too readily the judgement of his marshals or for investing too much in his faith in his 'star'. Most famously, as we have seen, Marbot expressed his anger when he recalled that 'we were made to manoeuvre like pumpkins' on the battlefield, while Napoleon stubbornly continued to wait for the arrival of Grouchy's reinforcements long after communication with the Marshal had been lost; as a consequence, he believed, he had needlessly handed the initiative in the battle to Blücher and Wellington.[39] Among his senior officers very few were prepared to express themselves so critically, even though most were realistic enough to recognize that the game was up and that they had no choice but to sue for peace. In the wider community, however, critical voices were less restrained. The years after 1815 were the high point of the black legend of Napoleon, when savage satires circulated in Paris and in some provincial cities, presenting him as a tyrant, an ogre, an unrepentant terrorist, a heartless squanderer of human lives, or a devoted disciple of Robespierre.[40] Among monarchist authors the most unrelenting was Chateaubriand, whose *De Buonaparte et des Bourbons* portrayed Napoleon as a general of limited talent who squandered the inexhaustible reserves of manpower which the system of conscription provided and abandoned the defensive strategies that had served France well since the time of Vauban.[41] In mid-century these criticisms were voiced anew, with some of his fiercest critics pointing to his failure to break the British squares at Waterloo as one of the most glaring examples of his tactical limitations. The successive crises on the battlefield were allowed to happen, Colonel Charras inferred, because Napoleon committed error after error and failed to provide the secure defences the army needed.[42] In the battle for history these attacks had a limited impact. Even after the near-despair of his last campaigns many old soldiers preferred to remain loyal to the man they still called, affectionately, 'their' Emperor.

A Glorious Defeat

The French troops who crossed the Ardennes in the wake of the battle knew that the war was lost; but they had no reason to blame themselves or to see in their defeat any cause for reproach. They had little to be ashamed of: they had fought well, with courage, against a series of coalitions and latterly against all the Great Powers of Europe. If there had been failures of communication, if they had made tactical errors, if they had misread Prussian manoeuvres, none of this besmirched their honour; throughout they had fought with the courage and *élan* on which French military identity was based. True, many of them wrote in the days following Waterloo expressing disappointment, disillusionment, occasionally a sense of despair born of sadness and exhaustion. But there was no sense of shame, as there was after wars when the French troops knew that they had not performed, or when they had been subjected to overwhelming losses and a rout on the battlefield: one only has to think of the public reaction to Napoleon III's army in the war of 1870 or to the French troops whose contribution to the Allied cause in the Second World War ended in capitulation in 1940. The contrast after 1815 could not have been greater, with many of Napoleon's soldiers eager to talk of their experiences, which, in spite of the danger and the suffering, they still counted among the most memorable of their lives. Some, indeed, were so inured to a life of adventure that they could not bring themselves to accept the dull routines of village life, preferring to offer their swords to others, especially where they were fighting in a cause that they could identify with freedom or throwing off tyranny. And so French veterans would welcome the chance to fight in Spain in 1823, just as they would be found in significant numbers in the southern United States (where anti-British feeling could be mobilized), and in the liberation struggles in Mexico, Bolivia, Peru, Ecuador, and across much of Central and South America.[43] Their quest for glory did not end at Waterloo.

Their reputation during the decades that followed would remain largely intact, and their tales of war inspired wide interest in the public at large. In French culture they had an assured place, not only in novels and history paintings, but in the various media of popular culture, ranging from the poetry of Pierre-Jean Béranger to the brightly coloured lithographs of Charles Pellerin and his fellow colourists of Épinal.[44] Patriotic images of Napoleon's soldiers, many of them by François Georgin, were widely distributed and highly prized, and under the July Monarchy they were to be found everywhere, from the Paris apartment to the peasant cottage, symbols of bravery and sacrifice in a lost cause.[45] The military prints of Raffet, which glorified the feats of the army and brought a certain humanity to the person of Napoleon, achieved a new vogue with the French public.[46] Under the Second Empire the representations of the battle become less naïve, more heroic, with a new wave of paintings that dwelt on the *élan* of the army, the bold charges of the cavalry, their courage under fire, or the Guard refusing to capitulate, fighting heroically to the end. By the end of the nineteenth century, following the humiliation at the hands of the Prussians at Sedan in 1871 and with French opinion bitterly divided over the Dreyfus Affair, the emphasis of this ever-changing iconography had switched again, from the nation to the military, an evolution that linked Waterloo to a cult of the army at a time when it found itself under political attack. Waterloo and the courage of the Guard became the perfect antidote to Sedan.[47]

And the exploits of Napoleon's armies were repeatedly celebrated in song, in the popular tunes of the period that were sung in bars and taverns wherever veterans assembled. For them Waterloo conjured up images of courage and tragedy, the end of a heroic era and—with the Second Restoration—a return to mediocrity. But few of these songs have survived. One that has, the rather unimaginatively entitled 'Épisodes de 1815', takes pleasure in recalling a moment of France's past when there was no Bourbon on the throne and when courage and the cause of liberty were, as its author saw it, still inextricably linked:

A Waterloo l'on vit la vieille garde
Plutôt périr que de suivre un tyran,
Et par amour de la vieille cocarde
Ils sont tous morts à l'affreux Mont-Saint-Jean.[48]

Another, Émile Debraux's 'La Bataille de Waterloo', perhaps the only song devoted entirely to the memory of the Battle, ended with its own unrestrained outpouring of admiration for the the men of Imperial Guard:

> Belliqueuse garde,
> L'Anglais te regarde,
> Admire et retarde
> Ses feux et ton sort,
> Ses lignes s'entr'ouvrent,
> Et vers toi, découvrent
> Cent bouches qui s'ouvrent
> Pour donner la mort.[49]

Unsurprisingly, these songs focused on the two moments of outstanding bravery in the face of defeat which eclipsed all others: the last stand of the Guard and the *mot de Cambronne*, both sharply etched on French patriotic memory. Like most of the popular lyrics written during the Restoration, they were strongly republican or Bonapartist in tone.

In France and beyond, Romantic writers ensured that the wars of Napoleon would be remembered not just for individual acts of courage, but for the values they upheld, the civil liberties they offered, and the grandeur of the imperial dream. For them the glorious defeat that was Waterloo was also a turning point, and a grim one, in modern European history, a turning back of European civilization that would have tragic consequences. It had killed off a dream and halted progress in its tracks. In 1825 Stendhal described Marengo as the battle that had opened Italy to liberty and modernity and had launched liberal ideas, a revolution in culture that had now been doomed to failure by Napoleon's removal. 'The Italians are right,' he wrote; 'Marengo advanced the civilization of their country by a hundred years, just as another battle has retarded it for a century.'[50] What Stendhal seeks to impart is his belief that Waterloo represented the end, not the beginning, the end of so much that was progressive: of an experiment in humanism, of secularism, of modern administration and accessible justice which France had come to represent and which through her victories she had offered to all of Europe. It was a defeat for mankind. He was not alone in seeing things in this light. Even in Britain, in the myriad responses to the battle in the year that followed, Philip Shaw can comment that 'it is a curious aspect of modern culture that Waterloo is best remembered as a tragic defeat rather than as a glorious triumph'.[51] So across Europe Waterloo would always be a *morne plaine*, which in defeat seemed greater than any victory. Later in the century Charles Péguy would sum up the feelings of his generation when he wrote: 'There are defeats, *Waterloo morne plaine*, which more than any victory, and more positively than any victory, fix themselves in the memory of men, in the common memory of humanity.'[52]

Waterloo would fix itself in the memory of generations of French schoolchildren, too, if only because it was the only Napoleonic battle that was narrated in any detail in the 'Petit Lavisse', that venerable republican textbook on the history of France which dominated the elementary school curriculum in the years before and after the First World War. Lavisse's account of the battle has little to say about the victors: it emphasizes the role of luck in determining the outcome of the battle and dwells on the tragedy that overcame the Emperor in the end. It is presented, as so often in France, as the victory that so nearly was, a victory snatched from Napoleon's grasp by the arrival, not once but twice, of a Prussian army. As he tells it, it is a touchingly simple tale:

> The Emperor went to attack an English army near Waterloo, a little village in Belgium. The English were on the point of being beaten when they heard rifle and cannon fire. It was a Prussian army which arrived to bring the English help.

The battle continued. Napoleon still hoped for victory. But again rifle and cannon fire rang out. And it was a second Prussian army which arrived.

For eight hours our soldiers fought on an extremely hot June day. They were overcome with fatigue.

Voices cried out: 'Sauve qui peut!' A troupe of the Emperor's oldest soldiers formed a square. They defended themselves with admirable courage. The remainder of the army fled.

Then the Emperor wanted to die. You see it at the moment when he had just drawn his sword. But an old soldier took hold of his horse's reins. His generals pleaded with him to leave the battlefield.

The Emperor allowed himself to be led away. He returned to Paris. But he could not remain there long. His enemies approached, and he had no more soldiers. He wanted to go to England, hoping that the English would allow him to live in their country.

But the English sent him very far away, to the Island of St Helena, where he died after suffering years of bad treatment at their hands.[53]

Bravery, misfortune, glory, and finally despair—Lavisse's account contains elements of them all. It is a classic celebration of the glorious defeat, and it would be repeated in edition after edition of Lavisse well into the twentieth century.

8

Waterloo in German and Dutch Memory

From reading some British accounts of the battle, and especially those written in the decades immediately following 1815, it is often difficult to remember that other nations were present on the battlefield and that Waterloo was an Allied rather than a purely British victory. Some historians, indeed, have implied that the British quite deliberately diminished the part played by others in order to arouse popular patriotism and extract maximum political advantage from the memory of the battle. Wellington, in particular, is accused of deliberate distortion, not only in his Despatch to the War Office, which may be seen as ambiguous, but also, more evidently, in his much fuller *Memorandum* of 1842.[1] It is certainly true that in Wellington's account of the battle little credit is given to the Prussians, nor yet to the German regiments in his own army, and the years after 1815 would be marked by some acrimonious exchanges between the Duke and members of the Prussian General Staff, who were indignant at the presumed slight which they had suffered at British hands. For Peter Hofschröer, indeed, Waterloo was first and foremost 'a German victory', a battle in which the troops of the King's German Legion (KGL) played a crucial role and where victory was gained only after the timely arrival of Blücher's Prussians out of the mist and smoke of battle. He backs this claim with statistics and with reference to cultural rather than political affiliations:

> In the theatre of the Low Countries, where most of the fighting of this campaign took place, the overwhelming majority of the Allied troops engaged spoke German as their native language. Of the 209,000 Allied soldiers in this theatre, 30,000 were English-speakers, 24,000 were Netherlanders, some of them Dutch- and some French-speaking; the remaining 155,000 were Germans.[2]

As he rightly acknowledges, Britain's Continental allies played a critical role, not only at Waterloo itself, but also in the wider campaign—in the earlier conflict at Ligny and in the pursuit of the French back to Paris. And it was not only Germans who were heavily involved. So were Dutch and Belgian troops, discrete units under their own commanders, who fought fiercely in their shared cause to defeat Napoleon and restore the balance of power that had been established at Vienna the previous year. They, too, played a significant part on the day. What is perhaps most surprising, given the extent of the celebration and self-congratulation emanating from London, is that Waterloo would play such a modest part in their own national narratives.

Figure 16. Copley,
William Prince of Orange

Figure 17. Blücher Memorial, Rostock

The figures for the men serving in the First and Second Corps and in the units of the Reserve at Waterloo are eloquent testimony to the international composition of Wellington's army and to the significance of the combined German contribution. By comparison, the contribution of British and Irish units, if this is seen from a purely numerical standpoint, was quite modest: some 20,000 infantry and fewer than 6,000 cavalry from a grand total of 68,900 and 14,500 respectively. The Dutch-Belgian divisions (which had 18,800 infantry and 3,400 cavalry) also made a substantial contribution to the Allied cause; and the Nassau battalions, which fought as part of the Dutch-Belgian army, provided a further 7,300 infantry. German soldiers at Waterloo fought in the colours of their different states and rulers: some in the Hanoverian Brigades, others in the Brunswick Corps, and others again in the KGL of the British army. In all the Hanoverians provided nearly 13,800 infantrymen to the army and the Brunswickers some 5,400, as well as significant contributions of cavalry and artillery.[3] These are not insignificant numbers, and their contribution was matched by units of the KGL, which, though it faced disbandment at the very moment when the Waterloo campaign was launched, responded immediately to the call to arms. In all, the KGL supplied eight battalions of infantry and four of cavalry for the Allied army as well as three batteries of artillery.[4] They played a critical role in the fighting, and might have expected to play a central part in the celebrations and commemorations that followed.

Prussian Memory: Waterloo and Leipzig

The totality of the Allied victory and the importance of the role played by Blücher in that victory appear to be ready-made for Prussia to appropriate the battle for propaganda purposes, not least at a moment, like 1815, when the first green shoots of German nationalism were sprouting so vigorously. It might seem to present the perfect opportunity to celebrate German manliness and military prowess, especially since the battle had led to Napoleon's final removal from the European arena and provided revenge for the painful humiliation that Prussia had suffered at Jena. Yet this did not happen. There was a logical connection between the two battles, as Prussia's most famous military theorist, Clausewitz, was quick to point out in his magisterial study *On War*. Jena had led to a rapid reappraisal of the condition of the Prussian army, the adoption of universal conscription, and the series of military reforms instituted by Hardenberg and Stein which lay at the heart of the effectiveness of the Prussian army, both at Waterloo and in the last years of the war. The reforms were widely praised, of course, and Clausewitz was rightly acclaimed as one of the greatest military thinkers of modern times. Clausewitz, it should be noted, devoted another study to Waterloo; indeed, he wrote the two works simultaneously, and his reflections on the Waterloo campaign were often incorporated in the more theoretical conclusions he outlined in *On War*.[5] Yet Waterloo, the battle, does not figure prominently in Prussian or German military memory. If in Britain it was fashioned into an iconic battle, a moment in the forging of British character and identity, in Prussia and more broadly across Germany it was accorded a relatively minor role. The German nation, even to its most ardent ideologues, was not born in 1815 in the mud of Belgium, and the attentions of German nationalists after 1815 quickly turned elsewhere.

It seems unlikely, indeed, that German nationalism played a significant role in any phase of the Napoleonic Wars, whatever nineteenth-century Romantics may have believed. Soldiers fought in these wars for their states and rulers, as Prussians or Hessians or Saxons, and these dynastic rulers had every interest in ensuring that war memories were forged around states, not cultural dreams. Though nationalism

Figure 18. John Everett Millais, *The Black Brunswicker*, 1860

unquestionably developed out of the so-called War of Liberation, a nationalism that evolved into liberalism and democracy but which was also deeply intertwined with ethnocentrism, there is little evidence to suggest that German nationalism was instrumental in motivating the troops, or that ridding themselves of the French brought the different armies any closer together as Germans.[6] Indeed, the idea that soldiers in these wars fought to defend the cause of Germany is part of a nineteenth-century narrative of the conflict which Prussia, in particular, sought to encourage as the cult of heroism became first nationalized, then increasingly democratized. As the German historian Karen Hagemann has recently expressed it, in the years after 1813 the cult of heroes was given a central role in 'cultural nation-building in Prussia and, more generally, throughout Germany'.[7] But what is interesting here is less the substance of the myth than its focus, the battle with which Prussia-Germany came to identify in the decades that followed. For if there was no place of honour for Waterloo in the Prussian-German national myth, there was for the Battle of the Nations fought in Leipzig two years earlier. Indeed, one of the earliest organizations set up to promote German cultural nationalism, the *Burschenschaft* movement of the immediate post-war years, wallowed in the memory of Leipzig even as they ignored Waterloo. At the festival they held in 1817 in Wartburg they selected two moments of Germany's past to celebrate, linking the victory at Leipzig to the tercentenary of the Reformation—in the historian James Sheehan's words, 'the freedom of the nation from foreign domination and the freedom of thought from doctrinaire restraints'.[8]

In nineteenth-century Germany Leipzig would be built into the totemic battle of modern times, inspiring a century of commemoration and leading to the construction of the huge and rather disturbing monument, the *Völkerschlachtdenkmal*, in the outskirts of Leipzig for the battle's centenary in 1913.[9] There was good reason for this choice, since it was at Leipzig that Napoleon's domination of Germany had been challenged, and then destroyed.[10] The battle was first claimed for the cause of German nationalism by the nationalist writer and propagandist Ernst Moritz Arndt, and it continued to figure in nation-alist speeches and writings throughout the following century. For Arndt it was a way of identifying the battle with a collective war effort against Napoleon, the spilling of German blood to drive a foreign usurper from German lands. The idea quickly caught the public mood, perhaps, as has recently been suggested, because this memory of the Battle of the Nations was one which 'constituted a critical, popular and sometimes *völkisch* alternative to the dynastically-oriented national memory preferred by the Hohenzollerns'.[11] But in the short term it received only muted expression because of the prevalence of state censorship in the years up to 1848, and it was not until the fiftieth anniversary in 1863 that commemoration began to have a bold, national dimension. In that year the city fathers of Leipzig sponsored a celebration of the battle that brought together 'hundreds of veterans from across Germany' and was attended by delegates from over two hundred towns and cities.[12]

Two years later, in 1865, no comparable event was staged to cele-brate the fiftieth anniversary of Waterloo, which was passed over in almost total silence. Indeed, the only monument to the Prussians who fell at Waterloo is the relatively modest memorial on the battlefield itself, the work of the sculptor Karl Friedrich Schinkel and dating from 1819. But by 1865 Prussian attentions were fixed on other struggles, and in particular the upcoming war with Austria that would mark a critical moment in the unification of the German people in a single state. And it is of course true that Waterloo was not fought on German soil, so that the impact on the civilian population was far less cruelly felt. The memory of 1815 played little part in the national *prise de conscience*, nor in the Prussian state's propaganda campaigns of the 1860s. Public attention was focused firmly elsewhere, and it was France's present-day emperor, Napoleon III, whose expansionist ambitions were arous-ing German fears.

As for the centenary in 1915, again circumstances hardly favoured it, with Germany in the throes of the Great War against both England and France and thoughts of alliance and friendship far from the public mind. The mood was entirely different from that of 1913, when noisy and enthusiastic celebrations had been held to mark the inauguration of the memorial in Leipzig. Where there were mentions of the centenary in the press, they could be slighting and resentful representations, often caricatures, of British accounts of the battle. The *Preussische Zeitung* in June 1915 is a good example of journalism that sought to link the centenary of Waterloo to the current situation across Europe. In an article entitled 'Waterloo and the "Entente"', they printed a column from the Greifswald professor Heinrich Spiess in which he railed at the extreme nationalism of the British and the propagandist use that they made of Waterloo in a world in which her former enemy, France, had been transformed into an ally, and in which historical memory had to be adjusted to accord with the needs of the present war. In the process no mention can be made of Prussia's role:

> Who has not, during historical discussions in England, had a battle of words about Waterloo and about Blücher's part in the battle? It is well known that the English systematically deny the importance of the Prussian intervention, which is naturally a consequence of their extremely nationalistic teaching of history.[13]

He notes, too, that the noisy clamour for a nationalistic public celebration of Waterloo which had been heard in parliament before the outbreak of war had given way to diplomatic silence.

It is not just that the battle played a relatively minor role in German historiography and national mythology. Outside of the occasional press article public acknowledgement of the German role at Waterloo was also fairly muted, and such commemoration as there was took place at local level. The Prussian general, Gebhard Leberecht von Blücher, was duly hailed as a war hero, though not exclusively, or principally, because of the part he played at Waterloo. His is a remarkable story. He had served in the French Revolutionary Wars in his younger days, had commanded the Prussian rearguard at Jena, and had then served out his remaining years until his retirement in the Prussian war ministry in Berlin. But when war resumed against Napoleon in 1813, Blücher returned to active service at the advanced age of 71. He fought in the battles of Lützen and Bautzen in May 1813, went on to defeat Marshal Macdonald at Wahlstatt, then led the Prussians against Napoleon at Leipzig in October, before pursuing the French back to Paris. For his part in the victory at Leipzig he was made a field marshal, and he accepted the title of Prince of Wahlstatt before retiring once more to his country estates. Then, when Napoleon escaped from Elba, Blücher came out of retirement for a second time to lead the Prussian army in Belgium. His boldness and commitment to attack won both the admiration of his king and the affection of ordinary Prussians, and his successes so late in life made him a natural war hero for Prussia and later for Germany as a whole. He was made an honorary citizen of Berlin and Hamburg, and after his death in 1819 memorials were erected to him in three German cities, Berlin, Kaub, and Breslau (today Wrocław), as well as in the city of his birth, Rostock in Mecklenburg. The statue in Rostock, which was inaugurated in 1819 just outside the main university buildings, attracted particular interest from, among others, Goethe, who wrote a series of twenty-four letters on the subject of Blücher's memorial.[14] The field marshal also has his place in the royal pantheon, or *Walhalla*, that was erected on the instructions of Ludwig I of Bavaria in the countryside near Regensburg, and which commemorates, along with other great Germans, the principal battles and military commanders of the Wars of Liberation.[15]

Waterloo itself is more sparingly commemorated, at least at national level, since it was not seen as a 'great battle' for either Prussia or Germany. Despite the large numbers of German soldiers who were involved in the battle and the tragically high losses they incurred, it was regarded as something of a footnote to the Napoleonic Wars, whose main action had taken place elsewhere. But that does not mean that it was forgotten entirely, and in some states and some cities, as in Britain, the battle is commemorated in the names of streets and squares, either as 'Waterloo' or in the name that the Prussians gave the battle after the name of the inn where Blücher supposedly met with Wellington on the previous evening, 'La Belle Alliance'. Much was left to local initiative, and, as in Britain, depended on extraneous factors like the growth of new neighbourhoods and the spread of suburban development in the years after 1815. The pattern is thus rather chequered. Berlin boasted a Belle-Alliance-Platz and a Belle-Alliance-Strasse throughout the nineteenth century, though both disappeared from the map in 1947 in the flurry of post-war rebranding; close by there is a Waterlooufer, as well as streets named after Blücher and Gneisenau. The choice of 'Belle-Alliance-Platz' for one of three geometrically shaped squares in new neighbourhoods of the city is perhaps most significant, as it shows that in this instance Waterloo was firmly integrated into the collective memory of the Napoleonic Wars: the other two squares were named Leipziger-Platz and Pariser-Platz, the second of these commemorating Prussian troops' entry into Paris in 1814 and 1815.[16] There is a Belle-Alliance-Strasse, too, in Hamburg, whose extension later in the century took the name of Waterloostrasse in an apparent nod in the direction of inclusivity.[17]

But Waterloo does not figure strongly in German public memory, and in the twentieth century, with Germany and Britain fighting each other in two world wars, there was little political will to resurrect a battle that recalled an alliance with London. After 1945 the new West German government, eager to erase any trace of Germany's militaristic past, had further reason to avoid acts of public commemoration. The former enemies of 1815, Prussia and France, had been reborn as allies at the heart of the new project for a European Union, and Germany's leaders had no desire to risk offending France by reviving memories of her past defeats. As a result, the 150th anniversary of Waterloo in 1965 passed virtually unnoticed in Germany. There were no parades, no official celebrations.[18] Indeed, when the Queen went on a state visit to Germany in that very year, the Federal government intervened to discourage any Waterloo celebrations, among them a proposal that she should lay a wreath at the foot of the Waterloo column in Hanover to honour the men of the KGL. Even such a simple ceremony was heavy with a symbolism that was seen as unnecessarily inflammatory in the diplomatic context of the 1960s. Waterloo, in Jasper Heinzen's crisp summation, 'laid bare political tensions and historical loyalties that shaped how citizens responded to the call for remembrance in 1965'.[19] Overall, it seemed, the battle was better forgotten.

Karl Grüne, it is true, made a film about the battle in 1928, though his choice of subject must be seen more in the context of German interest in Napoleon than as homage to the battle itself or to Wellington. It is surely significant that when Hagen Schulze and Étienne François drew up their list of key *lieux de mémoire* for modern-day Germany (*Deutsche Erinnerungsorte*), there was no place for Waterloo. The Napoleonic years are represented, as is Prussia's old enemy, France. There is an article on Napoleon himself; one on Versailles (and not exclusively in the context of the peace of 1919); even an article on Napoleon's personal nemesis, Madame de Staël, though principally as the author of *De l'Allemagne*. And there is, of course, an entry for the Battle of the Nations at Leipzig, *die Völkerschlacht*, which its author, Kirstin Schäfer, identifies as being the largest battle in European history to that point.[20] It is less the battle that people remember than the myth, the huge skein of nationalist ideology that has been woven around it. But the identification of Leipzig as a site of national memory only emphasizes the contrast between the Battle of the Nations, the battle that supposedly moulded the new Germany, and Waterloo, which unquestionably spelt the end of Napoleon's imperial ambitions.

Waterloo in Other German States

The German state which gave most prominence to the memory of Waterloo was, unsurprisingly, Hanover, George III's German electorate and the provider of so many men for the KGL. Hanover would retain its personal link with the British crown until 1837 (when the Salic law made it impossible for Queen Victoria to succeed to the throne), and the memory of Waterloo held greater personal and political significance for its rulers than was the case in other regions of Germany. It was this political interest and the desire of the King to associate Hanover with the Allied victory that proved crucial in the memorialization that followed. The former parade ground in the capital was renamed the Waterlooplatz, and on it was built a high, free-standing column, the *Waterloo Säule*, as a memorial to the battle against Napoleon. It is unashamedly a victory column, bedecked with the statue of a winged Victory and dedicated not to those who had died but to the 'victors of the battle'. The monarchy had reason to celebrate Napoleon's defeat: the former electorate of Hanover had been dissolved in 1803 and invaded by the French; and now, following the battle, it had re-emerged as a fully fledged kingdom. Like all such monuments it took some time to build: though planning began as early as 1816, the financing and construction took until 1832, when the column was duly inaugurated on the anniversary of the battle, 18 June.

Eighty miles to the west, in Osnabrück, stands another major monument—the *Waterloo Tor*, today the *Heger Tor*—commemorating the part played in the battle by the KGL. Again there is a clear political motive for the decision to build a triumphal arch in the city. Osnabrück had been much fought over during the Napoleonic Wars, with control of the previously independent city state passing in turn to the Elector of Hanover in 1803, the King of Prussia in 1806, and the King of Westphalia from 1807 till 1810, before being integrated into the French Empire. In 1815 it finally achieved new status as part the new Kingdom of Hanover, which was eager to celebrate the role of its troops in the recent fighting and to hail the city's new link to the British monarchy. The Waterloo Gate was a fitting and very public statement of the city's political loyalties as well as a tribute to the role of its fighting men.

Not all Germans viewed the political demise of Napoleon with undiluted pleasure, for there was a strong strand of admiration, and of political support, in those German provinces that had come most strongly under French sway, most notably in the four departments of the left bank of the Rhine and the territory of the Confederation of the Rhine. Here Napoleon continued to have his supporters, and something of a cult of the Emperor would develop in the nineteenth century, encouraged by France and following fairly closely on events in Paris. Its high points would coincide with the Return of the Ashes in 1840 and the Second Empire in the 1850s, and, as in France, it would find some of its staunchest support among the former officers and men of the Napoleonic legions. German Romantic writers, most notably Heinrich Heine, gave their backing to the cause. But Napoleonic sympathies were about more than simple nostalgia. Some of the bourgeois elite, those men who had been promoted under the Empire and enjoyed the trust of the imperial authorities, felt a bond of loyalty to the French and regretted their departure. Trading interests rallied, too, especially in those cities in the Rhineland which had gained commercial advantage from imperial protection: Cologne, which had benefited from the modernization of its port and the regulation of traffic on the Rhine; Mainz, which had seen considerable expansion under the Empire; or Düsseldorf, where Napoleon had ordered the demolition of the old fortifications and opened up the city to parks and walkways. Nor did everyone in Germany have an interest in seeing their old princes and electors return. There were Germans for whom Waterloo spelt the end of a rare period of progress and prosperity, and they felt little reason to join in the national mood of celebration after 1815.[21]

Holland and the House of Orange

It is striking, indeed, as we survey the capitals of those European states whose troops had participated in the battle, how far commemoration is linked to the political interest of the ruling dynasties. In the Netherlands, in particular, commemoration of Waterloo was from the beginning focused on dynastic issues, and on the House of Orange rather than on the Dutch people. The Orangists were well placed to exploit popular emotion and to identify their cause with Dutch national pride after the political disruption of the French period that had gone before. During the Revolution Holland had been invaded by

France and recreated as the Batavian Republic, one of a number of satellite states established with a constitution that closely mirrored the French constitution of the Year III. Then, between 1806 and 1813, the country had been officially ruled by the French, first as the Kingdom of Holland under King Louis, one of the Emperor's brothers, and later—once Louis had shown too much independence for Napoleon's taste—directly annexed as *départements* on the French model.[22] Though the period was generally peaceful, and Louis's rule set out to appease Dutch feeling, that does not mean that French administration, justice, policing, and conscription were accepted without demurral. As the Dutch historian Johan Joor shows, local groups did offer resistance to the invader, and the French period was marked by local disturbances, demonstrations, and occasional insurrections across Holland.[23] There was cultural resistance, too, as poets, writers, and literary societies produced patriotic works that praised the Dutch nation and the presumed qualities of the Dutch people. The result, as the literary scholar Lotte Jensen remarks, is 'an interesting paradox': 'just when the existence of the Dutch nation was seriously threatened it became omnipresent in poetry, theatre plays and novels'.[24] Public opinion in Holland was well prepared to celebrate Napoleon's downfall, first at Leipzig and then at Waterloo.

The primary importance that was attached to the battle lay in the fact that it confirmed not only the defeat of Napoleon but also the political solution that had been agreed the previous year in Paris, which authorized the incorporation of Belgium into the Kingdom of the Netherlands and the achievement of what had been one of the long-term ambitions of the House of Orange. Belgium's diplomatic position had been weakened by the invasion of the Spanish Netherlands and the occupation of Brussels in 1814, and the terms of the peace settlement reflected this. At the same time the treaty created a stronger monarchy than the Dutch had previously had and a bicameral system of government in which some 60,000 Belgians could vote alongside around 80,000 Dutchmen. This represented a considerable political coup for the Dutch, though it also spread resentment among the French-speaking Belgians. The Dutch therefore saw Waterloo differently from the other Allies. For them it was the battle which confirmed the 1814 settlement that had bestowed the throne on the Orangist claimant, William Frederick I of Orange-Nassau. In their memory of the Napoleonic Wars they, too, regarded 1814 as the critical year which had ended the period of foreign occupation. Leipzig rather than Waterloo was the determining moment in the war, but that did not mean that Waterloo should be forgotten.[25]

William went to visit the battlefield on 28 July, just forty days after the carnage of the battle, where he expressed the wish that the victory should be commemorated with due dignity. The King seems to have favoured a column of some kind, to be placed—and here historical opinion varies—either at the farm of La Belle Alliance, the spot where Wellington and Blücher met after the battle, or on the battlefield itself marking the spot where, at the age of 22, the young Prince William, the heir to the Dutch throne and the commander of the First Corps of the army of the Netherlands, had been wounded in the fighting. Stories about the Prince's heroism were already legion, and the King was keen to capitalize on them: how he had been wounded in the shoulder, had fainted in the arms of one of his officers, and had thrown one of his decorations among his troops, declaring that they all deserved to wear it. He was, in other words, the sort of a man who merited the status of a national hero, a worthy scion of the royal family who identified with his soldiers on the battlefield as the House of Orange identified with the subjects of its kingdom. Historians have tended to dismiss these claims to heroism. William, it is agreed, was slightly wounded in the battle and had to spend a week in hospital to recover; but his part in the victory should not be exaggerated. Wilhelm Aerts describes him as a bold young horseman, but one who 'had no other qualities than his bravura and whose only role at Waterloo was to serve as a living standard for his men'. But for the House of Orange, anxious to ingratiate itself to the people of Holland and Belgium, his part in the battle presented a golden opportunity to gain popularity. So, in recognition of his bravery William was given the palace of Soestdijk as his official residence, near to which was erected a monument to the victory, known as the Waterloo Needle (*de Naald*). In the same vein his father pressed for the country's memorial on the battlefield to be placed at the very spot where William had received his wound.[26] Though Waterloo would find its name on public streets and squares in various Dutch towns—the best-known is Waterlooplein in the heart of Amsterdam, a square that was created in 1882 on land retrieved from a former canal system and named in honour of the battle—it is more as a victory for the House of Orange that it is remembered than for the sacrifice that was made by the soldiers of Holland and Belgium or for the peace it brought to Europe.

So in art it is possible to see the reflection of a new national awareness, but nothing that could be called a widespread popular celebration of the Dutch victory. The years around 1815 were important ones in Dutch painting, not least because they saw the inauguration of the Rijksmuseum, but what is striking is how little emphasis there is in its collections on the recent war; indeed, there is relatively little that belongs to the genre of war painting, or to history painting more generally. There had been a glut of history painting during the French period, both for and against Napoleon's brother, Louis Bonaparte, after he had been given the Dutch throne. In contrast, the years following Waterloo were coloured by the return of the royal family of Orange, and in particular by King William I, who rather fancied himself as a patron of the arts and was concerned to guide artistic taste. Political paintings gave place to more traditional Dutch landscapes with cows and grasslands and to staged conversation pieces, genre tableaux, and scenes from Dutch history. Dutch artists came increasingly to hunt for their own national traditions and identity, and this took the form of a renewed interest in Holland's Golden Age, in traditional Dutch genres like landscapes and domestic interiors. 'Domesticity was an expression of the Dutch people's upstanding and virtuous character', notes one specialist, 'while the cow was of course a symbol of Dutch prosperity.'[27]

The year 1814 saw the growth of Dutch pockets of resistance to all forms of occupation and the emergence of the figures of patriotic heroes, and this found a reflection in artistic themes. At Waterloo the Dutch then played an active military role which Orangist artists, stimulated by royal favour and patronage, sought to commemorate. As a result, at the Brussels Salon in 1815 it was noted that 'there was talk of nothing except pictures of the Battle of Waterloo', whether by portrait painters, painters of the landscape, or even in watercolours.[28] Two memorable canvases were on display that presented aspects of the battle, both by the Dutch artist Jan Willem Pienemann: the life-size painting *The Battle of Waterloo* and an earlier scene of *The Prince of Orange near Quatre Bras*. In both, the Orange interest, shown through the gallantry of Prince William on the battlefield, was given due emphasis.[29] Today *The Battle of Waterloo* dominates one of the rooms in the Rijksmuseum, where it has the honour of being the largest canvas in the gallery. It depicts what to Dutch eyes was the turning point of the battle, the moment when Wellington hears that Prussian help is on its way. It is not actually a depiction of the battle itself, but rather a group portrait centred around the Duke of Wellington on horseback, with the wounded Prince of Orange lying on a stretcher off to the left. The Dutch saw him as the hero of the day, and the Prince is said to have been so proud of his part in the battle that he continued to sleep on an iron camp bed for many years. He was given the painting as a present from his father, King William I.[30]

Waterloo, it might seem, was more about the House of Orange than about the Dutch people. Perhaps for that reason, the construction of the memorial to the battle aroused little enthusiasm in the population at large, in spite of the scale and ambition of the enterprise. It is often forgotten that the great mound with the lion of Waterloo, the iconic landmark on the present-day battlefield, is a Dutch monument. Once the spot where William had made his sacrifice had been identified, the construction of the Butte began. Its conception and design were Dutch; the lion was sculpted by the Dutch artist Jean-Francois Van Geel to represent the martial spirit of the Dutch people. The monument took two years to build, from 1824 to 1826, and it was so placed that it dominated the flat landscape that surrounded it; 'this point', wrote the architect Jean-Baptiste Vifquain, the creator of one of a number of earlier plans for the monument, 'from where one looks out across the countryside seems to have been made expressly to bear such a weighty memory'.[31] Its dimensions are impressive, covering some 2 hectares and involving the removal of 300,000 cubic metres of soil from the battlefield to construct it. When it was completed, it required 226 steps to take visitors to the top to inspect it.[32] And yet it inspired little wonder or awe, especially among the local population. By the time when the statue of the lion was formally placed on the mound in October 1826, public apathy was such that the government did not arrange any official ceremony of inauguration and did not bring together representatives of the former Allies whose armies had conquered Napoleon and had ended his imperial dreams. Rather, the mound was topped off amidst general indifference; two medals were struck to celebrate the moment, but that was the extent of its public recognition. Even the local newspapers offered little comment. The appearance of the statue on its plinth looking down across the battle-field at Seraing was noted in a few laconic lines by those local papers across Belgium that bothered to report it. But beyond that there was a deafening silence.[33]

This silence was a reflection of what was seen by many as a partisan political gesture by the Dutch, a crude propagandist exercise by the Orange interest which had little to do with them and which did nothing to honour those who had served and died in the battle. Indeed, in Holland itself there was little knowledge of the extent of the Dutch engagement at Waterloo, and as the years passed no effort was made to correct the impression that this had been one man's war, a famous act of courage by the heir to the throne. The silence that was allowed to envelop the contribution of Dutch troops in the battle, the lack of any form of memorial or public testimony to their sacrifice, seemed almost to amount to open contempt, and it was an insult which many officers deeply resented. They would have to wait until

1865 and the celebration of the fiftieth anniversary of the battle before the survivors among them received some form of belated acknowledgement by the award of a silver *Croix de guerre*.[34]

Belgium and the Waterloo Battlefield

With the passage of time, of course, this would change as the battlefield was turned into a European *lieu de mémoire* and came to assume greater meaning for the population, especially for the Belgians on whose territory it stood. The Belgians, after all, had had no reason to feel grateful for the outcome of the battle or to celebrate their annexation by the House of Orange. After the creation of an independent Belgian state in 1830, anti-Dutch feeling was at height, and the lion became a bitterly disputed symbol, a specifically Dutch memorial to a victory that had led, as Belgians saw it, to the subjugation of their nation. Some called for it to be destroyed. The deputy Alexandre Gendebien, a member of the provisional government that was established after the 1830 Revolution in Belgium, favoured an alliance with France, not Holland, and did not disguise his contempt for Van Geel's monument. In the Chamber in December 1832 he expressed the feelings shared by many young Belgian nationalists when he described the lion as an 'emblem of violence and despotism...which perpetuates the passing triumph of brutal force over civilization'; and he talked of 'the fierce Dutch lion which threatened to devour us'.[35] Indeed, later demands for the destruction of the lion would be used as part of the campaign to assert a specific Walloon identity within a multilingual Belgium. The same lion that had started life as a memorial to the battle had been transformed into a symbol of Flemish domination and would later become the personification of German hatred of France. From 1928 Waterloo would become the site of an annual pilgrimage for French-speaking Belgians who were concerned less with preserving the memory of the past than with defining their own political future.[36]

Over time, too, the meaning of Waterloo for Belgian visitors would be transformed. Any lingering resentment of Waterloo that derived from its identification with the forced merger of 1815 faded, while the mound and its monument came to be more closely identified with Napoleon and the cult of a heroic French defeat. The tourist guide published in Brussels in 1907 by Fierens-Gevaert illustrates this attitude clearly when he explains the feelings that will overcome the visitor on climbing the stone staircase to the summit and standing atop the Butte:

> It of course commemorates the victory of Wellington and Blücher. But anyone who has climbed these steps feels, little by little, overwhelmed with respect for the genius of Napoleon, feels something of the sublimated admiration that his soldiers felt for him . . . and it is neither pity nor a childish regret for a battle lost that overcomes us at the top of this burial mound saturated in blood, but the serenity and religious calm that comes from a destiny fulfilled.[37]

Napoleon, as he would be for generations of Frenchmen, had become the principal focus of commemoration, a commemoration tinged with regret for the imperial glory of the past.

The same feeling was uppermost in the minds of those who took part in 1915 in what was necessarily a muted centenary commemoration at Waterloo, at a moment when the Great War was being fought all around them and when German troops were once more occupying Belgian soil. It had been anticipated that the centenary would be marked with a significant act of commemoration; plans had begun to be drawn up, indeed, in 1913, before hostilities had begun. These plans were quickly abandoned as the German authorities expressly forbade any ceremonies on the battlefield that might be used to revive Napoleon's memory. But, as articles in French newspapers noted, local people did celebrate, quietly, and pay their own private homage to the dead. The battlefield was empty on the morning of 18 June, windblown and echoing behind enemy lines. Individual Belgians, however, had not forgotten the victims, nor the traces of imperial glory that lay buried there, and though Frenchmen could not travel to Waterloo their thoughts were with their heroes. One French newspaper, *La Petite*

République, noted how the enemies of the former war now represented the 'coalition of civilization' and had become 'allies against Barbarism'; 'Frenchmen and Englishmen,' it reported, 'without a trace of hatred, met again yesterday on the tombs of their dead as their pilgrimages merged one with another.'[38] Four years later, in 1919, the same paper told its readers how a Belgian patriot, who lived in the farm at Le Caillou where Napoleon had established his headquarters, had defied the German order by walking the battlefield during the night and placing flowers and wreaths on the memorials to the British, French, and Belgian dead. Waterloo awoke, the report concluded, to find 'the colours of France and Belgium mingled on the stones on which is engraved the eternal glory of the Empire'.[39] It was a patriotic image, an image of Franco-Belgian friendship made more emotive by the events of the recent war; an image, moreover, that had not yet become harnessed to the political cause of Walloon nationalism.

By the twentieth century the battlefield had been turned into a memorial site for all the combatant nations, a compact landscape of cornfields to the south of Brussels that was easily accessible from the city and which bristled with graves and commemorative stones. In an age that popularized battlefield tourism Waterloo became a major heritage site, its graves and monuments visited by millions of tourists as well as by old soldiers who came to pay homage to their forebears in arms. In the early years the memorials had been erected only by the Allied side: exclusively by the British until 1818 when a Hanoverian memorial was added; there then followed monuments to the Prussians (1819) and the Dutch (1826). Until 1890 the English memorials were all erected to commemorate individual officers who had died in the battle, acts of piety by their families rather than official commemorations by the state. The two most famous were those to Lord Uxbridge and to Alexander Gordon, the brother of the Earl of Aberdeen, and others would follow. In contrast, the first collective British memorial dates only from 1890, and the French monument, as we have seen, was not built until 1904. The Hanoverian, Prussian, and Belgian monuments, on the other hand, were all collective memorials to their national dead.[40]

The challenge today, on the bicentenary of the battle, is to produce a fitting form of memorialization for the Europe of the twenty-first century, a Europe committed to peace and reconciliation. The plans for a new museum and visitor centre on the edge of the battlefield deliberately eschew the triumphalism of the past, and though Napoleon remains the most prominent single figure in the historical presentation, the displays deliberately avoid playing to the Great Man theory of history or wallowing in the glory of war. There is a refreshing internationalism in the manner in which they are structured, as visitors from all the combatant nations are able to follow the events of 18 June 1815 from their own national perspective, or from none. A wall of remembrance records the names and numbers of all the regiments that were present on the battlefield. There is a new emphasis on the battle as it was experienced and endured by the soldiers who took part in it, a willingness to see it from below as well as through the eyes of the various commanders. And due care is taken to see Waterloo as the prelude to peace and to the establishment of a balance of power that would help avoid another major European war until the Crimea in the 1850s.

The World beyond Europe

It was not only among the participating nations that Waterloo etched its presence on the public. For outsiders its significance was clear: it was the battle that finally destroyed the ambitions of the most feared aggressor of his day. That fear was not wholly restricted to Europe, nor yet to those of a deeply conservative political disposition. Among the new generation of freedom-fighters in South America, for instance, men consumed by their struggle against imperial Spain, the removal of Napoleon from the political stage was greeted with undisguised relief. Napoleon was commonly seen in the Americas not as a son of revolutionary France, bringing the gifts of liberty and fraternity across the Atlantic, but rather as an imperialist usurper, the man who had tried, and failed, to restore slavery to Haiti. It is interesting to note the degree of spleen which the very mention of Napoleon could conjure up in Simón Bolívar, who saw him as a conqueror and expansionist, a man who was dangerous precisely because there were no limits to his ambition. Bolívar knew Napoleonic Paris at first hand; in 1804 he had lived there, where he had visited its salons and had been introduced to its learned society by Alexander Humboldt. He had also gained from his time in Paris a sense of the direction of French policy, and was forewarned about the policies he might expect of Napoleon. In particular, he believed that the example of ruthless expansionism which the Emperor had set in Europe could only have dangerous consequences for his own country, and in a famous letter from Jamaica on 22 August 1815 he expressed himself of the view that

> The fate of the world was decided at Waterloo. Europe has been salvaged by this immortal battle whose consequences will prove to be more important than those of any other event in the annals of the universe.

Lest this judgement might seem a little exaggerated, Bolívar went on to explain the nature of the threat which Napoleon had represented for his country and for others in the Americas:

> His spirit of conquest is insatiable. He has scythed through the flower of European youth in the pursuit of his ambitious projects. Similar designs will lead him to the New World, where he will no doubt profit from the schisms that divide America in order to build himself a throne in this vast empire, when even the small amount of blood that remains in our veins will again be made to flow. As if America was not already sufficiently miserable, sufficiently destroyed by the war of extermination that is waged against her by Spain![41]

For at least some in the Americas what Napoleon appeared to promise was danger and the threat of endless aggrandizement; his final defeat at Waterloo came as a source of relief.

The newly independent United States presented a rather different profile, a country which had freed itself from British colonial control but which still had not rid itself of the sense that Britain was its principal rival and a continued source of threat. France, after all, was no longer directly present on the North American land mass following the loss of Canada in the Seven Years War and Napoleon's sale of Louisiana in 1803. But Britain remained a powerful maritime presence, and the War of 1812 was a recent reminder of the likelihood of future Anglo-American conflicts. This helps to explain the huge interest that Napoleon still aroused in American opinion in the nineteenth century—interest combined in many cases with unabashed enthusiasm. Napoleon divided American opinion. If more conservative writers, like Hyde de Neuville, continued to see him as a dangerous radical, he had his defenders, too, like Henry Banks from Virginia, for whom he would always be 'Europae pacificator et humani generis benefactor'.[42] Napoleon was not a distant or marginal figure to the American public; and when in the days after Waterloo the rumour spread that the former Emperor would like to settle in Virginia, there was even talk of sending a flotilla of American ships to St Helena to bring him back in triumph to New Orleans. Many Americans felt touched by the Emperor's exile on St Helena, and they showed no hostility when members of his family, most notably Joseph and the two sons of Lucien, sought refuge in the United States after 1815. Napoleon's relatives did not come alone. The French exile community in North America also included a significant number of former Napoleonic generals and marshals, among them Grouchy and Vandamme, men whose military record against Britain and consistent opposition to monarchy gave them special status in the American republic. Several, indeed, were received as guests of honour in 1816 at the national celebrations on 4 July in Baltimore, where a toast was very pointedly drunk in which Louis XVIII was mocked by the revellers as a 'foolish tyrant', to the extreme irritation of the Bourbons and their supporters.[43] The United States was one of the few countries outside France where the Napoleonic flame continued flickering brightly in the months following Waterloo, and where his defeat was a source of sorrow rather than of public rejoicing.

9

Postscript

B ritain turned to Waterloo after 1815 as a symbol of fortitude and stoical resistance in the face of attack, and it was not long before the word had entered the English language to encapsulate the idea of total victory, of irretrievable defeat. A person who overreached himself, only to be undone by his own ambition, was said to have 'met his Waterloo'. The expression has stood the test of time, and its use today is not restricted to high politics or the affairs of nations: it describes individual as well as collective setbacks, and it is as much a commonplace in conversation between neighbours as it is a mainstay of the sports pages of our newspapers. In a lecture given in Brooklyn in 1859 the American anti-slavery campaigner Wendell Phillips commented that 'every man meets his Waterloo at last'.[1] Better known to English audiences was the remark attributed to Sherlock Holmes by Arthur Conan Doyle and steeped in the military history of the period: 'We have not met our Waterloo, Watson, but this is our Marengo.'[2] The use of Waterloo in this context may seem peculiar to English; in French, the expression 'to meet one's Waterloo' is rendered by the more prosaic 'trouver son maître'. But Waterloo lives on in French, too, though references to the battle in modern-day speech refer almost entirely to personal setbacks. To describe collective disasters, be they in sport or in politics, another Napoleonic battle is the preferred point of reference: the Berezina in 1812, a disaster which could also, like Waterloo, be portrayed as a heroic defeat.[3] For while there is no doubting that the crossing of the Berezina spelt defeat for Napoleon—he lost somewhere between 25,000 and 40,000 men and most of his artillery, and his Old Guard was decimated, reduced to a mere 2,000 men—the outcome could have been worse. He got the rest of his army across the river safely and escaped more lightly than he had any right to expect.[4]

There is no way, either, in which Waterloo can be passed over in silence in French histories of the Napoleonic era: whether glorious or inglorious, it was the battle which ended Napoleon's reign for a second and final time, and which brought down the curtain, too, on France's centuries-old claim to European or world hegemony. And so it was only fitting, in 1964, when Gallimard launched its ambitiously titled series *Trente jours qui ont fait la France* (Thirty Days that Shaped France), 18 June 1815 should have figured among the thirty dates that were selected. Waterloo was the only one of Napoleon's battles to merit inclusion in the original list—there was no place for Jena, or Austerlitz, or Wagram—and it is one of only three days from the Napoleonic era to make the cut, the others being 9 November 1799 (the date of the coup of 18 Brumaire that brought the Consulate into being) and 2 December 1804 (the date of the Imperial Coronation). It was included not for its military significance but for the consequences for France that flowed from it, from the vengeance of the returning Bourbons to the costs of Allied requisitions and enemy occupation (costs which the book's author, Robert Margerit, estimates at not far short of 1,500 million francs), from the loss of territory and of half a million of its citizens in the East to its decline as a European and world power. Here the defeat at Waterloo would prove to be definitive.[5]

It is over thirty years since Thomas Nipperdey famously opened his history of modern Germany with the words, 'In the beginning was Napoleon'.[6] It was a beginning in the sense that the Empire heralded so much that seemed modern and futuristic: efficient administration, justice available to all, education, and above all the authority of the secular state. It was a beginning, too, in that it stimulated powerful reactions, including the forces of nationalism which Nipperdey believed to be so critical to modern German and European identity. But we should not forget that for many—and not only in France—the Napoleonic era had seemed to hold out promise and hope, and that

that hope finally died at Waterloo. By then, of course, the Empire was no longer the Empire of Napoleon's prime; historians are surely right to see the Hundred Days as a mere codicil to a glorious story. But it still took one final victory, and a huge, tragic level of human sacrifice, to topple him one last time. That is why, for many even in Britain, it is Napoleon, not Blücher or even Wellington, who is the central figure of the battle. His defeat was more significant in European history than their victory. Our use of language only serves to reflect this, for it was the Emperor, not any of the Allied leaders, who 'met his Waterloo' that day, as the battle set the seal on an era that had begun with the first stirrings of the French Revolution at the end of the 1780s. In the end, too, one might suggest, 'was Napoleon'.

NOTES

Chapter 1

1. Philip J. Haythornthwaite, *Invincible Generals: Gustavus Adolphus, Marlborough, Frederick the Great, George Washington, Wellington* (London, 1991).
2. John Keegan, *The Face of Battle: A Study of Agincourt, Waterloo and the Somme* (London, 1976), 117.
3. R. G. Grant, *Battle: A Visual Journey through 5000 Years of Combat* (London, 2005), 210–11.
4. Rory Muir, *Tactics and the Experience of Battle in the Age of Napoleon* (New Haven, 1998), 58.
5. Wellington to William Wellesley-Pole, 19 June 1815, in Antony Brett-James (ed.), *Wellington at War, 1794–1815* (London, 1961), 310.
6. Jacques Garnier, 'Waterloo', in Jean Tulard (ed.), *Dictionnaire Napoléon* (2 vols, Paris, 1999), ii. 961.
7. Wellington to Charles Stewart, 8 May 1815, quoted in Ian Fletcher, *A Desperate Business: Wellington, the British Army and the Waterloo Campaign* (Staplehurst, 2001), 11.
8. Wellington to Dr Hume, 19 June 1815, quoted in Fletcher, *A Desperate Business*. 168.
9. Jeremy Black, *Waterloo: The Battle that Brought Down Napoleon* (London, 2010), 157.
10. David A. Bell, *The First Total War: Napoleon's Europe and the Birth of Warfare as We Know It* (New York, 2007).
11. Jenny Macleod, *Reconsidering Gallipoli* (Manchester, 2004), 15.
12. Joseph Conrad, *Mirror of the Sea*, quoted in John Sugden, *Nelson: The Sword of Albion* (London, 2012), 853.
13. Richard Holmes, *Wellington, the Iron Duke* (London, 1996), 7–8.
14. Mark Wishon, *German Forces and the British Army: Interactions and Perceptions, 1742–1815* (Basingstoke, 2013), 165–6.
15. Peter Hofschröer, *The Waterloo Campaign: The German Victory* (London, 1999).
16. Walter Bruyère-Ostells, *Leipzig, 16–19 octobre 1813* (Paris, 2013), 131–46.
17. Jean-Marc Largeaud, *Napoléon et Waterloo: La Défaite glorieuse de 1815 à nos jours* (Paris, 2006), esp. ch. 6, 'Images et imaginaires de Waterloo', 273–343.

Chapter 2

1. Dominique de Villepin, *Les Cent Jours ou l'esprit de sacrifice* (Paris, 2001), 10.
2. Charles Esdaile, *Napoleon's Wars: An International History, 1803–1815* (London, 2007), 528; Clive Emsley, *The Longman Companion to Napoleonic Europe* (London, 1993), 19–20.
3. Paul Schroeder, *The Transformation of European Politics, 1763–1848* (Oxford, 1994), 495–6.
4. Schroeder, *The Transformation of European Politics*, 501.
5. Catherine Clerc, *La Caricature contre Napoléon* (Paris, 1985), 180.
6. Clerc, *La Caricature contre Napoléon*, 183.
7. Adam Zamoyski, *Rites of Peace: The Fall of Napoleon and the Congress of Vienna* (London, 2007), 201.
8. John Bew, *Castlereagh: A Life* (Oxford, 2012), 360–1.
9. Emmanuel de Las Cases, *Mémorial de Sainte-Hélène*, ed. Marcel Dunan (2 vols, Paris, 1951), ii. 578.
10. Stendhal, *Les Temps héroïques de Napoléon* (Paris, 1837), 15.
11. David Chandler, *The Campaigns of Napoleon* (London, 1998), 174.
12. Jean Tulard, *Napoléon chef de guerre* (Paris, 2012), 124.
13. Jeremy Black, *Introduction to Global Military History: 1775 to the Present Day* (London, 2005), 42.
14. Bernard Gainot, 'L'Emploi des régiments étrangers dans la Grande Armée: L'Exemple du régiment de La Tour d'Auvergne', in Hervé Drévillon, Bertrand Fonck, and Michel Roucaud (eds), *Guerres et armées napoléoniennes: Nouveaux regards* (Paris, 2013), 233.
15. Digby Smith, *1813: Leipzig. Napoleon and the Battle of the Nations* (London, 2001), 29.
16. Smith, *1813: Leipzig*, 30.
17. Jonathon Riley, *Napoleon as a General* (London, 2007), 199–200.
18. Arnaud Blin, *Iéna, octobre 1806* (Paris, 2003), 152–72.
19. Comment by Wellington, 2 November 1831, in Philip Henry Stanhope, *Notes of Conversations with the Duke of Wellington* (London, 1886), 12.
20. Michael Broers, *Europe after Napoleon: Revolution, Reaction and Romanticism, 1814–1848* (Manchester, 1996), 9–18.
21. Norman Mackenzie, *The Escape from Elba: The Fall and Flight of Napoleon, 1814–1815* (Oxford, 1982), 91.
22. Schroeder, *The Transformation of European Politics*, 548.
23. Mackenzie, *The Escape from Elba*, 189–99.
24. Mackenzie, *The Escape from Elba*, 212–15.
25. Thierry Lentz, *Nouvelle histoire du Premier Empire, iv. Les Cent-Jours* (Paris, 2010), 299.
26. Lentz, *Nouvelle histoire du Premier Empire*, iv, 291.
27. Sudhir Hazareesingh, *The Legend of Napoleon* (London, 2004), 219.

28. Henri Houssaye, *1815: Le Retour de l'Isle d'Elbe* (Paris, 1901), 200–365.
29. A detailed study of Napoleon's passage through Grenoble and Lyons can be found in Jordan Girardin, 'De l'aventurier au Prince: Le Retour de Napoléon de l'île d'Elbe: Le Vol de l'Aigle de Grenoble à Lyon, 7–13 mars 1815' (mémoire, Institut d'études politiques de Lyon, 2012), esp. 36–41. I should like to express my thanks to the author for pointing me to his work.
30. Mackenzie, *The Escape from Elba*, 268.
31. Lieutenant Henckens, *Mémoires se rapportant à son service militaire au 6ème régiment de chasseurs à cheval français de février 1803 à août 1816* (The Hague, 1912), 217–19.
32. Adam Zamoyski, *Rites of Peace: The Fall of Napoleon and the Congress of Vienna* (London, 2007), 457.
33. Lentz, *Les Cent-Jours*, 340–2.
34. I develop this theme at greater length in Alan Forrest, *Napoleon* (London, 2011), 283–5.
35. Robert S. Alexander, *Bonapartism and Revolutionary Tradition in France: The Fédérés of 1815* (Cambridge, 1991), 2.
36. Douglas Dakin, 'The Congress of Vienna, 1814–1815, and its Antecedents', in Alan Sked (ed.), *Europe's Balance of Power, 1815–1848* (London, 1979), 26–33.
37. Alessandro Barbero, *The Battle: A History of the Battle of Waterloo* (London, 2006), 2.
38. Schroeder, *The Transformation of European Politics*, 548–50.
39. A. F. Becke, *Napoleon and Waterloo: A Strategic and Tactical Study of the Emperor's Campaign with the Armée du Nord, 1815* (2 vols, London, 1914), i. 9.
40. Michael Glover, *Wellington as Military Commander* (London, 2001), 178.
41. Matthew Shaw, *The Duke of Wellington* (London, 2005), 72.
42. Zamoyski, *Rites of Peace*, 461.
43. Philip Dwyer, *Citizen Emperor: Napoleon in Power, 1799–1815* (London, 2013), 544.
44. Jeremy Black, *Waterloo, The Battle that Brought Down Napoleon* (London, 2011), 71.
45. Tim Blanning, *The Pursuit of Glory: Europe, 1648–1815* (London, 2007), 670.

Chapter 3

1. Hans Delbrück, *History of the Art of War* (4 vols, Lincoln, NE, 1990), iv. *The Dawn of Modern Warfare*, 438.
2. Jac Weller, *Wellington at Waterloo* (London, 1992), 29.
3. A. F. Becke, *Napoleon and Waterloo: A Strategic and Tactical Study* (London, 1914), 11.
4. Philip Dwyer, *Citizen Emperor: Napoleon in Power, 1799–1815* (London, 3013), 544–5.
5. Gunther E. Rothenberg, *The Napoleonic Wars* (London, 1999), 195.

6. David Chandler, *Waterloo: The Hundred Days* (London, 1980), 53.
7. Chandler, *Waterloo: The Hundred Days*, 26.
8. Rothenberg, *The Napoleonic Wars*, 196.
9. Philip J. Haythornthwaite, *The Armies of Wellington* (London, 1994), 262.
10. Wellington to Bathurst, 4 May 1815, in Antony Brett-James (ed.), *Wellington at War, 1794–1815* (London, 1961), 306.
11. William Tomkinson, *The Diary of a Cavalry Officer in the Peninsular and Waterloo Campaigns, 1809–1815* (Staplehurst, 1999), 295.
12. Mike Robinson, *The Battle of Quatre Bras, 1815* (Stroud, 2009), 19–25; Dwyer, *Citizen Emperor*, 545–6.
13. Letter of 17 August 1815, quoted in Peter Hofschröer, *1815: The Waterloo Campaign: The German Victory* (London, 2004), 2.
14. Baron von Müffling, *Passages from my Life*, quoted in Michael Glover, *Wellington as a Military Commander*, 181.
15. Peter Hofschröer, *Waterloo 1815: Quatre Bras and Ligny* (Barnsley, 2005), 12–17.
16. Black, *Waterloo*, 82.
17. Peter Hofschröer, 'Battle of Quatre Bras, 16 June 1815', in Gregory Fremont-Barnes (ed.), *The Encyclopedia of the French Revolutionary and Napoleonic Wars: A Political, Social and Military History* (3 vols, Santa Barbara, CA, 2006), ii. 799–802.
18. Jacques Logie, *Waterloo: The 1815 Campaign* (Stroud, 2003), 59.
19. Alessandro Barbero, *The Battle: A History of the Battle of Waterloo* (London, 2006), 19.
20. Andrew Uffindell, *The Eagle's Last Triumph: Napoleon's Victory at Ligny, June 1815* (London, 1994); Peter Hofschröer, 'Battle of Ligny, 16 June 1815', in Fremont-Barnes (ed.), *The Encyclopedia of the French Revolutionary and Napoleonic Wars*, ii. 570–2.
21. R. E. Foster, *Wellington and Waterloo: The Duke, the Battle and Posterity* (Stroud, 2014), 59.
22. Logie, *Waterloo*, 67–8.
23. Jean-Baptiste Lemonnier-Delafosse, *Souvenirs militaires*, quoted in Andrew W. Field, *Waterloo: The French Perspective* (Barnsley, 2012), 34.
24. Edward Sabine (ed.), *Letters of Colonel Sir Augustus Simon Frazer, KCB, commanding the Royal Horse Artillery in the Army under the Duke of Wellington* (London, 1859), 544.
25. Barbero, *The Battle*, 81.
26. Foster, *Wellington and Waterloo*, 57.
27. Philip J. Haythornthwaite, *Napoleon's Military Machine* (Staplehurst, 1995), 18–23.
28. Field, *Waterloo: The French Perspective*, 262–3.
29. Andrew Roberts, *Waterloo: Napoleon's Last Gamble* (London, 2006), 69–70.
30. David Howarth, *Waterloo, A Near-Run Thing* (London, 1968), 100–2.
31. Roberts, *Waterloo: Napoleon's Last Gamble*, 89.

32. William Siborne, *The Waterloo Campaign, 1815* (London, 1848), 320–2.
33. Howarth, *Waterloo, A Near-Run Thing*, 108–10.
34. Michael Leggiere, 'Waterloo', in John Merriman and Jay Winter (eds), *Europe, 1789–1914* (5 vols, New York, 2006), v. 2443.
35. Barbero, *The Battle*, 380.
36. Roberts, *Waterloo: Napoleon's Last Gamble*, 120.
37. Christopher Hibbert, *The Destruction of Lord Raglan: A Tragedy of the Crimean War, 1854–1855* (Boston, 1961), 218–20.
38. Gordon Corrigan, *Waterloo: A New History of the Battle and its Armies* (London, 2014), 295.
39. Delbrück, *History of the Art of War*, iv. 439.

Chapter 4

1. Reginald Colby, *The Waterloo Despatch: The Story of the Duke of Wellington's Official Despatch on the Battle of Waterloo and its Journey to London* (London, 1965), 9–32.
2. R. E. Foster, *Wellington and Waterloo: The Duke, the Battle and Posterity* (Stroud, 2014), 74.
3. C. M. Woolgar, 'Writing the Despatch: Wellington and Official Communication', in Woolgar (ed.), *Wellington Studies*, ii (Southampton, 1999), 1.
4. Wellington to Aberdeen, quoted in John Scott, *Paris Revisited in 1815, by way of Brussels* (London, 1817), 160.
5. Wellington to Bathurst, Despatch from Waterloo, 19 June 1815.
6. Elizabeth Longford, *Wellington: The Years of the Sword* (London, 1969), 486.
7. Andrew Uffindell and Michael Corum, *On the Fields of Glory: The Battlefields of the 1815 Campaign* (London, 1996), 47–8.
8. Hansard, *The Parliamentary Debates from the Year 1803 to the Present Time* (London, 1803–20), session of 23 June 1815.
9. Hansard, *Parliamentary Debates*, session of 23 June 1815.
10. Hansard, *Parliamentary Debates*, session of 23 June 1815.
11. Hansard, *Parliamentary Debates*, session of 23 June 1815.
12. Hansard, *Parliamentary Debates*, session of 23 June 1815.
13. Hansard, *Parliamentary Debates*, session of 29 June 1815.
14. Hansard, *Parliamentary Debates*, session of 29 June 1815.
15. Hansard, *Parliamentary Debates*, session of 29 June 1815.
16. *The Times*, Wednesday 28 June 1815.
17. *The Times*, Thursday 29 June 1815.
18. *The Times*, Friday 30 June 1815.
19. *The Times*, Thursday 6 July 1815.
20. *The Times*, Thursday 6 July 1815.
21. Rory Muir, *Britain and the Defeat of Napoleon, 1807–1815* (New Haven, 1996), 372–3.

22. Exhibition catalogue, *Helden nach Mass: 200 Jahre Völkerschlacht bei Leipzig* (Leipzig, 2013), 236.
23. Jean-Paul Bertaud, Alan Forrest, and Annie Jourdan, *Napoléon, le monde et les Anglais: Guerre des mots et des images* (Paris, 2006), 187.
24. *Buonaparte on the 17th of June, Buonaparte on the 17th of July—1815*, British Museum, Catalogue of Political and Personal Satires, no. 12592.
25. *L'écolier Battant la Retraite devant son maître*, BNF, Collection De Vinck tome 73, no. 9581; Catherine Clerc, *La Caricature contre Napoléon* (Paris, 1985), 232.
26. *Sacrifice de Napoléon Buonaparte (18 juin 1815)*, BNF, Collection De Vinck tome 73, no. 9576; Clerc, *La Caricature*, 243.
27. *Le Diable l'emporte: Souhait de la France*, BNF, Collection De Vinck tome 80, no. 10386; Clerc, *la Caricature*, 250.
28. Paul Schroeder, *The Transformation of European Politics, 1763–1848* (Oxford, 1994), 552.
29. John Bew, *Castlereagh: A Life* (New York, 2012), 406.
30. Jeremy Black, *Waterloo: The Battle that Brought Down Napoleon* (London, 2010), 152.
31. Huw J. Davies, *Wellington's Wars: The Making of a Military Genius* (New Haven, 2012), 214–16.
32. Arthur Benoît, *Waterloo: Récits de la campagne de 1815 par le Général Drouot et le Maréchal Ney* (Metz, 1869), 3–28.
33. Declaration of Napoleon on 22 June 1815, *Le Moniteur universel* (1815), 715.
34. Resolution of the Chamber of Deputies, 22 June 1815, *Le Moniteur universel* (1815), 716.
35. Speech of Duchesne, 22 June 1815, *Le Moniteur universel* (1815), 716.
36. Speech of Macdonald (Duke of Otranto), 22 June 1815, *Le Moniteur universel* (1815), 717.
37. Speech by Regnault de Saint-Jean-d'Angély, 22 June 1815, *Le Moniteur universel* (1815), 718.
38. *Bulletin des armées*, 28 June 1815.
39. *Bulletin des armées*, 25 June 1815.
40. Las Cases, *Mémorial*, i. 488.
41. Didier Le Gall, *Napoléon et le Mémorial de Sainte-Hélène: Analyse d'un discours* (Paris, 2003), 177.
42. Caleb Carr, 'Napoleon Wins at Waterloo', in Robert Cowley (ed.), *What If? The World's Foremost Historians Imagine What Might Have Been* (New York, 1999), 220.
43. Duff Cooper, *Talleyrand* (London, 1958), 219.
44. Despatch from Macdonald (Duke of Otranto) to Wellington, 27 June 1815, *Le Moniteur universel* (1815), 720.
45. Munro Price, *The Perilous Crown: France between Revolutions, 1814–1848* (London, 2007), 89.

46. Harold Nicholson, *The Congress of Vienna: A Study in Allied Unity* (London, 1946), 236–7; Bew, *Castlereagh*, 408.

47. The generals and army officers were to be taken before a *conseil de guerre* in their respective military divisions. In addition to those who were executed the following officers were named in the decree; the two Lallemant brothers, Drouet d'Erlon, Lefebvre-Desnouettes, Ameilh, Brayer, Gilly, Mouton-Duvernet, Grouchy, Clausel, Laborde, Debelle, Bertrand, Drouot, Cambronne, Lavalette, and Rovigo.

48. A. Combier, *Mémoires du Général Radet* (Saint-Cloud, 1892), 344.

Chapter 5

1. Catriona Kennedy, 'Bayonets across the Hedges: British Civilian Diaries and the War at Home, 1793–1815', in Alan Forrest, Étienne François, and Karen Hagemann (eds), *War Memories: The Revolutionary and Napoleonic Wars in Modern European Culture* (Basingstoke, 2012), 88.

2. Samuel Hynes, *The Soldiers' Tale: Bearing Witness to Modern War* (London, 1997), 11.

3. Erckmann-Chatrian (Émile Erckmann and Alexandre Chatrian), *The History of a Conscript of 1813 and Waterloo*, trans. Russell Davis Gillman (London, 1909), 329.

4. W. D. King, *Henry Irving's Waterloo: Theatrical Engagements with Arthur Conan Doyle, George Bernard Shaw, Ellen Terry, Edward Gordon Craig* (Berkeley and Los Angeles, 1993), 5.

5. King, *Henry Irving's Waterloo*, 259.

6. Edward Costello, *Adventures of a Soldier* (London, 1852).

7. Edward Costello, *The Peninsular and Waterloo Campaigns*, ed. Antony Brett-James (London, 1967), 150–1.

8. James Tomkinson (ed.), *The Diary of a Cavalry Officer in the Peninsular War and the Waterloo Campaign, 1809–1815* (London, 1971), 286–7.

9. Tomkinson (ed.), *The Diary of a Cavalry Officer*, 297.

10. For a remarkable collection of British soldiers' journals and letters of the Waterloo campaign, see Gareth Glover (ed.), *The Waterloo Archive* (5 vols, Barnsley, 2010–13), vols i, iii, and iv.

11. Andrew Uffindell, *The National Army Museum Book of Wellington's Armies* (London, 2005), 306.

12. Alexander Cavalié Mercer, *Journal of the Waterloo Campaign* (London, 1969), 176–7.

13. George R. Gleig, *The Subaltern* (Edinburgh, 1825); John Kincaid, *Adventures in the Rifle Brigade, in the Peninsula, France and the Netherlands from 1809 to 1815* (London, 1830).

14. Neil Ramsay, *The Military Memoir and Romantic Literary Culture, 1780–1835* (Aldershot, 2011), 109; Catriona Kennedy, *Narratives of the Revolutionary and*

Napoleonic Wars: Military and Civilian Experience in Britain and Ireland (Basingstoke, 2013), 194–5.

15. John Howell, 'Preface' to Thomas, *Journal of a Soldier of the Seventy-First or Glasgow Regiment* (Edinburgh, 1819); Ramsay, *The Military Memoir*, 112.

16. David Miller, *The Duchess of Richmond's Ball, 15 June 1815* (Staplehurst, 2005).

17. Nick Foulkes, *Dancing into Battle: A Social History of the Battle of Waterloo* (London, 2006), p. xii.

18. Charlotte Ann Eaton, *Waterloo Days: The Narrative of an Englishwoman Resident at Brussels in June 1815* (London, 1817); Fanny Burney, 'Waterloo Journal', in *The Journals and Letters of Fanny Burney (Madame d'Arblay)*, viii. *1815*, ed. Peter Hughes et al. (Oxford, 1980).

19. Kennedy, *Narratives of the Revolutionary and Napoleonic Wars*, 189.

20. Glover (ed.), *Waterloo Archive*, ii. 121–2.

21. Glover (ed.), *Waterloo Archive*, ii. 168.

22. Glover (ed.), *Waterloo Archive*, v. 16.

23. Glover (ed.), *Waterloo Archive*, ii. 168.

24. Glover (ed.), *Waterloo Archive*, ii. 208.

25. Carl von Müffling, *The Memoirs of Baron von Müffling: A Prussian Officer in the Napoleonic Wars* (London, 1997), 242.

26. Müffling, *The Memoirs*, 246.

27. Müffling, *The Memoirs*, 250.

28. Mark Wishon, *German Forces and the British Army: Interactions and Perceptions, 1742–1815* (Basingstoke, 2013), 73.

29. Jean Tulard, *Nouvelle bibliographie critique des mémoires sur l'époque napoléonienne, écrits ou traduits en français* (Geneva, 1991), 312.

30. Pierre Nora, 'Les Mémoires d'État: De Commynes à de Gaulle', in Nora (ed.), *Les Lieux de mémoire* (3 vols, Paris, 1986), ii. *La Nation*, 356–9.

31. Philip G. Dwyer, 'Public Remembering, Private Reminiscing: French Military Memoirs and the Revolutionary and Napoleonic Wars', *French Historical Studies* 22/2 (2010), 234.

32. Dwyer, 'Public Remembering, Private Reminiscing', 240–2.

33. Damien Zanone, *Écrire son temps: Les Mémoires en France de 1815 à 1848* (Lyons, 2006), 283.

34. Zanone, *Écrire son temps*, 293–4.

35. Jean-Roch Coignet, *Les Cahiers du Capitaine Coignet, publiés d'après le manuscrit original*, ed. Lorédan Larchey (Paris, 1907), 258.

36. A. Combier (ed.), *Mémoires du Général Radet d'après ses papiers personnels et les Archives de l'État* (Saint-Cloud, 1892), 330.

37. Natalie Petiteau, *Lendemains d'Empire: Les Soldats de Napoléon dans la France du 19ᵉ siècle* (Paris, 2003), 131.

38. Andrew W. Field, *Waterloo: The French Perspective* (Barnsley, 2012), 216.

39. Field, *Waterloo*, 222.

40. *Mémoires du Général Baron de Marbot* (3 vols, Paris, 1891), iii. 403–4.

41. *Mémoires du Maréchal de Grouchy* (5 vols, Paris, 1874), v. 55–237.
42. Savary was tried in his absence in 1815 by a *conseil de guerre* and sentenced to death on 24 July 1815. He had left France for England at Napoleon's side after Waterloo, was separated from him when Napoleon embarked for St Helena, and was taken to Malta where he benefited from the protection of British law. In 1816 he took refuge in Smyrna, from where he was expelled by the Porte, and left for exile in the United States in 1816. See the printed text of the trial, *Procès du Lieutenant-général Savary, Duc de Rovigo, contumax* (Paris, 1817).
43. Emmanuel de Grouchy, *Réfutation de quelques articles des Mémoires du Duc de Rovigo, par le Marquis de Grouchy: Première lettre* (Paris, 1829), 13–14.
44. Emmanuel de Grouchy, *Campagne de 1815: Fragments historiques réunis pour établir le fait de calomnie répandue dans un libelle du Général Berthezène* (Paris, 1840).

Chapter 6

1. *The Times*, 29 June 1815, quoted in Philip Shaw, *Waterloo and the Romantic Imagination* (Basingstoke, 2002), 1.
2. Robert Southey, *The Poet's Pilgrimage to Waterloo* (London, 1816), 17–18; Tim Blanning, '18 Juni 1815: Waterloo', in Étienne François and Uwe Puschner (eds), *Erinnerungstage: Wendepunkte der Geschichte von der Antike bis zur Gegenwart* (Munich, 2010), 163.
3. John Jolliffe (ed.), *Neglected Genius: The Diaries of Benjamin Robert Haydon, 1808–1846* (London, 1990), 36–7.
4. Donald D. Horward, 'Wellington as a Strategist, 1808–1814', in Norman Gash (ed.), *Wellington: Studies in the Military and Political Career of the First Duke of Wellington* (Manchester, 1990), 113.
5. Walter Scott, *The Field of Waterloo: A Poem* (Edinburgh, 1815), 14–15.
6. Thomas R. Dale, 'The Shaping of History: Scott's Life of Napoleon Buonaparte', in J. H. Alexander and David Hewitt (eds), *Scott in Carnival: Selected Papers from the Fourth International Scott Conference* (Aberdeen, 1993), 394.
7. Philip Shaw, *Waterloo and the Romantic Imagination* (Basingstoke, 2002), 59.
8. Charles Campbell, *The Traveller's Complete Guide through Belgium, Holland and Germany, etc.* (London, 1815), 72.
9. John Booth, *Battle of Waterloo: Circumstantial Details of the Memorable Event* (London, 1815).
10. John Scott, *Paris Revisited in 1815, by way of Brussels: Including a walk over the field of battle at Waterloo* (London, 1816).
11. James Simpson, *A Visit to Flanders, in July, 1815: Being chiefly an account of the field of Waterloo* (London, 1816).
12. Scott, *Paris Revisited*, 201–2.
13. Arthur Gore, *An Historical Account of the Battle of Waterloo* (London, 1817).

14. Christopher Kelly, *A Full and Circumstantial Account of the Memorable Battle of Waterloo: The second restoration of Louis XVIII; and the deportation of Napoleon Buonaparte to the island of St. Helena and every recent particular relative to his conduct and mode of life in his exile. Together with an interesting account of the affairs of France, and biographical sketches of the most distinguished Waterloo heroes* (London, 1817).

15. William Siborne, 'Preface to the second edition (1844)', in *The Waterloo Campaign 1815* (4th edn, London 1895), 13.

16. Wellington, *Supplementary Despatches, Correspondence and Memoranda of Field Marshal Arthur Duke of Wellington* (16 vols, London, 1857–72); Herbert T. Siborne, *Waterloo Letters* (London, 1891).

17. For a fuller discussion of nineteenth-century historiography of the battle across Europe, see Barbero, *The Battle*, 435.

18. Andrew Roberts, for example, divides the battle into five distinct phases: see Roberts, *Waterloo: Napoleon's Last Gamble* (London, 2005).

19. Linda Colley, *Britons: Forging the Nation, 1707–1837* (New Haven, 1992), esp. 7–9.

20. John Cookson, *The British Armed Nation, 1793–1815* (Oxford, 1997), 126–7.

21. Hugh Trevor-Roper, 'The Invention of Tradition: the Highland Tradition of Scotland', in Eric Hobsbawm and Terence Ranger (eds), *The Invention of Tradition* (Cambridge, 1983), 15–41.

22. David French, *Military Identities: The Regimental System, the British Army and the British People, 1870–2000* (Oxford, 2005), 240.

23. Susan Pearce, 'The *matériel* of War: Waterloo and its Culture', in John Bonehill and Geoff Quilley (eds), *Conflicting Visions: War and Visual Culture in Britain and France, 1700–1830* (Guildford, 2005), 218.

24. Cookson, *The British Armed Nation*, 146.

25. Simpson, *A Visit to Flanders, in July, 1815*, 34.

26. Blanning, '18 Juni 1815: Waterloo', 167.

27. Donald Read, *Peterloo: The 'Massacre' and its Background* (Manchester, 1958), 5–24.

28. Peter Hofschröer, *Wellington's Smallest Victory: The Duke, the Model Maker and the Secret of Waterloo* (London, 2004), *passim*.

29. Holger Hoock, *Empires of the Imagination: Politics, War and the Arts in the British World, 1750–1850* (London, 2010), 354.

30. Colin White, 'Official and Popular Commemoration of Nelson in 1805–06', in Holger Hoock (ed.), *History, Commemoration and National Preoccupation: Trafalgar, 1805–2005* (London, 2007), 46.

31. R. F. Foster, *Wellington and Waterloo: The Duke, the Battle and Posterity* (Stroud, 2014), 118.

32. Melvyn Thompson, *St George's (Kidderminster): A Waterloo Church* (Kidderminster, 2009), 14.

33. Holger Hoock, *Empires of the Imagination: Politics, War and the Arts in the British World, 1750–1850* (London, 2010), 364.

34. T. F. Bowerbank, *A Sermon Preached in the Parish Church of Chiswick, Middlesex, July 30 1815* (London, 1815).

35. Henry Cotes, *To the members of the Westminster Waterloo Association: A Sermon preached in the parish church of Bedlington in the County of Durham, 20 August 1815* (Newcastle, 1815), 18.

36. Holger Hoock, *The King's Artists: The Royal Academy of Arts and the Politics of British Culture, 1760–1840* (Oxford, 2003), 254.

37. Foster, *Wellington and Waterloo*, 97.

38. Hew Strachan, *Wellington's Legacy: The Reform of the British Army, 1830–1854* (Manchester, 1984), 101–2.

39. David Chandler, *Marlborough as Military Commander* (London, 1979).

40. Foster, *Wellington and Waterloo*, 153.

41. Shaw, *Waterloo and the Romantic Imagination*, 24.

42. Colley, *Britons*, 365.

43. Hoock, *Empires of the Imagination*, 359–61.

44. Philip Shaw, *Suffering and Sentiment in Romantic Military Art* (Farnham, 2013), 167.

45. Shaw, *Waterloo and the Romantic Imagination*, 78–91.

46. Martin Meisel, *Realizations: Narrative, Pictorial and Theatrical Arts in Nineteenth-Century England* (Princeton, 1983), 214–15.

47. W. D. King, *Henry Irving's Waterloo: Theatrical Engagements with Arthur Conan Doyle, George Bernard Shaw, Ellen Terry, Edward Gordon Craig* (Berkeley and Los Angeles, 1993), 112–13.

48. Pamela Pilbeam, *Madame Tussaud and the History of Waxworks* (London, 2003), 224.

49. Matthew Craske, 'Making National Heroes? A Survey of the Social and Political Functions and Meanings of Major British Funeral Monuments to Naval and Military Figures, 1730–1770', in Bonehill and Quilley (eds), *Conflicting Visions*, 42–3.

50. Holger Hoock, 'The British Military Pantheon in St Paul's Cathedral: The State, Cultural Patriotism and the Politics of National Monuments, 1790–1820', in Richard Wrigley and Matthew Craske (eds), *Pantheons: Transformations of a Monumental Idea* (Aldershot, 2004), 83.

51. Craske, 'Making National Heroes?', 46–7.

52. Martin van Creveld, *The Culture of War* (New York, 2008), 239.

53. Alison Yarrington, *The Commemoration of the Hero, 1800–1864: Monuments to the British Victors of the Napoleonic Wars* (New York, 1988), 168.

54. Holger Hoock, *Empires of the Imagination*, 361–4.

55. Christine Sutherland, *Marie Walewska: Napoleon's Great Love* (London, 1979), 247.

56. <http://www.britishlistedbuildings.co.uk/sc-17312-waterloo-monument-new-abbey>

57. Willard Bissell Pope (ed.), *The Diary of Benjamin Robert Haydon* (6 vols, Cambridge, MA, 1960), ii. 199.

58. Yarrington, *The Commemoration of the Hero, 1800–1864*, 220–30.

59. Yarrington, *The Commemoration of the Hero, 1800–1864*, 215.

60. My thanks are due to Geraint Thomas for drawing my attention to this Waterloo Bridge.

61. Uffindel and Corum, *On the Fields of Glory*, 320.

62. Serge Joyal, *Le Mythe de Napoléon au Canada français* (Montreal, 2013), 173–5.

63. A. J. Youngson, *The Making of Classical Edinburgh, 1750–1840* (Edinburgh, 1966), 148.

64. These references are taken from the A–Z for Manchester (Sevenoaks, 1987), 53–4.

65. A. V. Seaton, 'War and Thanatourism: Waterloo, 1815–1914', *Annals of Tourism Research* 26 (1999), 133.

66. Philip Shaw, 'Shocking Sights of Woe: Charles Bell and the Battle of Waterloo', in Bonehill and Quilley (eds), *Conflicting Visions*, 192–9.

67. Scott, *Paris Revisited*, 201.

68. Philip Shaw, 'Shocking Sights of Woe', 190.

69. Scott, *Paris Revisited*, 202–3.

70. Scott, *Paris Revisited*, 214.

71. Pearce, 'The *matériel* of War: Waterloo and its Culture', 212.

72. Scott, *Paris Revisited*, 216.

73. *Blackwood's Edinburgh Magazine* (July 1835), 115.

74. *Blackwood's Edinburgh Magazine* (July 1835), 114.

75. Michael L. Bush, *The Casualties of Peterloo* (Lancaster, 2005), 45.

76. Bush, *The Casualties of Peterloo*, 50.

77. Christopher Woodward, 'Napoleon's Last Journey', in Margarette Lincoln (ed.), *Nelson and Napoleon* (London, 2005), 243.

78. Peter Spence, *The Birth of Romantic Radicalism: War, Popular Politics and English Radical Reformism, 1800–1815* (Aldershot, 1996), 208.

79. E. Tangye Lean, *The Napoleonists: A Study in Political Disaffection* (Oxford, 1970), 262–6.

80. Walter Scott, *Life of Napoleon Bonaparte* (Edinburgh, 1828).

81. Richard Whately, *Historical Doubts Relative to Napoleon Bonaparte* (London, 1819). The text that is used here, published in London in 1985, was edited with a critical introduction by Ralph S. Pomeroy.

82. Whately, *Historical Doubts*, 23.

83. Whately, *Historical Doubts*, 35.

84. Brian Bond, *The Victorian Army and the Staff College, 1854–1914* (London, 1972), 17–18.

85. Bond, *The Victorian Army*, 55–6.

86. Bond, *The Victorian Army*, 166–7.

Chapter 7

1. Emmanuel de Las Cases, *Le Mémorial de Sainte-Hélène* (2 vols, Paris, 1951), ii. 6.
2. Wolfgang Schivelbusch, *The Culture of Defeat: On National Trauma, Mourning and Recovery* (London, 2003), 3.
3. Christopher Bayly, *The Birth of the Modern World, 1780–1914* (Oxford, 2004), 125–38.
4. Jacques Hantraye, *Les Cosaques aux Champs-Élysées: L'Occupation de la France après la chute de Napoléon* (Paris, 2005).
5. Alan Forrest, *The Legacy of the French Revolutionary Wars: The Nation-in-Arms in French Republican Memory* (Cambridge, 2009), 63; Hantraye, *Les Cosaques aux Champs-Élysées*, 46–8.
6. Sergio Luzzatto, *Mémoire de la Terreur: Vieux Montagnards et jeunes républicains au 19e siècle* (Lyons, 1988), 13–20.
7. Daniel Resnick, *The White Terror and the Political Reaction after Waterloo* (Cambridge, MA, 1966); Nora Hudson, *Ultra-Royalism and the French Restoration* (New York, 1973).
8. Price, *The Perilous Crown*, 68.
9. Natalie Petiteau, *Guerriers du Premier Empire: Expériences et mémoires* (Paris, 2011), 57–73.
10. Alan Forrest, *Napoleon's Men: The Soldiers of the Revolution and Empire* (London, 2002), 133–59.
11. André Zeller, *Soldats perdus: Des armées de Napoléon aux garnisons de Louis XVIII* (Paris, 1977), 319–41.
12. Frédéric Bluche, *Le Bonapartisme—aux origines de la droite autoritaire* (Paris, 1980); Robert Gildea, 'Bonapartism', in *The Past in French History* (New Haven, 1994), 62–111.
13. Bernard Ménager, *Les Napoléon du peuple* (Paris, 1988), 39.
14. Lucien Bonaparte, *Réponse de Lucien Bonaparte, prince de Canino, aux mémoires du Général Lamarque* (London, 1835), 7.
15. Roger Price, *People and Politics in France, 1848–1870* (Cambridge, 2004), 68–9.
16. Maurice Agulhon, *Marianne into Battle: Republican Imagery and Symbolism in France, 1789–1880* (Cambridge, 1981), 45.
17. Sudhir Hazareesingh, *The Legend of Napoleon* (London, 2004), 155.
18. Hazareesingh, *The Legend of Napoleon*, 242–59.
19. The stated goal of 'La Sabretache' was 'to contribute to the development of a museum of the French Army and to propagate the taste for and the study of French military history'.
20. Céji-Hesse, *Notice sur le mémorial français à Waterloo: L'Aigle expirant de Gérôme* (Braine-l'Alleud, 1904).
21. Jean-Marc Largeaud, *Napoléon et Waterloo: La Défaite glorieuse de 1815 à nos jours* (Paris, 2006), 219.
22. Pierre Larousse, *Le Mot de Cambronne* (Paris, 1862), 3–15.

23. Larousse, *Le Mot de Cambronne*, 318–23.
24. Archives Départementales Loire-Atlantique, 1J 351, Monument du Général Cambronne à Nantes.
25. Jacques Garnier, 'Pierre-Jacques-Étienne Cambronne, vicomte', in Jean Tulard (ed.), *Dictionnaire Napoléon* (2 vols, Paris, 1999), i. 355.
26. Stéphane Calvet, *Les Officiers charentais de Napoléon au 19e siècle: Destins de braves* (Paris, 2010), 33.
27. Forrest, *Napoleon's Men*, 21–52.
28. Quoted in Thomas R. Dale, 'The Shaping of History: Scott's Life of Napoleon Buonaparte', 398.
29. Natalie Petiteau, *Napoléon de la mythologie à l'histoire* (Paris, 1999), 84.
30. Gérard Gengembre, *A vos plumes, citoyens! Écrivains, journalistes, orateurs et poètes, de la Bastille à Waterloo* (Paris, 1988), 127.
31. Victor Hugo, *Les Misérables*, trans. Isabel Hapgood (London, 1929), pt. 2, p. 10.
32. Hugo, *Les Misérables*, trans. Hapgood, pt. 2, p. 28.
33. Victor Hugo, 'L'Expiation', in *Les Châtiments* (Paris, 1853).
34. John Lynn, *Battle: A History of Combat and Culture* (Cambridge, MA, 2003), 196.
35. Gita May, *Stendhal in the Age of Napoleon* (New York, 1978), 114.
36. Stendhal, *Les Temps héroïques de Napoléon* (Paris, 1837), 15.
37. Marcel Heisler, *Stendhal et Napoléon* (Paris, 1969), 137.
38. Heisler, *Stendhal et Napoléon*, 193.
39. *Mémoires du Général Baron de Marbot* (3 vols, Paris, 1891), iii. 403.
40. Jean Tulard, *L'Anti-Napoléon* (Paris, 2013), 35–49.
41. Jean Tulard, *Napoléon chef de guerre* (Paris, 2012), 255–6.
42. Colonel Charras, *Histoire de la campagne de 1815* (Brussels, 1857), cited in Tulard, *Napoléon chef de guerre*, 265.
43. Jean-Claude Lorblanchès, *Soldats de Napoléon aux Amériques* (Paris, 2012), *passim*.
44. David Hopkin, *Soldier and Peasant in French Popular Culture, 1766–1870* (Woodbridge, 2003), 253–5.
45. Barbara Ann Day-Hickman, *Napoleonic Art: Nationalism and the Spirit of Rebellion in France, 1815–1848* (Newark, DE, 1999); they included several images of Waterloo (p. 53).
46. Bruno Foucart, 'Napoléon et l'inspiration napoléonienne', in *Raffet, 1804–1860*, catalogue of exhibition at the Bibliothèque Marmottan (Paris, 1999), 38–51.
47. Largeaud, *Napoléon et Waterloo*, 333–4.
48. Dérémy, 'Épisodes de 1815', in Pierre Barbier et France Vernillat (eds), *Histoire de France par les chansons*, v. *Napoléon et sa légende* (Paris, 1958), 153.
49. Émile Debraux, 'La Bataille de Waterloo', in Barbier et Vernillat (eds), *Histoire de France par les chansons*, v. 152.
50. Stendhal, *Voyages en Italie* (Paris, 1973), 83.

51. Philip Shaw, *Waterloo and the Romantic Imagination* (Basingstoke, 2002), 1.
52. Michel Arrous (ed.), *Actes du Colloque Napoléon, Stendhal et les Romantiques: L'Armée, la guerre, la gloire* (Paris, 2002), 9.
53. Ernest Lavisse, *Histoire de France: Cours élémentaire* (Paris, 1913), 155–6.

Chapter 8

1. Wellington, *Supplementary Despatches, Correspondence and Memoranda of Field Marshal Arthur Duke of Wellington* (16 vols, London, 1857–72), x. 513–31.
2. Peter Hofschröer, *1815: The Waterloo Campaign* (2 vols, London, 1998–9), ii. 336.
3. Ian Fletcher, 'A Desperate Business': Wellington, the British Army and the Waterloo Campaign* (Staplehurst, 2001), 189.
4. Fletcher, 'A Desperate Business', 17.
5. Carl von Clausewitz, *On Waterloo: Clausewitz, Wellington and the Campaign of 1815*, ed. Christopher Bassford, Daniel Moran, and Gregory W. Pedlow (Charleston, SC, 2010); Bruno Colson, 'Clausewitz on Waterloo', *War in History* 19 (2012), 400.
6. Georg G. Iggers, 'Nationalism and Historiography, 1789–1996: The German Example in Historical Perspective', in Stefan Berger, Mark Donovan and Kevin Passmore (eds), *Writing National Histories: Western Europe since 1800* (London, 1999), 17.
7. Karen Hagemann, 'National Symbols and the Politics of Memory: The Prussian Iron Cross of 1813, its Cultural Context and its Aftermath', in Alan Forrest, Étienne François, and Karen Hagemann (eds), *War Memories: The Revolutionary and Napoleonic Wars in Modern European Culture* (Basingstoke, 2012), 229.
8. James J. Sheehan, *German History, 1770–1866* (Oxford, 1989), 406.
9. An interesting overview of the development of the myth surrounding the Battle of Leipzig can be found in *Helden nach Mass: 200 Jahre Völkerschlacht bei Leipzig: Katalog zur Ausstellung des Stadtgeschichtlichen Museums Leipzig* (Leipzig, 2013).
10. Christopher Clark, *Iron Kingdom: The Rise and Downfall of Prussia, 1600–1947* (London, 2006), 371; Blanning, '18 Juni 1815: Waterloo', 178.
11. Jason Tebbe, 'Revision and "Rebirth": Commemoration of the Battle of the Nations in Leipzig', *German Studies Review* 33 (2010), 619–23.
12. Tebbe, 'Revision and "Rebirth"', 624.
13. *Preussische Zeitung*, 17 June 1915. I should like to thank Peter Hofschröer for drawing my attention to this article.
14. Gebhard Leberecht von Blücher, *Das Blücherdenkmal in Rostock und Goethes Teilnahme an diesem Werke* (Leipzig, 1862).
15. Eveline G. Bouwers, *Public Pantheons in Revolutionary Europe: Comparing Cultures of Remembrance, 1790–1840* (Basingstoke, 2012), 162.

16. Étienne François, 'The Revolutionary and Napoleonic Wars as a Shared and Entangled European *lieu de mémoire*', in Forrest et al. (eds), *War Memories*, 390.

17. For the topographical information of German street names in this paragraph I am grateful once again to Peter Hofschröer, who generously sent me a list of the names he was able to locate and has kindly given me permission to cite from it.

18. Brendan Simms, *The Longest Afternoon: The Four Hundred Men who Decided the Battle of Waterloo* (London, 2014), 74–5.

19. Jasper Heinzen, 'A Negotiated Truce: The Battle of Waterloo in European Memory since the Second World War', *History and Memory* 26 (1974), 48–51.

20. Étienne François and Hagen Schulze (eds), *Deutsche Erinnerungsorte* (3 vols, Munich, 2001); see the articles by Michel Espagne, '"De l'Allemagne"' (i. 225–41), Hagen Schulze, 'Versailles' (i. 407–21), Hagen Schulze, 'Napoleon' (ii. 28–46), and Kirstin Schäfer, 'Die Völkerschlacht' (ii. 187–201).

21. J. Saint-Mathurin, 'Le Culte de Napoléon en Allemagne de 1815 à 1848', *Revue des études napoléoniennes*, 11 (1917), esp. 48–52.

22. Annie Jourdan (ed.), *Louis Bonaparte, roi de Hollande* (Paris, 2010), *passim*.

23. Johan Joor, '"A very rebellious disposition": Dutch Experience and Popular Protest under the Napoleonic Regime (1806–1813)', in Alan Forrest, Karen Hagemann, and Jane Rendall (eds), *Soldiers, Citizens and Civilians: Experiences and Perceptions of the Revolutionary and Napoleonic Wars, 1790–1820* (Basingstoke, 2009), 181–204; for a fuller treatment see Joor, *De Adelaar en het Lam: Onrust, opruiing en onwilligheid in Nederland ten tijde van het Koninkrijk Holland en de Inlijving bij het Franse Keizerrijk, 1806–1813* (Amsterdam, 2000).

24. Lotte Jensen, 'The Dutch Against Napoleon: Resistance Literature and National Identity, 1806–1813', *Journal of Dutch Literature* 2/2 (2012), 5–26.

25. E. H. Kossmann, *The Low Countries, 1780–1940* (Oxford, 1978), 103–13.

26. Georges Jacquemin, *Les Boteresses liégeoises à la Butte du Lion de Waterloo (1826)?* (Braine-l'Alleud, 2002), 78–80.

27. Wiepke Loos, Guido Jansen, and Wouter Kloek (eds), *Waterloo, Before and After: Paintings from the Rijksmuseum in Amsterdam, 1800–1830* (Amsterdam, 1997), 11.

28. Dominique Poulot, 'Conservation et mémoire d'une bataille: Quelques réflexions', in Marcel Watelet, Pierre Couvreur, and Philippe de Villelongue (eds), *Waterloo: Monuments et représentations de mémoires européennes, 1792–2001* (Louvain-la-Neuve, 2003), 14.

29. Poulot, 'Conservation et mémoire d'une bataille', 15–16.

30. See the Rijksmuseum website, <https://www.rijksmuseum.nl/en/explore-the-collection/timeline-dutch-history/1813-1815-king-william-i-and-waterloo>.

31. Anne Buyle, 'Un projet inédit de monument à Waterloo', in Marcel Watelet and Pierre Couvreur (eds), *Waterloo, lieu de mémoire européenne, 1815–2000* (Louvain-la-Neuve, 2000), 142.

32. Jacquemin, *Les Boteresses liégeoises à la Butte du Lion de Waterloo (1826)?*, 82.

33. Jacquemin, *Les Boteresses liégeoises à la Butte du Lion de Waterloo (1826)?*, 96–101.
34. I should like to thank Annie Jourdan who most helpfully drew my attention to recent Dutch scholarship on Waterloo and on the reception given to those who had fought in the battle. The classic Dutch source is E. Van Löben Sels, *Bijdragen tot de Krijgsgeschiedenis van Napoleon Bonaparte* (4 vols, 'S Gravenhage, 1842).
35. Philippe Raxhon, 'Le Lion de Waterloo, un monument controversé', in Watelet and Couvreur (eds), *Waterloo, lieu de mémoire européenne, 1815–2000*, 156–7.
36. Raxhon, 'Le Lion de Waterloo', 158.
37. Fierens-Gevaert, *Figures et sites de Belgique* (Brussels, 1907), quoted by Raxhon, 'Le Lion de Waterloo', 159.
38. *La Petite République* (June 1915), in 'Comment fut célébré le centenaire de Waterloo pendant la guerre de 1914–1918', *Société belge d'études napoléoniennes* 50 (1965), 17.
39. *La Petite République* (June 1915), 19.
40. Marcel Watelet, 'L'Après-Waterloo: Cartographie et paysage mémorial', in Watelet et al. (eds), *Waterloo: Monuments et représentations de mémoires européennes, 1792–2001*, 282–4.
41. G. F. Pardo de Leygonier, 'Napoléon et les libérateurs de l'Amérique latine', *Revue de l'Institut Napoléon* 82 (1962), p. 32.
42. Lee Kennet, 'Le Culte de Napoléon aux États-Unis jusqu'à la guerre de Sécession', *Revue de l'Institut Napoléon* 125 (1972), p. 146.
43. Kennet, 'Le Culte de Napoléon', 146–7.

Chapter 9

1. Wendell Phillips, 'Lecture at Brooklyn, NY, 1 November 1859', in *The Oxford Dictionary of Quotations* (London, 1956), 378.
2. Arthur Conan Doyle, 'The Return of Sherlock Holmes', in *The Oxford Dictionary of Quotations*, 188.
3. Jean-Marc Largeaud, *Napoléon et Waterloo: La Défaite glorieuse de 1815 à nos jours* (Paris, 2006), 11 n.
4. Dominic Lieven, *Russia Against Napoleon: The Battle for Europe, 1807–1814* (London, 2009), 281–2.
5. Robert Margerit, *Waterloo: 18 juin 1815* (Paris, 1964), 569–73.
6. Thomas Nipperdey, *Deutsche Geschichte, 1800–1866: Bürgerwelt und starker Staat* (Munich, 1983), 11.

BIBLIOGRAPHY

Agulhon, Maurice, *Marianne into Battle: Republican Imagery and Symbolism in France, 1789–1880* (Cambridge, 1981).

Alexander, J. H., and Hewitt, David (eds), *Scott in Carnival: Selected Papers from the Fourth International Scott Conference* (Aberdeen, 1993).

Alexander, Robert S., *Bonapartism and Revolutionary Tradition in France: The Fédérés of 1815* (Cambridge, 1991).

Anon., 'Comment fut célébré le centenaire de Waterloo pendant la guerre de 1914–1918', *Société belge d'études napoléoniennes* 50 (1965), 16–20.

Arrous, Michel (ed.), *Actes du Colloque Napoléon, Stendhal et les Romantiques: L'Armée, la guerre, la gloire* (Paris, 2002).

Barbero, Alessandro, *The Battle: A History of the Battle of Waterloo* (London, 2006).

Barbier, Pierre, and Vernillat, France, *Histoire de France par les chansons*, v. *Napoléon et sa légende* (Paris, 1958).

Bayly, Christopher, *The Birth of the Modern World, 1780–1914* (Oxford, 2004).

Becke, A. F., *Napoleon and Waterloo: A Strategic and Tactical Study of the Emperor's Campaign with the Armée du Nord, 1815* (2 vols, London, 1914).

Bell, David A., *The First Total War: Napoleon's Europe and the Birth of Warfare as We Know It* (New York, 2007).

Benoît, Arthur, *Waterloo: Récits de la campagne de 1815 par le Général Drouot et le Maréchal Ney* (Metz, 1869).

Bertaud, Jean-Paul, Forrest, Alan, and Jourdan, Annie, *Napoléon, le monde et les Anglais: Guerre des mots et des images* (Paris, 2006).

Bew, John, *Castlereagh: A Life* (Oxford, 2012).

Black, Jeremy, *Introduction to Global Military History: 1775 to the Present Day* (London, 2005).

Black, Jeremy, *Waterloo: The Battle that Brought Down Napoleon* (London, 2010).

Blackwood's Edinburgh Magazine, July 1835.

Blanning, Tim, *The Pursuit of Glory: Europe, 1648–1815* (London, 2007).

Blanning, Tim, '18. Juni 1815: Waterloo', in Étienne François and Uwe Puschner (eds), *Erinnerungstage: Wendepunkte des Geschichte von der Antike bis zur Gegenwart* (Munich, 2010), 163–85.

Blin, Arnaud, *Iéna, octobre 1806* (Paris, 2003).

Bluche, Frédéric, *Le Bonapartisme—aux origines de la droite autoritaire* (Paris, 1980).

Blücher, Gebhard Leberecht von, *Das Blücherdenkmal in Rostock und Goethes Teilnahme an diesem Werke* (Leipzig, 1862).

Bonaparte, Lucien, *Réponse de Lucien Bonaparte, prince de Canino, aux mémoires du Général Lamarque* (London, 1835).

Bond, Brian, *The Victorian Army and the Staff College, 1854–1914* (London, 1972).

Bonehill, John, and Quilley, Geoff (eds), *Conflicting Visions: War and Visual Culture in Britain and France, 1700–1830* (Guildford, 2005).

Booth, John, *Battle of Waterloo: Circumstantial Details of the Memorable Event* (London, 1815).

Bouwers, Eveline G., *Public Pantheons in Revolutionary Europe: Comparing Cultures of Remembrance, 1790–1840* (Basingstoke, 2012).

Bowerbank, T. F., *A Sermon Preached in the Parish Church of Chiswick, Middlesex, July 30 1815* (London, 1815).

Brett-James, Antony (ed.), *Wellington at War, 1794–1815* (London, 1961).

Broers, Michael, *Europe after Napoleon: Revolution, Reaction and Romanticism, 1814–1848* (Manchester, 1996).

Bruyère-Ostells, Walter, *Leipzig, 16–19 octobre 1813* (Paris, 2013).

Bulletin des armées, 1815.

Burney, Fanny, 'Waterloo Journal', in *The Journals and Letters of Fanny Burney (Madame d'Arblay)*, viii. 1815, ed. Peter Hughes, Joyce Hemlow, Althea Douglas, and Patricia Hawkins (Oxford, 1980).

Bush, Michael, *The Casualties of Peterloo* (Lancaster, 2005).

Calvet, Stéphane, *Les Officiers charentais de Napoléon au 19e siècle: Destins de braves* (Paris, 2010).

Campbell, Charles, *The Traveller's Complete Guide through Belgium, Holland and Germany, etc.* (London, 1815).

Carr, Caleb, 'Napoleon Wins at Waterloo', in Robert Cowley (ed.), *What If? The World's Foremost Historians Imagine What Might Have Been* (New York, 1999).

Céji-Hesse, *Notice sur le mémorial français à Waterloo: L'Aigle expirant de Gérôme* (Braine-l'Alleud, 1904).

Chandler, David, *Marlborough as Military Commander* (London, 1979).

Chandler, David, *Waterloo: The Hundred Days* (London, 1980).

Chandler, David, *The Campaigns of Napoleon* (London, 1998).

Clausewitz, Carl von, *On Waterloo: Clausewitz, Wellington and the Campaign of 1815*, ed. Christopher Bassford, Daniel Moran, and Gregory W. Pedlow (Charleston, SC, 2010).

Clerc, Catherine, *La Caricature contre Napoléon* (Paris, 1985).

Coignet, Jean-Roch, *Les Cahiers du Capitaine Coignet, publiés d'après le manuscrit original*, ed. Lorédan Larchey (Paris, 1907).

Colby, Reginald, *The Waterloo Despatch: The Story of the Duke of Wellington's Official Despatch on the Battle of Waterloo and its Journey to London* (London, 1965).

Colley, Linda, *Britons: Forging the Nation, 1707–1837* (New Haven, 1992).

Colson, Bruno, 'Clausewitz on Waterloo', *War in History* 19 (2012), 397–400.

Combier, A., *Mémoires du Général Radet d'après ses papiers personnels et les Archives de l'État* (Saint-Cloud, 1892).

Cookson, John, *The British Armed Nation, 1793–1815* (Oxford, 1997).

Cooper, Duff, *Talleyrand* (London, 1958).

Costello, Edward, *Adventures of a Soldier* (London, 1852).

Costello, Edward, *The Peninsular and Waterloo Campaigns*, ed. Antony Brett-James (London, 1967).

Cotes, Henry, *To the members of the Westminster Waterloo Association: A Sermon preached in the parish church of Bedlington in the County of Durham, 20 August 1815* (Newcastle, 1815).

Creveld, Martin van, *The Culture of War* (New York, 2008).

Davies, Huw J., *Wellington's Wars: The Making of a Military Genius* (New Haven, 2012).

Day-Hickman, Barbara Ann, *Napoleonic Art: Nationalism and the Spirit of Rebellion in France, 1815–1848* (Newark, DE, 1999).

Drévillon, Hervé, Fonck, Bertrand, and Roucaud, Michel (eds), *Guerres et armées napoléoniennes: Nouveaux regards* (Paris, 2013).

Dwyer, Philip, 'Public Remembering, Private Reminiscing: French Military Memoirs and the Revolutionary and Napoleonic Wars', *French Historical Studies* 22/2 (2010), 231-58.

Dwyer, Philip, *Citizen Emperor: Napoleon in Power, 1799–1815* (London, 2013).

Eaton, Charlotte Ann, *Waterloo Days: The Narrative of an Englishwoman Resident at Brussels in June 1815* (London, 1817).

Emsley, Clive, *The Longman Companion to Napoleonic Europe* (London, 1993).

Erckmann-Chatrian [Erckmann, Émile, and Chatrian, Alexandre], *The History of a Conscript of 1813 and Waterloo*, trans. Russell Davis Gillman (London, 1909).

Esdaile, Charles, *Napoleon's Wars: An International History, 1803–1815* (London, 2007).

Field, Andrew W., *Waterloo: The French Perspective* (Barnsley, 2012).

Fletcher, Ian, *'A Desperate Business': Wellington, the British Army and the Waterloo Campaign* (Staplehurst, 2001).

Forrest, Alan, *Napoleon's Men: The Soldiers of the Revolution and Empire* (London, 2002).

Forrest, Alan, *The Legacy of the French Revolutionary Wars: The Nation-in-Arms in French Republican Memory* (Cambridge, 2009).

Forrest, Alan, *Napoleon* (London, 2011).

Forrest, Alan, François, Étienne, and Hagemann, Karen (eds), *War Memories: The Revolutionary and Napoleonic Wars in Modern European Culture* (Basingstoke, 2012).

Forrest, Alan, Hagemann, Karen, and Rendall, Jane (eds), *Soldiers, Citizens and Civilians: Experiences and Perceptions of the Revolutionary and Napoleonic Wars, 1790–1820* (Basingstoke, 2009).

Foster, R. E., *Wellington and Waterloo: The Duke, the Battle and Posterity* (Stroud, 2014).

Foulkes, Nick, *Dancing into Battle: A Social History of the Battle of Waterloo* (London, 2006).

François, Étienne, and Schulze, Hagen (eds), *Deutsche Erinnerungsorte* (3 vols, Munich, 2001).

Fremont-Barnes, Gregory (ed.), *The Encyclopedia of the French Revolutionary and Napoleonic Wars: A Political, Social and Military History* (3 vols, Santa Barbara, CA, 2006).

French, David, *Military Identities: The Regimental System, the British Army and the British People, 1870–2000* (Oxford, 2005).

Garnier, Jacques, 'Waterloo', in Jean Tulard (ed.), *Dictionnaire Napoléon* (2 vols, Paris, 1999).

Gash, Norman (ed.), *Wellington: Studies in the Military and Political Career of the First Duke of Wellington* (Manchester, 1990).

Gengembre, Gérard, *A vos plumes, citoyens! Écrivains, journalistes, orateurs et poètes, de la Bastille à Waterloo* (Paris, 1988).

Gildea, Robert, 'Bonapartism', in *The Past in French History* (New Haven, 1994).

Girardin, Jordan, 'De l'aventurier au Prince: Le Retour de Napoléon de l'île d'Elbe: Le Vol de l'Aigle de Grenoble à Lyon, 7–13 mars 1815' (mémoire, Institut d'études politiques de Lyon, 2012).

Gleig, George R., *The Subaltern* (Edinburgh, 1825).

Glover, Gareth (ed.), *The Waterloo Archive* (5 vols, Barnsley, 2010–13).

Glover, Michael, *Wellington as Military Commander* (London, 2001).

Gore, Arthur, *An Historical Account of the Battle of Waterloo* (London, 1817).

Grant, R. G., *Battle: A Visual Journey through 5000 Years of Combat* (London, 2005).

Grouchy, Emmanuel de, *Réfutation de quelques articles des Mémoires du Duc de Rovigo, par le Marquis de Grouchy: Première lettre* (Paris, 1829).

Grouchy, Emmanuel de, *Campagne de 1815: Fragments historiques réunis pour établir le fait de calomnie répandue dans un libelle du Général Berthezène* (Paris, 1840).

Grouchy, Emmanuel de, *Mémoires du Maréchal de Grouchy* (5 vols, Paris, 1874).

Hansard, *The Parliamentary Debates from the Year 1803 to the Present Time* (London, 1803–20).

Hantraye, Jacques, *Les Cosaques aux Champs-Élysées: L'Occupation de la France après la chute de Napoléon* (Paris, 2005).

Haythornthwaite, Philip J., *Invincible Generals: Gustavus Adolphus, Marlborough, Frederick the Great, George Washington, Wellington* (London, 1991).

Haythornthwaite, Philip J., *The Armies of Wellington* (London, 1994).

Hazareesingh, Sudhir, *The Legend of Napoleon* (London, 2004).

Heisler, Marcel, *Stendhal et Napoléon* (Paris, 1969).

Helden nach Mass: 200 Jahre Völkerschlacht bei Leipzig: Katalog zur Ausstellung des Stadtgeschichtlichen Museums Leipzig (Leipzig, 2013).

Henckens, Lieutenant, *Mémoires se rapportant à son service militaire au 6e régiment de chasseurs à cheval français de février 1803 à août 1816* (The Hague, 1912).

Heinzen, Jasper, 'A Negotiated Truce: The Battle of Waterloo in European Memory since the Second World War', *History and Memory* 26 (1974), 39–74.

Hibbert, Christopher, *The Destruction of Lord Raglan: A Tragedy of the Crimean War, 1854–1855* (Boston, 1961).

Hobsbawm, Eric, and Ranger, Terence (eds), *The Invention of Tradition* (Cambridge, 1983).

Hofschröer, Peter, *The Waterloo Campaign: The German Victory* (London, 1999).

Hofschröer, Peter, *Wellington's Smallest Victory: The Duke, the Model Maker and the Secret of Waterloo* (London, 2004).

Hofschröer, Peter, *Waterloo 1815: Quatre Bras and Ligny* (Barnsley, 2005).

Holmes, Richard, *Wellington—the Iron Duke* (London, 1996).

Hoock, Holger, *The King's Artists: The Royal Academy of Arts and the Politics of British Culture, 1760–1840* (Oxford, 2003).

Hoock, Holger (ed.), *History, Commemoration and National Preoccupation: Trafalgar, 1805–2005* (London, 2007).

Hoock, Holger, *Empires of the Imagination: Politics, War and the Arts in the British World, 1750–1850* (London, 2010).

Hopkin, David, *Soldier and Peasant in French Popular Culture, 1766–1870* (Woodbridge, 2003).

Houssaye, Henri, *1815: Le Retour de l'Isle d'Elbe* (Paris, 1901).

Howarth, David, *Waterloo, A Near-run Thing* (London, 1968).

Hudson, Nora, *Ultra-Royalism and the French Restoration* (New York, 1973).

Hugo, Victor, 'L'Expiation', in *Les Châtiments* (Paris, 1853).

Hugo, Victor, *Les Misérables*, trans. Isabel Hapgood (London, 1929).

Hynes, Samuel, *The Soldiers' Tale: Bearing Witness to Modern War* (London, 1997).

Jacquemin, Georges, *Les Boteresses liégeoises à la Butte du Lion de Waterloo (1826)?* (Braine-l'Alleud, 2002).

Jensen, Lotte, 'The Dutch Against Napoleon: Resistance Literature and National Identity, 1806–1813', *Journal of Dutch Literature* 2/2 (2012), 5–26.

Jolliffe, John (ed.), *Neglected Genius: The Diaries of Benjamin Robert Haydon, 1808–1846* (London, 1990).

Joor, Johan, *De Adelaar en het Lam: Onrust, opruiing en onwilligheid in Nederland ten tijde van het Koninkrijk Holland en de Inlijving bij het Franse Keizerrijk, 1806–1813* (Amsterdam, 2000).

Joor, Johan, '"A very rebellious disposition": Dutch Experience and Popular Protest under the Napoleonic Regime (1806–1813)', in Alan Forrest, Karen Hagemann, and Jane Rendall (eds), *Soldiers, Citizens and Civilians: Experiences and Perceptions of the Revolutionary and Napoleonic Wars, 1790–1820* (Basingstoke, 2009), 181–204.

Jourdan, Annie (ed.), *Louis Bonaparte, roi de Hollande* (Paris, 2010).

Joyal, Serge, *Le Mythe de Napoléon au Canada français* (Montreal, 2013).

Keegan, John, *The Face of Battle: A Study of Agincourt, Waterloo and the Somme* (London, 1976).

Kelly, Christopher, *A Full and Circumstantial Account of the Memorable Battle of Waterloo: The second restoration of Louis XVIII; and the deportation of Napoleon Buonaparte to the island of St. Helena and every recent particular relative to his conduct and mode of life in his exile. Together with an interesting account of the affairs of France, and biographical sketches of the most distinguished Waterloo heroes* (London, 1817).

Kennedy, Catriona, *Narratives of the Revolutionary and Napoleonic Wars: Military and Civilian Experience in Britain and Ireland* (Basingstoke, 2013).

Kennet, Lee, 'Le Culte de Napoléon aux États-Unis jusqu'à la guerre de Sécession', *Revue de l'Institut Napoléon* 125 (1972), 145–56.

Kincaid, John, *Adventures in the Rifle Brigade, in the Peninsula, France and the Netherlands from 1809 to 1815* (London, 1830).

King, W. D., *Henry Irving's Waterloo: Theatrical Engagements with Arthur Conan Doyle, George Bernard Shaw, Ellen Terry, Edward Gordon Craig* (Berkeley and Los Angeles, 1993).

Kossmann, E. H., *The Low Countries, 1780–1940* (Oxford, 1978).

Largeaud, Jean-Marc, *Napoléon et Waterloo: La Défaite glorieuse de 1815 à nos jours* (Paris, 2006).

Larousse, Pierre, *Le Mot de Cambronne* (Paris, 1862).

Las Cases, Emmanuel de, *Mémorial de Sainte-Hélène*, ed. Marcel Dunan (2 vols, Paris, 1951).

Lavisse, Ernest, *Histoire de France: Cours élémentaire* (Paris, 1913).

Lean, E. Tangye, *The Napoleonists: A Study in Political Disaffection* (Oxford, 1970).

Le Gall, Didier, *Napoléon et le Mémorial de Sainte-Hélène: Analyse d'un discours* (Paris, 2003).

Leggiere, Michael, 'Waterloo', in John Merriman and Jay Winter (eds), *Europe, 1789–1914* (5 vols, New York, 2006), vol. v.

Lentz, Thierry, *Nouvelle histoire du Premier Empire*, iv. *Les Cent-Jours* (Paris, 2010).

Lieven, Dominic, *Russia Against Napoleon: The Battle for Europe, 1807–1814* (London, 2009).

Lincoln, Margarette (ed.), *Nelson and Napoleon* (London, 2005).

Logie, Jacques, *Waterloo: The 1815 Campaign* (Stroud, 2003).

Longford, Elizabeth, *Wellington: The Years of the Sword* (London, 1969).

Loos, Wiepke, Jansen, Guido, and Kloek, Wouter (eds), *Waterloo, Before and After: Paintings from the Rijksmuseum in Amsterdam, 1800–1830* (Amsterdam, 1997).

Lorblanchès, Jean-Claude, *Soldats de Napoléon aux Amériques* (Paris, 2012).

Luzzatto, Sergio, *Mémoire de la Terreur: Vieux Montagnards et jeunes républicains au 19e siècle* (Lyons, 1988).

Lynn, John, *Battle: A History of Combat and Culture* (Cambridge, MA, 2003).

Mackenzie, Norman, *The Escape from Elba: The Fall and Flight of Napoleon, 1814–1815* (Oxford, 1982).

Macleod, Jenny, *Reconsidering Gallipoli* (Manchester, 2004).

Marbot, Marcellin de, *Mémoires du Général Baron de Marbot* (3 vols, Paris, 1891).

Margerit, Robert, *Waterloo: 18 juin 1815* (Paris, 1964).

May, Gita, *Stendhal in the Age of Napoleon* (New York, 1978).

Meisel, Martin, *Realizations: Narrative, Pictorial and Theatrical Arts in Nineteenth-Century England* (Princeton, 1983).

Ménager, Bernard, *Les Napoléon du peuple* (Paris, 1988).

Mercer, Alexander Cavalié, *Journal of the Waterloo Campaign* (London, 1969).

Miller, David, *The Duchess of Richmond's Ball, 15 June 1815* (Staplehurst, 2005).

Moniteur universel, 1815.

Müffling, Carl von, *The Memoirs of Baron von Müffling: A Prussian Officer in the Napoleonic Wars* (London, 1997).

Muir, Rory, *Britain and the Defeat of Napoleon, 1807–1815* (New Haven, 1996).

Muir, Rory, *Tactics and the Experience of Battle in the Age of Napoleon* (New Haven, 1998).

Nicholson, Harold, *The Congress of Vienna: A Study in Allied Unity* (London, 1946).

Nipperdey, Thomas, *Deutsche Geschichte, 1800–1866: Bürgerwelt und starker Staat* (Munich, 1983).

Nora, Pierre, 'Les Mémoires d'État: De Commynes à de Gaulle', in Nora (ed.), *Les Lieux de mémoire*, ii. *La Nation* (3 vols, Paris, 1986).

Pardo de Leygonier, G. F., 'Napoléon et les libérateurs de l'Amérique latine', *Revue de l'Institut Napoléon* 82 (1962).

Petiteau, Natalie, *Napoléon de la mythologie à l'histoire* (Paris, 1999).

Petiteau, Natalie, *Lendemains d'Empire: Les Soldats de Napoléon dans la France du 19e siècle* (Paris, 2003).

Petiteau, Natalie, *Guerriers du Premier Empire: Expériences et mémoires* (Paris, 2011).

Pilbeam, Pamela, *Madame Tussaud and the History of Waxworks* (London, 2003).

Pope, Willard Bissell (ed.), *The Diary of Benjamin Robert Haydon* (6 vols, Cambridge, MA, 1960).

Preussische Zeitung, 17 June 1915.

Price, Munro, *The Perilous Crown: France between Revolutions, 1814–1848* (London, 2007).

Price, Roger, *People and Politics in France, 1848–1870* (Cambridge, 2004).

Procès du Lieutenant-général Savary, Duc de Rovigo, contumax (Paris, 1817).

Raffet, 1804–1860, catalogue of exhibition at the Bibliothèque Marmottan (Paris, 1999).

Ramsay, Neil, *The Military Memoir and Romantic Literary Culture, 1780–1835* (Aldershot, 2011).

Read, Donald, *Peterloo: The 'Massacre' and its Background* (Manchester, 1958).

Resnick, Daniel, *The White Terror and the Political Reaction after Waterloo* (Cambridge, MA, 1966).

Riley, Jonathon, *Napoleon as a General* (London, 2007).

Roberts, Andrew, *Waterloo: Napoleon's Last Gamble* (London, 2006).

Robinson, Mike, *The Battle of Quatre-Bras, 1815* (Stroud, 2009).

Rothenberg, Gunther E., *The Napoleonic Wars* (London, 1999).

Sabine, Edward (ed.), *Letters of Colonel Sir Augustus Simon Frazer, KCB, commanding the Royal Horse Artillery in the Army under the Duke of Wellington* (London, 1859).

Saint-Mathurin, J., 'Le Culte de Napoléon en Allemagne de 1815 à 1848', *Revue des études napoléoniennes* 11 (1917), 48–87.

Schivelbusch, Wolfgang, *The Culture of Defeat: On National Trauma, Mourning and Recovery* (London, 2003).

Schroeder, Paul, *The Transformation of European Politics, 1763–1848* (Oxford, 1994).

Scott, John, *Paris Revisited in 1815, by way of Brussels: Including a walk over the field of battle at Waterloo* (London, 1817).

Scott, Walter, *The Field of Waterloo: A Poem* (Edinburgh, 1815).

Scott, Walter, *Life of Napoleon Bonaparte* (Edinburgh, 1828).

Seaton, A. V., 'War and Thanatourism: Waterloo, 1815–1914', *Annals of Tourism Research* 26 (1999), 130–58.

Sels, E. Van Löben, *Bijdragen tot de Krijgsgeschiedenis van Napoleon Bonaparte* (4 vols, 'S Gravenhage, 1842).

Shaw, Matthew, *The Duke of Wellington* (London, 2005).

Shaw, Philip, *Waterloo and the Romantic Imagination* (Basingstoke, 2002).

Shaw, Philip, *Suffering and Sentiment in Romantic Military Art* (Farnham, 2013).

Sheehan, James J., *German History, 1770–1866* (Oxford, 1989).

Siborne, William, *The Waterloo Campaign, 1815* (London, 1848).

Siborne, Herbert T., *Waterloo Letters* (London, 1891).

Simms, Brendan, *The Longest Afternoon: The Four Hundred Men who Decided the Battle of Waterloo* (London, 2014).

Simpson, James, *A Visit to Flanders, in July, 1815: Being chiefly an account of the field of Waterloo* (London, 1816).

Sked, Alan (ed.), *Europe's Balance of Power, 1815–1848* (London, 1979).

Smith, Digby, *1813: Leipzig—Napoleon and the Battle of the Nations* (London, 2001).

Spence, Peter, *The Birth of Romantic Radicalism: War, Popular Politics and English Radical Reformism, 1800–1815* (Aldershot, 1996).

Stanhope, Philip Henry, *Notes of Conversations with the Duke of Wellington* (London, 1886).

Stendhal, *Les Temps héroïques de Napoléon* (Paris, 1837).

Stendhal, *Voyages en Italie* (Paris, 1973).

Strachan, Hew, *Wellington's Legacy: The Reform of the British Army, 1830–1854* (Manchester, 1984).

Sugden, John, *Nelson: The Sword of Albion* (London, 2012).

Sutherland, Christine, *Marie Walewska: Napoleon's Great Love* (London, 1979).

Tebbe, Jason, 'Revision and "Rebirth": Commemoration of the Battle of the Nations in Leipzig', *German Studies Review* 33 (2010), 618–40.

Thomas, *Journal of a Soldier of the Seventy-First or Glasgow Regiment* (Edinburgh, 1819).

Thompson, Melvyn, *St George's (Kidderminster): A Waterloo Church* (Kidderminster, 2009).

The Times, 1815.

Tomkinson, James (ed.), *The Diary of a Cavalry Officer in the Peninsular and Waterloo Campaigns, 1809–1815* (Staplehurst, 1999).

Tulard, Jean, *Nouvelle bibliographie critique des mémoires sur l'époque napoléonienne, écrits ou traduits en français* (Geneva, 1991).

Tulard, Jean (ed.), *Dictionnaire Napoléon* (2 vols, Paris, 1999).

Tulard, Jean, *Napoléon chef de guerre* (Paris, 2012).

Tulard, Jean, *L'Anti-Napoléon* (Paris, 2013).

Uffindell, Andrew, *The Eagle's Last Triumph: Napoleon's Victory at Ligny, June 1815* (London, 1994).

Uffindell, Andrew, *The National Army Museum Book of Wellington's Armies* (London, 2005).

Uffindell, Andrew, and Corum, Michael, *On the Fields of Glory: The Battlefields of the 1815 Campaign* (London, 1996).

Villepin, Dominique de, *Les Cent Jours ou l'esprit de sacrifice* (Paris, 2001).

Watelet, Marcel, and Couvreur, Pierre (eds), *Waterloo, lieu de mémoire européenne, 1815–2000* (Louvain-la-Neuve, 2000).

Watelet, Marcel, Couvreur, Pierre, and Villelongue, Philippe de (eds), *Waterloo: Monuments et représentations de mémoires européennes, 1792–2001* (Louvain-la-Neuve, 2003).

Weller, Jac, *Wellington at Waterloo* (London, 1992).

Wellington, *Supplementary Despatches, Correspondence and Memoranda of Field Marshal Arthur Duke of Wellington* (16 vols, London, 1857–72).

Whately, Richard, *Historical Doubts Relative to Napoleon Bonaparte* (London, 1819); edited with a critical introduction by Ralph S. Pomeroy (1985).

Wishon, Mark, *German Forces and the British Army: Interactions and Perceptions, 1742–1815* (Basingstoke, 2013).

Woolgar, C. M., 'Writing the Despatch: Wellington and Official Communication', in Woolgar (ed.), *Wellington Studies*, ii (Southampton, 1999).

Wrigley, Richard, and Craske, Matthew (eds), *Pantheons: Transformations of a Monumental Idea* (Aldershot, 2004).

Yarrington, Alison, *The Commemoration of the Hero, 1800–1864: Monuments to the British Victors of the Napoleonic Wars* (New York, 1988).

Youngson, A. J., *The Making of Classical Edinburgh, 1750–1840* (Edinburgh, 1966).

Zamoyski, Adam, *Rites of Peace: The Fall of Napoleon and the Congress of Vienna* (London, 2007).

Zanone, Damien, *Écrire son temps: Les Mémoires en France de 1815 à 1848* (Lyons, 2006).

Zeller, André, *Soldats perdus: Des armées de Napoléon aux garnisons de Louis XVIII* (Paris, 1977).

PICTURE ACKNOWLEDGEMENTS

1. Napoleon at Fontainebleau During the First Abdication - 31 March 1814, (1845). Artist: Paul Delaroche. © Heritage Images/Glow Images.com
2. Courtesy of The Lewis Walpole Library, Yale University
3. Field-Marshal Gebhardt von Blucher, 1814 (oil on canvas), Lawrence, Sir Thomas (1769–1830) / The Royal Collection © 2014 Her Majesty Queen Elizabeth II / The Bridgeman Art Library
4. The Battle of Waterloo, 18th June 1815 (coloured engraving), French School, (19th century) / Bibliotheque Nationale, Paris, France / Giraudon / The Bridgeman Art Library
5. A Soldier relating his exploits in a tavern, 1821 (oil on panel), Cawse, John (1779–1862) / National Army Museum, London / Acquired with assistance of National Art Collections Fund / The Bridgeman Art Library
6. The Chelsea Pensioners Reading the Waterloo Dispatch, 1822 (oil on wood), Wilkie, Sir David (1785–1841) / Apsley House, The Wellington Museum, London, UK / The Bridgeman Art Library
7. © Mary Evans Picture Library
8. © York & Son / English Heritage / Arcaid/Corbis
9. © PhotoNonStop/Glow Imgaes.com
10. The Field of Waterloo, c.1817 (w/c over pencil on paper), Turner, Joseph Mallord William (1775–1851) / Fitzwilliam Museum, University of Cambridge, UK / The Bridgeman Art Library
11. Scotland For Ever! 1881 (oil on canvas), Butler, Lady (Elizabeth Southerden Thompson) (1846–1933) / Leeds Museums and Galleries (Leeds Art Gallery) U.K. / The Bridgeman Art Library
12. The Waterloo Banquet, 1836 (oil on canvas), Salter, John William (fl.1848–75) / Private Collection / Photo © Philip Mould Ltd, London / The Bridgeman Art Library
13. © Photononstop/Glow Images.com
14. © Maurice Savage / Alamy
15. Courtesy of The Lewis Walpole Library, Yale University
16. William II, King of Holland, when Prince of Orange, c.1812 (oil on canvas), Copley, John Singleton (1738–1815) (after) / The Royal Collection © 2014 Her Majesty Queen Elizabeth II / The Bridgeman Art Library

Index